War, Wine, and Taxes

THE POLITICAL ECONOMY
OF ANGLO-FRENCH
TRADE, 1689–1900

John V. C. Nye

PRINCETON UNIVERSITY PRESS

PRINCETON AND OXFORD

Copyright © 2007 by Princeton University Press

Published by Princeton University Press, 41 William Street, Princeton, New Jersey 08540

In the United Kingdom: Princeton University Press, 3 Market Place, Woodstock, Oxfordshire OX20 1SY

LIBRARY OF CONGRESS CATALOGING-IN-PUBLICATION DATA

Nye, John V. C.
    War, wine and taxes : the political economy of Anglo-French trade, 1689–1900 / John V. C. Nye.
        p. cm. — (The Princeton economic history of the western world)
    Includes bibliographical references and index.
    ISBN-13: 978-0-691-12917-4 (hardcover : alk. paper)
    ISBN-10: 0-691-12917-7 (hardcover : alk. paper)
    1. Great Britain—Commercial policy—History.   2. Tariff on wine—Great Britain—History.   3. Great Britain—Foreign economic relations—France.   4. France—Foreign economic relations—Great Britain.   I. Title.
    HF1536.5.F8N94   2007
    3828.456632009440903—dc22   2006032179

British Library Cataloging-in-Publication Data is available

This book has been composed in Sabon

Printed on acid-free paper.

pup.princeton.edu

Printed in the United States of America

10 9 8 7 6 5 4 3 2 1

THIS WORK IS DEDICATED TO THE MEMORY OF MY PARENTS

Walter Nye and Pacita Cañizares-Nye

Contents

Preface

Economic historians have always been in something of an insecure position in the academic world. Torn between the demands of history with its emphasis on archival research, textual sophistication, and commitment to context, and economics with its technical language and structure, abundant use of statistical techniques, and pretensions to emulate the natural sciences, the economic historian often finds it difficult to come up with an acceptable synthesis. It is well known that in the world of North American economic history, economics and social scientific rigor have come to dominate research methodology. This shift in emphasis was highlighted over four decades ago by the coming of the New Economic History, or cliometrics, which sought to marry economic models and statistical testing of hypotheses with the descriptive work of traditional economic historians. The belief was that careful hypothesis testing would lead to a more precise and reliable understanding of the causes of economic growth and the development of the modern industrial economy. In contrast, some of the grand schemas of historians seemed little more than vague storytelling.

But something unfortunate happened on the way to the revolution. Aside from the fact that many historians chose to pointedly ignore work in the new field—often dismissing the various hypotheses posed as irrelevant or ahistorical—the cliometricians found themselves boxed in by the demands of the academic market for economists. If every work in economic history was to be framed in terms of existing mathematical models or was constructed to test a well-elaborated hypothesis amenable to quantification, then the questions that economic historians could ask would be constrained by the demands of the larger economics community. Furthermore, economists were limited by the fact that neoclassical economics—at least as it was studied circa 1960—allowed for a narrower range of theoretical models than we see today. The first generation of cliometricians worked within the narrow confines of social scientific testing but had the benefit of questions generated by an earlier generation of historians more attuned to the problems of the long term. Without the freedom to make historical questions paramount as history, subsequent generations found themselves only working on the topics that would fit conveniently into the mold of conventional applied economics. This has had the most unsalutary effect of further marginalizing the field within economics itself, for if economic history is simply applied economics, what special claim can it have as a discipline with something to teach all economists?

Fortunately, a generation's worth of research in a variety of fields—including economic history, but also encompassing property rights theory, transactions cost economics, the study of the law, and the public choice revolution in political economy—has led to a renewed interest in broader historical and institutional issues in tandem with a desire to sort out the more easily testable claims of cliometric history. In particular, Douglass North has championed what we might call New Institutional Economic History and the use of the analytical or institutional narrative in which descriptive history interacts with a broader analytic structure that seeks to tie together the many static snapshots that more rigorous quantification presents to us as we consider the longer run evolution of political economy.

I have conducted this short review for the purposes of explaining the evolution in my conception of this book. Initially I was trained as a cliometrician who saw my job as digging up historical data that could be used to test well-specified hypotheses or to elaborate counterfactuals that would enhance our understanding of some historical event or process. When I began this work over a decade ago, my initial interest was in analyzing the course of Anglo-French trade from a French perspective, making full use of statistical and econometric reasoning to trace out the patterns of trade and to study its responses to changes in the politics of cross-Channel commerce. But along the way a bigger story began to poke its nose through the mass of notes I had begun to accumulate on Anglo-French history.

My discovery that nineteenth-century Britain was not quite the free trader the textbooks have made it out to be, coupled with my interest in finding out why this fact had been ignored for so long, caused me to focus on the history of the hotly contested wine trade between Britain and France. Research into the wine trade eventually resulted in this book, which is not just an economic history but also a meditation on the complicated interaction between fiscal and commercial policy as well as the problems of strategic interest in international politics during the rise of the modern state.

What began as a narrow study focusing on a few well-specified issues became a much bigger story with something to say to historians, economists, political scientists, and anyone interested in the political economy of trade policy or of trade liberalization in general. I have been inspired, as have many other authors, by the seminal work of Douglass North and Barry Weingast (1989), which argued that institutional innovations after the Glorious Revolution made it possible to increase taxation and hence to borrow much more at favorable rates, thus enabling a remarkable expansion of the British state in the eighteenth century. Yet despite my admiration for their work, my own research has called into question some aspects of their explanation, in particular the inadequacy of mere institutional innovation in explaining the British ability to both tax and spend at historically unprecedented levels. It complements their work by presenting changes in the political economy that allowed the British state not simply to raise tax rates but more importantly to effectively collect more in total revenue (a distinction that is often overlooked in the historical literature). At the same time, I raise some doubts about the wisdom of these policies and show what a pernicious effect they may have had on British economic policy. Indeed, it is arguable that Britain succeeded economically despite its ability to raise revenues.

So it is proper that I acknowledge the unstinting support I have received from Douglass North throughout the long gestation of this work. North has both commented on the manuscript many times and engaged in friendly debate with me as I have sought to develop my own theses and at times to challenge his. I owe him a debt of gratitude that may be impossible to repay.

Along the way I have also benefited from the in-depth comments and criticisms of Joel Mokyr, who has followed this work over many years. I also want to thank Deirdre McCloskey, who made detailed comments on an early draft.

I am also grateful for the extraordinary opportunity provided me by the Mercatus Center, where Paul Edwards organized a seminar in 2004 entirely devoted to a discussion of an early version of this manuscript. There I had the benefit not only of the suggestions of North and Mokyr, but also from the comments of Phil Hoffman, John Wallis, Barry Weingast, Avner Greif, Pete Boettke, Jack Goldstone, and Lynne Kiesling, as well as other participants from the Mercatus Center and from George Mason University.

Over the years I have also appreciated the advice and comments of many other individuals, including but not confined to Lee Benham, Norman Schofield, Sukkoo Kim, Francois Crouzet, Marc Flandreau, Ellen Paul, Jean Ensminger, Peter Lindert, Ken Shepsle, Jim Alt, Jack Knight, Andy Sobel, Phil Keefer, Randy Calvert, Jean-Laurent Rosenthal, Margaret Levi, Julian Simon, Russ Roberts, Sami Dakhlia, as well as participants from workshops and seminars at Stanford, Northwestern, Harvard, UC Davis, University of Alabama, University of Hawaii, University of Massachusetts, University of Illinois-Chicago, the Institut d'Etudes Politiques de Paris, ATOM in Paris, Pompeu Fabra, and various workshop presentations for the Ronald Coase Institute and the Institute for Humane Studies. Early on I also benefited from a year as a National Fellow at the Hoover Institution. Later drafts of this work were completed during extended visits to the Institut d'Études Politiques de Paris and the Social Philosophy and Policy Center at Bowling Green State University. I wish to acknowledge having received support for parts of this research from the Bradley Foundation and INRA, France. I also wish to thank an anonymous reader for Princeton University Press for a number of constructive suggestions.

I should note that chapter 1, "The Myth of Free Trade Britain and Fortress France," is partially drawn from an article with the same title originally published in the *Journal of Economic History* (Nye, 1991b). The appendix is based on joint work with Sami Dakhlia (Dakhlia and Nye, 2004).

I have also benefited from the comments of my many students over the years, including Art Carden, Peter Grossman, Michael Haupert, Tawni Hunt, Noel Johnson, Phil Keefer, Janice Kinghorn, Randy Nielsen, and Werner Troesken. I especially benefited from the detailed research assistance of Jeremy Meiners from 2004 to 2006. I also received help from Terence Watson in 2005.

I should state the obvious. None of the persons cited or mentioned bears the slightest responsibility for any mistakes or erroneous claims that I may make.

Above all, I am grateful to my wife Lirong and to my two sons, Michael and Andrew, for supporting me during the long process of writing this book. If anyone has paid a price for the hours I devoted to this project, it is they. I thank them for their patience and their constant encouragement of my efforts.

Introduction

The idea that Britain was the leading free trader of the nineteenth century is one of those rare stylized facts in economic history that resonates with the public as much as it commands the attention of historians and other scholars. In the conventional wisdom, Britain's move to free trade was the triumph of the Scottish Enlightenment, an outgrowth of the Industrial Revolution, and a political and ideological movement that converted the whole world—or at least the major European powers—to the virtues of what is now called "globalization." Nineteenth-century free trade is at once credited with the success of the Western economy and at the same time vilified for its promotion of the ills of economic integration and its apparent support for European imperialism. The subjects that swirl around British free trade and its significance for economics, politics, the history of ideas, sociocultural change, and long-run transformation of all sorts are so numerous that they could (and indeed have) filled hundreds of books and thousands of articles.

It is therefore surprising to learn that until fairly recently no detailed attention has been paid to the validity of the claims of British free trade. Nor have economic historians, eager to quantify most subjects, done much to place British trade policy in a wider international context. There was little done to separate claims about lower British tariffs over time, from lower tariffs in comparison to other nations to the uses to which the tariffs had been put and their effects on the economy. Despite occasional forays into quantitative speculation, (e.g. McCloskey, 1980), British claims of trade liberalization were taken at face value.

A comparative analysis of British and French trade policy (Nye, 1991b) showed that the standard fables about Britain moving unilaterally to free trade after the Repeal of the Corn Laws were misleading if not outright false. This required a further rethinking of the conventional wisdom surrounding the political economy of nineteenth-century trade policy (cf. Nye, 1991a) and necessitated further research into understanding why scholars have mischaracterized the core features of these policies.

Subsequent work indicated that the problems of nineteenth-century tariff reform had their roots in conflicts going back to the reign of Louis XIV in the closing decades of the seventeenth century. The discovery of the ways in which a flourishing trade in French wine was destroyed at the end of the 1600s by a long war between Britain and France caused me to focus more intensively on the political economy of British trade policy and on the long history of Anglo-French commerce. The political economy of customs led me to the more general question of the evolution of modern British fiscal policy. From there it was an easy step to a surprising story that intermingled commercial and foreign policy with issues of domestic tax policy, the rise of the British excise, the development of the modern London brewing industry, and changes in British consumption and French production arising from the massive distortions in international trade introduced by the new anti-French tariff structure.

The argument is essentially this: a British government eager to reduce the trade deficit with France at the end of the seventeenth century was presented with a special opportunity arising out of the period of war from 1689 to 1713. These conflicts provided the protectionists with the opportunity that they sought to cut off almost all commerce with France, thus eliminating the trade deficit. This created a powerful class of protected interests both at home (brewers and distillers) and abroad (notably in the form of British merchants and investors in Portuguese wine) and led to the imposition of prohibitively high tariffs on French imports—notably on wine and spirits—when trade with France resumed in 1714. The implicit threat of lower tariffs allowed the state to raise domestic excises on alcoholic beverages and other consumables that might otherwise have been uncollectible, thus leading to increased government revenues with almost no increases in the tax rates on land and income. The state ensured compliance not simply through the threat of lower tariffs on foreign substitutes, but also through the encouragement of a trend toward monopoly production in brewing and the restricted retail sales of beer, which began around 1700 and continued throughout the eighteenth century.

The net result was an expansive British state with revenues collected by central tax authorities and backed by a cooperative domestic industry shielded from foreign competition that found it easy to shift much of the burden of taxation onto the consumers. The centuries' old trade with France was permanently deformed and cheap wine was kept out of the British Isles during the century and a half that saw the coming of the Industrial Revolution and the rise of the middle-class British consumer.

Chapter 1 provides the core empirical findings that motivate this entire book: the demonstration that Britain was not as much of a free trader in the nineteenth century as has been previously perceived, especially in comparison to France. It will go into some detail about the nature of the evidence in support of this thesis and will tie this to the conventional historiography of the nineteenth century.

Chapter 2 jumps back to the beginning of our story and gives a quick overview of British commercial history from the late seventeenth to the mid-nineteenth century that touches on the received wisdom of the period but that also points to the links between foreign policy, trade restrictions, and domestic demands for revenue.

Chapters 3 and 4 are given over to a more detailed discussion of the history of commercial relations in the eighteenth century that show us the origins of the trade war between Britain and France that led to the tariffs and prohibitions on French wine, which shaped policy over the next century and a half.

Chapter 5 is a brief counterfactual discussion designed to discuss what might have happened had the British permitted the French wines to enter with a more liberal economic policy. The object here is not to precisely re-run history—such an exercise is both impossible and implausible. Rather, the goal is to give the reader some idea of the magnitude of the trade that was foregone and its potential effects on the structure of consumption and production.

Chapter 6 argues that the protection of domestic brewing interests and the technical revolution in the London beer industry led to a situation in which the government and the leading brewers entered into a symbiotic relationship in which protection from foreign competition was granted in exchange for substantially higher beer revenues. This led to a surge in total British revenues as well as a shift in the composition of British taxes away from land to various excises that made possible government expansion in the eighteenth century. A later section shows how domestic politics in the early eighteenth century can be better understood by taking this relationship to account and by explaining the political economy of sustainable revenue collection support through protection and the promotion of oligopoly in production.

Because the history of British commercial policy has been such an important component of debates in politics as well as in history and economics, chapter 7 discusses the implications of this work for political economy. Indeed, the story of the so-called Pax Britannica and the British domination of commerce through the promotion of free trade is so central to so many different theories that it behooves us to explore how changing the underlying story would change the leading hypotheses. Theorists of political hegemony, international cooperation, or what is known to political scientists as international political economy (e.g. Keohane, 1984; Gilpin, 1987) have relied on a conventional reading of changing trade regimes that is not supported by this historical research. Consequently, I hope that many political theorists will find this historical analysis of some interest.

The final section not only sums up the complete argument of the book but extends the analysis by considering how this might lead us to rethink the existing historical generalizations about Britain's rise to power and wealth. It will also give space to discuss how reconsideration of the role of fiscal policy in Hanoverian Britain actually leaves unanswered many questions of great importance to the rise of the liberal state and shows how misleading conventional wisdom has been. It calls into question the easy link we tend to make between fiscal success and economic development and allows us to question recent attempts to justify mercantile policy on the grounds that state expansion paved the way for modern growth.

It is unlikely that any one work or single empirical test will serve to make people reject theses that have been built up over the years. In addition to the complex welter of arguments that have accumulated in the literature, all sorts of caveats and cautions will have been worked into the analysis. Nonetheless no one should be able to read through this material and ponder its particular reading of commercial history without feeling obligated to rethink many of the ideas in international political economy: the rise of the modern state; the role of fiscal policy in development; the struggle over free trade; the problem of market reform; the political economy of interest groups in times of rapid change; policy perception versus economic reality. These are some of the most important and the most central problems in history and the social sciences.

The story of British development and the evolution of its trade policy has long stood at the center of these investigations. This is not just a story about the past; it is the beginning of a fundamental reassessment of our understanding of commercial policy in economic history. More importantly, it is the hope that this will serve as a small lesson in how history can inform more static economic analysis and vice versa. The limitations of our models can be overcome by recourse to a narrative that fills in the dynamic elements of the problem. It provides the context without which any analysis is hopelessly obscure, or worse, pointless. And ultimately, it makes for a more interesting read.

Let us begin with the end of our story.

War, Wine, and Taxes

CHAPTER 1

Problems of Perspective: The Myth of Free Trade Britain and Fortress France

WHY do the British drink beer and not wine? How did commercial tariff policy designed to protect domestic interests help the British state raise revenues to the point where Britain emerged as the leading European power of the eighteenth century? These two seemingly unrelated issues are at the heart of the one of the most important and underexplored cases in modern economic history. To understand the political economy of British wine tariffs is to open a window onto the ways in which small policy decisions can have large, long-term consequences. It provides us with an exceptional historical case with which to see how patterns of trade, consumption, and taxation are shaped by international geopolitics and the economics of special interests. But before discussing the arguments contained in this book, it might be helpful to understand something about its intellectual genesis.

This chapter lays out how British trade policy was neither so free nor so selfless as many had thought. This is done by not simply looking at British average tariffs over time but also by comparing them to the tariffs of France, who by most accounts was both less enthusiastic about free trade and more desirous of protecting domestic production interests. Furthermore the analysis in this chapter looks closely at which tariffs British chose to lower or remove, and which remained after the reforms of the 1840s. It will then be seen that British liberalism was wanting when measured against the yardstick of protectionist France. More significant is the fact that most of the goods that continued to be taxed were precisely those products that had been the source of mercantilist conflict a century and a half earlier. And many of the tariffs of the mercantile system that Adam Smith had so vigorously denounced remained in place and continued to serve many of the protectionist goals that had been sought as early as the mid-1600s.

Why these tariffs have been ignored and still tend to be dismissed by those making use of the story of British free trade will then be discussed. The analysis will then move to why interpreting the tariffs illustrates different conceptions of the role of trade policy and the nature of protection. All this will then serve as the starting point for the rest of the book's move backwards in time to the beginnings of the Anglo-French trade wars.

The last two decades have witnessed serious revisions in our views of modern English and French economic history. For instance, our views of the relative sizes of the state in late seventeenth and eighteenth century Britain and France have been altered by the work on the relative tax burdens in the two countries (Mathias and O'Brien, 1976a, 1976b; O'Brien, 1988). Without overturning the conventional findings of Eli Heckscher (1935), regarding the interventionist character of the French relative to the British governments, the more recent research has reversed the received wisdom concerning the relative size of the state and the average tax burden in the two nations.

Conventional wisdom still treats the nineteenth century from a perspective of strong contrasts between the two nations. England is still viewed as having had the liberal, virtually minimalist state par excellence with small government, laissez-faire at home, and free trade abroad, while France had the backward economy, dirigiste government, and was closed to trade. Why such a difference? How can we reconcile the conflicting views and what changes must have been wrought to bring about this transformation? The problems of reconciling these interpretations are made greater still when taking into account the revisionist work in economic history that has done much to diminish the perception of French economic failure in the nineteenth century.[1] The revisions narrow the development gap between the two nations and have stimulated new thinking about the course of economic growth in the two wealthiest European nations.

The conventional literature has stressed the ideological changes in English governance beginning in the early to mid-1800s, in particular the embrace of laissez-faire as an overarching principle. Under no circumstances are the importance of this intellectual shift and its influence on the thinking of other national elites contested. But in policy terms, the changes were more gradual. The major change is supposed to have come in the area of international trade and in the move to free trade in the nineteenth century.

Paul Bairoch writes the following of the period in the *Cambridge Economic History of Europe*:

> The situation as regards trade policy in the various European states in 1815–20 can be described as that of an ocean of protectionism surrounding a few liberal islands.
>
> The three decades between 1815 and 1846 were essentially marked by the movement towards economic liberalism in Great Britain. This remained a very limited form of liberalism until the 1840s, and thus only became effective when this country had nearly a century of industrial development behind it and was some 40–60 years ahead of its

neighbors. A few small countries, notably The Netherlands, also showed tendencies towards liberalism. But the rest of Europe developed a system of defensive, protectionist policies, directed especially against British manufactured goods. (Bairoch, 1989, p. 6)

But an examination of British and French commercial statistics suggests that the conventional wisdom is simply wrong. There is little evidence that Britain's trade was substantially more open than that of France. Very little of the existing work on British or French trade has taken a comparative perspective, and there has been little economic as opposed to political analysis of the commercial interaction between nations. Most of the economic work has focused on the volume of trade in the two nations and has taken the changing tariffs for granted as an interesting stylized fact.

When the comparison is made, the trade figures suggest that France's trade regime was more liberal than that of Great Britain throughout most of the nineteenth century, even in the period from 1840 to 1860. This is when France was said to have been struggling against her legacy of protection while Britain had already made the decision to move unilaterally to freer trade. Although some have recognized that Napoleon III had begun to liberalize France's trade regime even before the 1860 treaty of commerce, both current and contemporaneous accounts treat the period before the 1860s as protectionist in France and relatively free in Britain.

A proper reading of the evidence would suggest a more balanced, less heroic view of British trade policy, and it would underline the links between government policy in the eighteenth century and its constraining influence on government action in the nineteenth century. The demonstration that all is not well with the traditional picture of a uniquely free trade Britain in the nineteenth century rests on a simple comparison that had never been made previously. The simplest and most basic index of overall tariff levels is the nominal average tariff—that is, total tariff revenue as a fraction of the value of all imports. On the basis of the conventional stories of free trade in Britain and high tariffs in France, what would you expect the outcome to be?

The average tariff levels of both France and Britain are given from 1820 to 1900 in figure 1.1. These figures are based on the work of Imlah for the United Kingdom and Lévy-Leboyer and Bourguignon for France. They indicate quite dramatically that British average tariffs were substantially higher than those in France for the greater part of the nineteenth century. This is especially startling for the period from 1840 to 1860 after Britain began the repeal of her Corn Laws and the move to freer trade and before the 1860 Anglo-French Treaty of Commerce, thus

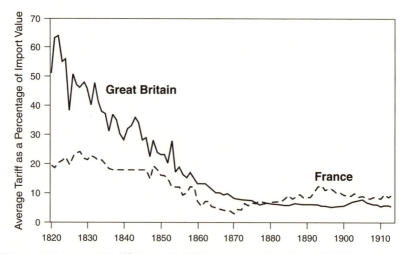

Figure 1.1. Average Tariff Rates: Tariff Revenue as a Fraction of All Imports (Imlah, 1958; Lévy-Leboyer and Bourguignon, 1985).

refuting the traditional stories of a lone free trade Britain surrounded by hostile, anti–free trade nations such as France. In fact, not only was Britain's tariff higher than that of France until 1860, it was about on a par with the average tariff of the United States—a nation not known in the nineteenth century for its devotion to free trade.

Average French tariffs in the earlier period were comparable to, but lower than those in Britain after she had begun her move to free trade with the abolition of the Corn Laws. Judging by the absolute size of the fall in average tariff levels, Britain seems to have shown a much greater change in tariff levels than France.[2] But Britain started out from much higher levels—over 50 percent—than did France, which never exceeded 25 percent in any single year. Bearing in mind the high point from which British tariff levels fell, one notes that the changes in tariffs seemed to fit the conventional chronology, beginning in the late 1820s and falling rapidly from the 1840s onward.[3] Similarly, French tariffs steadily declined until the early 1850s and then plummeted to a low of around 3 percent in 1870—well below the minimum for Britain at any time in the nineteenth century. French tariff levels remained at quite low levels until the move back toward protection in the last ten or fifteen years of the century. British average tariff levels did not compare favorably with those of France until the 1880s and were not substantially lower for much of the time. The view of Britain as the principled free trader is most consistent with the tariff averages from the end of the nineteenth century, indicating Britain's commitment to keeping tariffs low in opposition to rising protectionist sentiment both at home and abroad. Furthermore, her movements toward free trade were magnified by the scale of her involvement in the world economy. In fact, Britain's rapid shift to freer trade was fully matched in timing and extent—and even anticipated (in the French discussions of tariff rationalization before 1830)—by the commercial restructuring taking place in France.

There is no widely accepted and perhaps no possible universal index of "partially free" trade. Either a nation admits all goods without taxes, restrictions, and supplementary domestic distortions of any sort or it deviates from the pure ideal of free trade. Into the latter category all nations fall. Thus there will always be room for argument regarding what is an "acceptable degree" of "unfree" trade. Moreover, it will always be difficult (many economists believe it to be impossible) to rank countries whose choice of restrictions are quite dissimilar. This problem plagues any comparison of Britain and France. So the point of this chapter is to demonstrate that using a number of reasonable and varied measures, France's trading regime emerges as freer than that of Britain for most of the nineteenth century. It does *not* argue that France's trade was freer than Britain's on every relevant margin.

The nominal average tariff is not a perfect measure of a nation's deviation from free trade, but do note that it is the common first measure (and is often the final measure) used by many authorities to discuss the relative openness or freedom of a nation's trade. Notably, both Imlah (1958) and McCloskey (1980) used just this measure in their seminal and influential discussions of Britain's move to free trade.[4] Their common use however, does not free us from confronting the weaknesses of the measure. In particular, high tariffs on some items may lead to such a drop in their importation (as was the case with British tariffs on French wine and spirits, and French tariffs on finished textiles) that these tariffs do not receive much weight in the calculation of the averages.

A first response to this is straightforward. Reweight the tariff measures making different assumptions about the distribution of import quantities. This follows an existing adjustment in the literature; McCloskey's (1980) study of British trade policy wherein a given year's tariff was recomputed using import quantity weights from other periods, in particular, years with very low tariffs. This more fully approximated the weight of a given tariff under nearly free trade conditions. In the case of prohibitions, differences in the domestic and foreign prices of certain goods were used as the upper-bound implicit weights and then applied the highest reasonable number to each category of items. In addition, one can test for the sensitivity of the French figures to large swings in import composition and tariff rates by applying the rates in every period to the import shares in every other period. Furthermore, the weights were

TABLE 1.1
Alternative Calculations of the British Tariff Rate: 1841, 1854, and 1881

Using Individual Tariff Rates from the Year:	Weighted by Each Commodity's Share from the Year:		
	1841	1854	1881
1841	35%	30%	27%
1854	25%	18%	16%
1881	13%	10%	6%
Total decline	22%	21%	21%

Source: McCloskey, 1980, p. 309

TABLE 1.2
Alternative Calculations of French Tariff Rates using Different Decadal Import Weights

Decade	Percentages, Using Weights in the Decade:				
	1827–36	1837–46	1847–56	1857–66	1867–76
1827–36	20.82	19.10	19.97	21.43	19.96
1837–46	18.73	16.86	17.55	19.05	17.67
1847–56	14.63	13.41	13.03	14.33	13.10
1857–66	8.89	7.35	7.17	6.89	5.81
1867–76	8.74	6.76	6.40	6.02	4.93

Source: France, Administration des Douanes, 1878

selected in all cases to bias the calculations only *against* the French, choosing to ignore similar problems in Britain.[5] When the recalculations are made, the findings are clear and unambiguous: France's average tariffs are lower by decade than those of Britain until the late 1870s and the new averages are very insensitive to changes in the weights used, often changing by only a few percentage points even if the tariff weights on textiles are biased upwards. Under no set of reasonable assumptions could the French averages be made so high as to match those of Great Britain before around 1870.[6]

Table 1.1 presents the table used by Deirdre McCloskey, in examining the fall of British tariffs under different assumptions. Table 1.2 shows a variety of alternative calculations of French tariff rates using the trade weights from different decades drawn from the official trade statistics. (The reader may note that the figures used were actually lower than the tariff averages reported by Lévy-Leboyer and Bourguignon I used to construct the figure comparing British and French tariff rates. I cannot reconstruct their figures and so revert to material in the Tableau Décennal du Commerce.)

The French figures are robust to fairly substantial respecification. In contrast to the British figures, which change greatly depending on which weights are used, the French averages are fairly stable, partly a testimony to the low French rates and the extent to which so much of French trade was not subject to any tariff at all. In no case do the average tariffs increase by more than two to four percentage points. The numbers used in calculations were selected to bias the results upward. To deal with the problem of prohibitions on textiles, the effective tariff was assumed to be 50 percent. This figure was derived from the comparative prices on cotton yarn for the period from 1825 to 1864, calculated by O'Brien and Keyder (1978, p. 46) using an exchange rate of 25 francs to the pound. O'Brien and Keyder's figures show cotton yarn in France to be some 30 to 40 percent higher than in Britain during this period; 50 percent would seem to be a reasonable upper bound. This number is consistent with the writings of even the most fervent French protectionists who argued that a rate of 30 to 40 percent, consistently applied, would have been sufficient to defend existing producers against foreign competition.[7] Most of the textiles excluded had fairly elastic demands and therefore faced much smaller effective tariffs.[8] No easily comparable price series are available for wool, but woolen textile prices did not seem to be systematically higher in France than in Britain. Jean Marczewski's numbers show even a lower average price for raw wool in France than in Britain throughout the century (1965, p. xxii). At any rate, using the 50 percent markup from cotton yarn for wool is certainly an overestimate. Besides my using a high tariff rate in these cases, the use of the import composition of the 1860s and 1870s with the tariff rates for the earlier periods ignores any changes in income or responses to lowered textile prices that would have increased consumption of such products (so long as they could be imported), thus tending to overstate the weight of textiles in the recalculations. Any further adjustments that minimize the upward bias would only serve to confirm that French tariff levels averaged 10 to 15 percent for the 1840s and 1850s and 4 to 8 percent for the 1860s and 1870s.[9]

Another common concern centers around the problem of "openness," and rejects tariff levels as an inappropriate measure to begin with. This view would use a measure such as imports or total trade as a fraction of national product to indicate trade openness. The underlying idea is interesting, but the simple application is probably misleading. Given the resource bases and degree of trade specialization of the two countries, it is

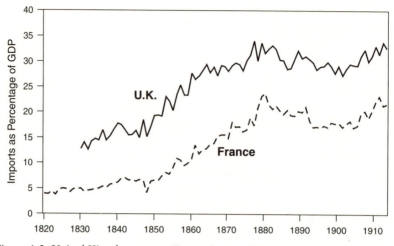

Figure 1.2. United Kingdom versus France Imports/GDP (Mitchell, 1988).

likely that Britain would have imported more goods and engaged in trade more heavily than France even if both nations had moved to "pure" free trade in the early 1800s, so the direct cross-sectional comparison would not be helpful. Thus, that the British ratio of imports to GDP is higher than that of the French throughout the nineteenth century might be evidence either of greater openness *or* of Britain's economy being less diversified in production than France's.

The change in the import/GDP ratio, however, can be a useful indicator of openness in a comparative static sense. All else being equal, a substantial liberalization in a country's trade regime should lead to a rise in its import/GDP ratio. In this regard, figure 1.2 is revealing. As you can observe, the import/GDP ratios for the two countries moved surprisingly in parallel throughout the nineteenth century, confirming the evidence from the nominal average tariff levels that the trade in imports of both countries was similarly improving and that both countries had liberalized around the same time. Had Britain been more vigorous or more successful in the pursuit of freer trade than the French, it is likely that the two ratios would have diverged more.

These ratios are particularly interesting for what they say about the insufficient comparisons heretofore undertaken in evaluating French and British performance. Examining the export/GDP ratio, the curves are quite similar. In fact the French and British ratios are virtually identical by the 1870s, belying the view that France was an unsuccessful trader and in particular the judgment of some that the French export sector underperformed in the last third of the nineteenth century (as argued in

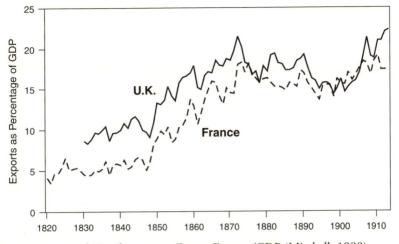

Figure 1.3. United Kingdom versus France Exports/GDP (Mitchell, 1988).

Lévy-Leboyer and Bourguignon, 1985). While the export/GDP ratio fell in France in the 1880s, the same was true for Great Britain—still acknowledged to be the world's leading trading nation. Thus, in structural terms, rather than reasoning from the absolute levels of trade, there is no reason to suppose that the French export sector and the French economy in general did not benefit fully from the worldwide liberalization of trade begun during the reign of Napoleon III. The increased stimulus of greater international competition almost certainly contributed to the enhanced efficiency and global competitiveness of French exporters.

Other potential objections to the comparison of average tariffs have to do with the role of effective protection, and more generally, the problem surrounding the different uses of the terms "free trade" and "protection." Although effective protection (that is the nominal tariff minus the weighted tariffs on inputs into the production of the items) is a useful and common measure of the productive distortions induced by a particular set of tariff policies (introduced by W. Max Corden, 1971), I believe that it is inappropriate in this context. Leaving aside entirely the difficulties in classifying and measuring all relevant intermediate inputs, the greatest concern I have with using effective protection to rank the two countries' trade policies is that it focuses on only one class of distortions resulting from tariffs—those concerning the effects of a tariff on domestic production.

In the discussions of trade policy in Britain and France, the one recurring problem is the difficulty of disentangling the various uses of the terms "free trade" and "protection." In particular, while protection is often viewed as simply the opposite of free trade, it is often defined more narrowly and simultaneously as something less than "unfree" trade. For some observers, protection involves only those instances in which tariffs are used to permit domestic industries producing import substitutes to survive by charging higher than competitive market prices. If this is protection then it does not come anywhere near exhausting what most of us instinctively understand as unfree trade. Ultimately, our interest should not be in protection so narrowly defined but in determining how far nations deviate from some ideal standard of free trade. Tariffs induce a variety of distortions both in consumption and production patterns at home and abroad. An index that gives us a rough idea of these barriers without focusing on any one set of distortions would be ideal; nominal average tariffs (appropriately weighted) do this more clearly than effective tariffs. A high tariff on items not produced at home should rightly be considered a deviation from free trade even if it does not thereby serve to "protect" a specific domestic industry.

Taking a cue from the public finance aspects of trade policy, some scholars tend to separate tariffs into those for protection and those for revenue. Ostensibly "protective" tariffs protect local producers while "revenue" tariffs merely tax consumption. Thus for these scholars it should not matter that Britain had high tariffs for revenue purposes because these were not "protective" tariffs but merely effective means of extracting revenue.

But in guessing at the intent and perhaps the reality of British tax collection, they miss the point of the debate on free trade. One should not confound issues of optimal tax policy with the very different question of which nation was more of a free trader. Questions of intent or of the political and economic effectiveness of a tariff structure should be separate from discovering the truth behind the existing stories of free trade Britain. Surely (to take a hypothetical extreme case), a nation with high (say 200 percent) average tariffs would not be a free trader whatever the reason for such tariffs. Conversely, we could have a nation (such as nineteenth-century France) that consciously sought to design and implement a tariff system that protected and aided various industries; yet, this same country also imposed tariffs in such a manner that the overall tariff level was low and trade was quite open despite the severity of restrictions on some items that were of limited importance to the overall trade. Yet it was precisely the trade in those items (such as textiles or other newer manufactures) that—given their political and historical significance—helped to shape our impressions of overall trade policy in the two countries. We can debate the importance of the types of restrictions imposed by the two nations, and we might choose to assert that some sorts of restrictions were worse than others, but we would now have to make the case explicitly. Moreover, we would not be allowed to assert that nineteenth-century Britain was the great free trader variously lauded and vilified in scholarship and popular mythology.[10]

Such distinctions between "protective" and "revenue" measures are ingenuous because they get the history of British-French commercial relations wrong. Most of the so-called British revenue tariffs were originally protectionist measures specifically designed to punish the French because of war and as reprisals for the commercial policies against the British dating from Louis XIV. As O'Brien has noted:

> Britain's tariffs were never mere devices for raising revenue. In their range and legal complexity they reflected a penumbra of objectives related to the nation's stance towards foreign, friendly and imperial countries within an evolving international economy. . . . As far as the Exchequer was concerned, navigation acts, codes for the regulation of imperial commerce and bilateral treaties with friendly powers represented real constraints on the possibility of raising more revenue in the form of duties on retained imports (O'Brien 1988, pp. 23–24).[11]

If French average trade levels were lower than, and at worst comparable to, those of Great Britain for virtually the whole of the nineteenth century (and particularly for the first part of the century and for the late Second Empire) how can such a pattern have been ignored for so long? Many conjectures are possible; the analysis will be confined to the most obvious.

Trade formed a much larger proportion of British production than it did in France for most of the century. This fact coupled with the much larger absolute level of total British trade was bound to make British trade policy seem more important to the world at large.[12] Given the high starting level of British tariffs, the steady and ultimately dramatic drop in the average level of British tariffs would have seemed doubly impressive to outside observers focusing on government action that affected very large volumes of trade. In contrast, much of France's commerce was internal and was more seriously affected by domestic economic developments than by trade policy. Tariff reform was a prominent and important accomplishment of Napoleon III, but it was only one part of a large-scale effort to modernize and stimulate the French economy. Furthermore, and despite discussion that has focused on the exogenous politics of the 1860 Treaty of Commerce, the falling average tariff rates show that there were substantial changes in France's overall trading regime even before the treaty came under discussion. Some of these changes were unplanned; others were simply unheralded. Other French reforms in the quarter century before the 1860 treaty did a great deal to improve trading conditions in France through the removal of older prohibitions and a

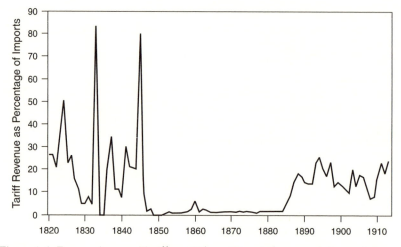

Figure 1.4. France: Average Tariffs on Wheat (Lévy-Leboyer and Bourguignon, 1985).

tariff "rationalization" (imposition of more uniform tariff rates). Like those promoted with only limited success by Huskisson in 1820s Britain, these improvements may not have received as much attention as did the 1860 treaty.

Certainly a large part of the impressions that have been retained about Britain's shift to free trade was owing to the intensity of the debates over the Corn Laws. Large drops in the tariffs on agricultural items were bound to affect British trade, and the ideological nature of the debate stamped commercial discussions in England henceforth. The spotlight on Corn Law repeal obscured the important, though less publicized, changes occurring in France. The graph of average tariffs in French wheat imports (see figure 1.4) shows the dramatic drop in rates around the time of the Corn Law repeal. Although the changes moved in parallel, the British talked of free trade while the French, even under Napoleon III, always spoke of going no further than moderate protection.

Free traders in both England and France were much more concerned with free trade for specific classes of goods they felt were vital to industry rather than with the generalized free trade favored by neoclassical economists. Lucy Brown writes in her study of the free trade movement that the free traders were not averse to tariffs of all kinds:

> It should be emphasized again that Radical free-traders of this kind expressed no objections to the general principle of deriving a large proportion of the public revenue from import duties. To the regressive

character of taxation which leant heavily on duties on tea, coffee, and sugar they were, as has been shown, largely indifferent, perhaps on the grounds that they were not necessities. There is also a final point. None of these duties, except those on timber, which were strongly attacked, and the duty on Swedish iron, were levied on raw materials used in industry, so that they could not be said directly to raise the price of exports. But in criticizing the corn laws a great deal of emphasis was placed on the argument, which was itself based on a subsistence theory of wages, that the corn laws raised wages and therefore indirectly the price of exports. This line of argument could equally well be applied to duties on tea, coffee, and sugar, but it was not used. The reason for this distinction was probably the commonsense one that there is a large degree of difference between the effects on the cost of living of the price of bread and the effects of the price of tea. Altogether then, there was nothing in the Board of Trade in 1840 comparable to the late Victorian propaganda for the "free breakfast table." (Brown, 1958, p. 157)

France too maintained high tariffs on items of consumption such as sugar, coffee, and olive oil, which made up the largest portion of French tariff revenues. What is striking is how relatively important the limited prohibitions on textiles and tariffs seem to have been in French trade overall. Opening up trade with Britain did increase French imports a bit, but not enough to matter in the overall scheme of things. For the most part that is because France's international trade was fairly open to begin with.

A substantial fraction of French imports were duty free and, though prohibitions may have distorted this figure in the first half of the nineteenth century, the proportion of duty-free items did not change much and even grew in the period when prohibitions were replaced with tariffs.[13] This runs counter to the intuitive notion that the existence of prohibitions masked the true extent of protection by biasing the fraction of duty-free imports upward relative to the years of freer trade. Table 1.3 shows that the proportion of French imports by value that were duty free stood at around 61 percent in 1849 and increased to 65 percent by 1869. What is remarkable is the stability of the shares of dutiable and duty-free items in value terms through periods of widely varying tariff levels and trade restrictions. Thus, with only a third of all imports being dutiable even in the period when moderate tariffs replaced all prohibitions, it should come as no surprise that even fairly large adjustments in the composition of earlier imports would not do much to raise the average tariff levels by more than a few percentage points. Certainly these are not enough to eliminate the 8 to 15 percent gap in average tariff

TABLE 1.3
Percentage of All French Imports Broken Down by Tariff Classification
using Current Values

	1849	1859	1869	1857–59	1867–69
Duty-free	20.82	19.10	19.97	21.43	19.96
Dutiable	18.73	16.86	17.55	19.05	17.67

Source: France, Direction Générale des Douanes, 1870

rates between Britain and France in the 1830s and 1840s, nor the larger gap that existed in the 1820s and early 1830s.

Perhaps the oddest aspect of received wisdom is that the high British tariffs on French products were simply anomalies, unrelated to the mercantilism of earlier centuries. The British tariffs on French wine were at the heart of mercantilist policy and can be traced back to trade struggles between Britain and France during the long reign of Louis XIV. Even in the nineteenth century the British recognized that the tariffs that remained were protectionist, as is evidenced by the report of the customs officials.

That the wine tariffs were at the heart of the commercial disputes between Britain and France is not in doubt. It was at the center of all negotiations for a century before the 1860 treaty. The leading historian of British commercial diplomacy of the period, Judith Williams, has written that, "the keys to commercial relations between France and Britain were war, political hostility, and commercial rivalry. Commercially each country tried to hurt the other, Britain by preferential duties for Portuguese wines as against French and by protective duties against French silks and woolens, and France by prohibitions and high duties directed against British staple products" (Williams, 1972, pp. 186–87). After negotiating the abortive 1786 treaty between Britain and France, Eden had fretted to the British ambassador to France that British manufacturers wanted, "to exact from this country the terms of the most favored nation as to all the manufactures in case we excel in them; but not to give those terms to wines because our climate does not produce them" (p. 189, citing F.O. 27/20).

Wine remained a problem throughout the nineteenth century after the earlier free trade experiment collapsed in the wake of the French Revolution and the continental wars. By the 1820s the issue of a possible treaty reappeared but as Williams notes:

Huskisson's plan in 1824 to remove prohibitions on French silks in favor of a duty of 30 percent seemed an opportunity for renewing the offer to reduce duties on French wines, in hopes that now France might be willing to lower her duties in steel, iron, copper, and brass, and if possible coal and tin. Instead France added prohibitions on more varieties of woollens and linens, but when Britain proposed an additional 20 percent on French products, which would keep out French wines, a convention for reciprocity in shipping was agreed upon on 26 January 1826. (pp. 191–92)

The British Parliamentary papers document both the extent of British tariffs and prohibitions in the earlier half of the century, and the extent to which the so-called revenue tariffs on wine, spirits, tea, sugar, and tobacco survived throughout the period of "free trade" and were used to protect both domestic and colonial industry.

The British parliamentary report speaks of "the long list of articles which were altogether prohibited to be imported, or could be imported under severe restrictions" lasting virtually unchanged until at least the 1830s, with a few surviving well into the 1860s (Great Britain, 1898, p. 38). In certain cases the prohibitions were said to have been holdovers from British rivalry with the Dutch and reflect the political influence of the East India Company.[14]

It was the commendable accomplishment of the British government to have simplified their tariff structure and eliminated most of these tariffs and prohibitions in the period from the late 1840s to the 1870s. But such measures were also being undertaken by the French, who attracted less notice (perhaps because they had less need of drastic reform in the first place). Moreover, the British emphasis on removing tariffs on *manufactured goods* and not on other "non-essential items" has caused us to ignore the protectionist aspects of those duties augmented "upon purely fiscal considerations" (Williams, 1972, p. 40).

More significant is the fact that the tariffs on wine and liquor imposed by Britain before the 1860 treaty by Britain were levied by volume of wine rather than by alcoholic content or value. This had the effect of favoring Spanish and Portuguese products in which British merchants had a direct interest over the products of Bordeaux and Burgundy.[15] The British Parliamentary report contains this query:

> In the present day, when the duty is levied according to alcoholic strength, it strikes the enquirer as curious that until 1831, French wine, which is alcoholically amongst the lightest of wines, should have been saddled with the highest duty of any description [per gallon]. But so it was, until the year mentioned, when the Wine Duties were greatly simplified, a duty of 5s. 6d. per gallon being then levied on all foreign wine without discrimination, and 2s. 9d. on Cape Wine. In 1840, by the addition of 5 percent to the duties, the two rates became severally 2s. 10 13/20 d. and 5s. 9 6/20 d. and so remained until 1860. (Great Britain, 1898, p. 141)

The French had long complained of the pernicious effects of the British tariff system on the French wine trade. Duties and excises on French alcohol to favor Portugal and Spain were initiated in 1667 and 1685 and had been augmented and refined since then both to protect British beverage interests and to generate revenue. A French report to the minister of commerce in 1858 remarked that French wines had been the British drink of choice in the seventeenth century, but that the preferential tariff treatment of Portugal and Spain and the British investment on the continent that followed had led to the French wines being displaced so that French exports to Britain had barely changed in the last hundred years. They were less in the mid-1840s than they had been in the late 1600s, and British per-capita wine consumption from all foreign countries had actually declined in the first half of the nineteenth century. Moreover, even after the tariffs on wine by volume were "equalized" in 1831, the French bore the brunt of the tariffs; the average barrel had a value of 300 or 400 francs whereas the Portuguese wines with higher alcoholic content were valued at 1,500 or even 2,000 francs (France, Archives Nationales, 1858). Other reports complained that the British were in the anomalous position relative to other nations (taking into consideration the dominance of French wine in world production and trade) of importing ten to twenty times as much wine from Portugal and Spain as from France and consuming substantially less wine in general than would have been warranted by growth in income and population.[16]

The degree to which French wines had been kept out of the British market and the degree of substitution of other wines can be seen from the fact that after the 1860 treaty, when the tariff on all liquor remained high but the gap between French and other wines was partly closed by duties set according to alcoholic strength, imports of French wine rose fivefold in the first decade. This matched the quantities imported from Portugal, and Spanish imports grew from a sixth to a half of in the same period; by 1882 French wine imports to Britain surpassed those from either Portugal or Spain (Great Britain, 1898, p. 156). Complaints that the British tariffs and excises still biased consumption toward the more expensive wines and protected British beer and tea, however, caused growth in total wine consumption from all foreign sources to proceed at a more measured pace.[17]

The section on spirits is equally revealing in that it explicitly discusses the problems of multiple discrimination employed in the British tariff system—with French products at one end, United Kingdom products at the other, and other foreign and colonial spirits in between. Foreign spirits, and especially French brandies, were either prohibited or taxed at a high rate to favor domestic and colonial spirits.[18] Although rum from the colonies enjoyed protection vis-à-vis foreign spirits, colonial producers complained of being excluded by tariffs designed to protect local British products such as gin and whiskey (p. 166). Protection of domestic and colonial producers extended further in the century than even the wine tariffs, which were substantially revised and lowered after the 1860 treaty while those for spirits were even raised. As France was a major producer of both wine and spirits, all this customs activity would have seemed quite exclusionary regardless of the fiscal motivation.[19]

One group, however, did notice that there was a British double standard with respect to free trade: the protectionists. In the vigorous battles over the first attempt at major tariff reform in 1856, a number of writers in France denounced British unwillingness to lower the duties on wine and spirits while vigorously promoting free trade. *Le Moniteur Industriel*, the leading protectionist newspaper, editorialized as follows on its front page:

> The wine-producing nations now know that they are the dupes in this great British market that should enrich them; they know that Great Britain will never sacrifice either their distilleries or their pubs for them. She [Britain] does not go so far in her devotion to the theories of free trade. From competition that she does not fear, she is willingly faithful [to free trade]. But free trade that touches her domestic production is another matter: she will hear none of it. . . . In Spain, as in France, the diplomats of liberalism have shamed the Spanish for their backward ideas regarding the protectionist system and have generously proposed establishing free trade between their two nations. Unfortunately, the Spanish asked if the free introduction of their wines was also included. They responded that that was a separate issue; that it touched too great a number of English interests; that Great Britain drew large revenues from her production of beer and of spirits; that these industries represented vast sums of capital, were the livelihood of masses of workers, and that England could never agree to make such a sacrifice on the altar of her principles. That is how the English understand the regime of free trade! . . . Everything to one side and nothing to the other. (*Le Moniteur Industriel, 1856, p. 1*)

These arguments have been forgotten partly because the protectionists used such rhetoric to bolster unsound and discredited theories, but mainly because trade reform eventually triumphed in France with the coming of the 1860 Anglo-French Treaty of Commerce. Still, however misguided their defense of protectionism may have been, their observations regarding the limitations of British tariff policy were accurate.

Although wine and spirits were the major focus of continental dissatisfaction over British trade policy, protectionist vestiges survived in other high-revenue products such as tobacco. For example, even when "reforming" the duties on raw tobacco and cigars in 1863 (which involved increased duties), the chancellor of the Exchequer spoke of trying "to avoid extending a protective duty to the British manufacturer" (Great Britain, 1898, p. 87). Yet on the average there was a "cover" to the British manufacturer (effective protection in making cigars) of 11 pence per pound. Said cover was an underestimate, established so that the laborers "who were employed in manufacture, amongst whom were women and children, might be well looked after" (p. 186).

Sugar duties were not done away with until 1874. Before then British manufacturers and British colonies had been well protected. Imports of raw sugar came almost exclusively from the West Indies before 1844, and refined sugar was derived entirely from domestic British production. In 1844 raw sugar imports were opened up, but protection was prolonged as a result of extraneous political concerns having to do with a bill designed to distinguish between free sugar and slave-produced sugar from foreign countries. After 1846 these distinctions were eliminated by Sir Robert Peel, but British refiners were protected until 1874 (p. 211).

In the final analysis, the paradoxical gap between historical perception and commercial reality is explained by the observation that writers who talked about trade policy did not really consider the economy as a whole. For the thousandth time it seems, scholars have confused the process of growth and development with industrialization most narrowly defined within a few areas of production: notably, textiles, machinery, iron, and steel. They have confused what was politically important with what was economically significant. When writers from John Clapham to A. L. Dunham spoke of the benefits of free trade they often looked to what was happening in the crucial "leading" sectors. Because France had prohibitions on textiles, for example, they were economically backward in relation to England. That France had no comparative advantage in mass-market cotton textiles, consumed large masses of raw cotton and wool for home production, and generally had a comparative advantage in agriculture and expensive silk and linens rather than spun cotton seems to have been overlooked.

The importance of certain traded commodities to the political debate has misled scholars into confusing trade and protection in these few areas with overall trade and protection.[20] Protection from the imports of French silks (in Britain) and English cottons (in France) dominated much of the political discussion of protectionism in the two nations, despite the fact that consumption of both items was always low in relation to total trade.[21] In contrast, agricultural products were important to both economies, so the British Corn laws and wine duties did increase the gap in the average tariff between France and Britain before the mid-nineteenth-century. In addition, both France and Britain derived many of their import revenues from coffee and tea, assorted foreign manufactures, and construction materials such as wood. These items were always a significant fraction of revenues, and fluctuations in demand for them were more dependent on changing incomes than on changing tariffs. Most of these imports came from nations outside the circle of the half-dozen world trading leaders and were likely to have been left out of discussions of policy designed to increase direct trade between France and Britain. In addition, the problems of colonial protection were an important determinant of trade policy.

Ultimately, there is no way to understand the nature and origin of British tariff policy toward France without focusing specifically on wine and beer (and corresponding taxes on brandy and spirits). The history of policy toward imports of French wine cannot be understood without going back to the period before the British tried to cut off most trade with France and went from imposing moderate tariffs with some protection to prohibitive tariffs that had large distortionary effects that colored both foreign and domestic policy for nearly two centuries.

The next few chapters explore the evolution of British trade history, particularly in relation to the wine trade with France, and demonstrate how the struggle over trade that began in the seventeenth century continued to exert a powerful influence on the history of both countries for the next two centuries, and arguably, down to the present day.

CHAPTER 2

The History of British Economic Policy

THE PURPOSE of this chapter is to provide a short chronology of British trade policy from 1689 to the end of the nineteenth century. It should serve as an overview of those historical events that are of particular significance to the problem of British commercial policy toward France, and whose legacy is central to the evolution of fiscal and commercial policy in the eighteenth and nineteenth centuries. It is also meant to highlight the fact that anti-French policy was not a late development. Indeed it was a recurrent, even persistent, feature of an evolving struggle that saw Britain and France emerge as rivals in the eighteenth century.

From an economic perspective, the Glorious Revolution has as good a claim as any of being the pivotal event in the founding of the modern era (cf. North and Weingast, 1989).

The ill-timed passage of the two Acts of Indulgence in 1687 and 1688—which in hindsight seem like moderate steps toward religious tolerance—aroused concern on the parts of Protestant partisans that King James was to be used as a means of Catholic influence by foreign powers. Growing concerns by the English over the possible establishment of a Catholic dynasty were followed by a usurpation of the throne by James II's son-in-law Willem van Oranje (William of Orange). William came from Holland to take the throne of England and, after the fact, convened Parliament in 1689 to provide the pretext that he had been invited to rule by the English people.

Much has been written of the political, cultural, and social ramifications of the ascension of William and Mary. The Glorious Revolution became the opportunity to establish a system that came remarkably close to a constitutional monarchy with the balance of power shared between the Crown and Parliament. The power to tax passed primarily to the Parliament. Although the King had the power to make war, he could not finance such ventures for the most part without the consent of the members of Parliament. These restraints on the Crown combined with the establishment of the Bank of England and resulted in improved financial discipline and a greater respect for private property rights. Moreover it ensured that spending would be tied to the capacity of Crown and Parliament to raise the appropriate funds to pay for the expenditures.

The deposition of James also had the effect of reshaping English foreign policy. As Louis XIV of France had been supporting, indeed, had openly subsidized the Catholic James II on a regular basis, so James's overthrow sharpened the enmity between Protestant England and Catholic France. Undoubtedly realizing that Louis would not tolerate this Protestant "takeover" of England, William preemptively declared war on France at the head of a coalition of England, the Netherlands, Spain, and the Holy Roman Empire.

Though France had emerged in the seventeenth century as the dominant power in Europe, the rise of a powerful, Protestant England guaranteed that these two nations would find themselves often at war. The rivalry between the two nations came to a head during the period from 1689 to 1713.

The period from 1688 to 1697 was dominated by conflict between France and a coalition of nations led by England (known as the Grand Alliance from 1689). Officially this was designed to resist French expansion in the Rhine but it was also seen by the English as a means of forestalling any French attempts to reinstall James as King. The end of the war was quickly followed in 1701 by a greater conflict upon the death of the Spanish Habsburg King Charles II. Since Philip V, his successor, was also a grandson of Louis XIV, there was a great deal of concern about French dominance of the Continent. The British and Dutch entered the war on the side of the Holy Roman Empire, which worked to preserve the rights of their claimants on the Spanish throne. The war would last for over a decade and would range over Europe and North America and only came to an end with treaties in 1713 and 1714. Philip V continued as King of Spain but gave up claims to the French throne.

Britain and France were therefore officially in conflict for a quarter of a century. During this time, in England there was almost always a ban on trade with France with only a brief interval of limited commerce between the two major wars. These conflicts would only come to an end with the death of Louis XIV. To a large extent this would turn out to be a temporary reprieve, as Britain and France would continue to be in conflict for much of eighteenth century. Their trade policies remained antagonistic in times of peace as in war.

War with France was not simply a military or political matter. Trade, and the struggles for greater access to world markets that would erupt into the pursuit of empire in the eighteenth or nineteenth centuries were to be preceded by a transformation in which Britain would have the capacity to protect and promote the interests of its exporters. Its principal expression was the direct defense of British ships and trade routes from French predation and on occasion from the participation of other nations such as Holland or Spain. But as Crowhurst (1977) has shown, the bulk of the raids were not seen in direct challenges from the official naval fleets but from the French privateers who were authorized to operate from St. Malo or Dunkirk. But if privateering was the most visible and concrete expression of the struggle for commercial supremacy, at a more abstract level, the "trade wars" that preceded and outlasted the military struggles were about the possibilities of taxation, the promotion of exports, and the regulation of trade at home and imports from abroad.

It was long a staple of British policy that commerce should be used as a means of furthering the political ends of the state. Notable among these attempts to subsume external commerce to the needs of state were the various navigation acts of the seventeenth and eighteenth centuries. Beginning in 1651, when the Parliament under Oliver Cromwell decided to restrict trade to England by banning foreign ships outside Europe from bringing imports, and then in 1660, when exports came under similar rules, the navigation acts were specifically designed to reserve trade for British ships, promote trade with friendly nations, and generally prohibit, regulate, or tax trade with rival powers. These acts and related commercial disputes were considered a major factor in the First Dutch War, 1652–54. Further acts and their amendments were to be a central feature of British commercial policy until their abolition in 1849. Notable among the later acts was the 1733 Molasses Act, which forced traders to forego the sugar trade with the French Indies in favor of the British colonies. The preference against France in favor of Portugal extended back to the seventeenth century, when Madeira had been exempted from crown duty in exporting alcohol to the Americas (cf. Hancock, 2000, p. 111). The Tories made an attempt to return to freer trade with France through the Treaty of Utrecht in 1713. But those efforts were in vain. The clauses that dealt with liberalization were defeated and the victorious Whig government of Walpole saw to it that protectionism would be continued.

In many ways the period from 1689 to 1815 can be viewed as an extended struggle between the major European powers and particularly between Britain and France. Officially, the struggles with France were about preserving the Protestant monarchy and staving off the influence of popish nations, but in practice religious fervor took a backseat to more mundane issues of state influence, colonial expansion, and international power politics. Though there were decades in which conflict was muted, the British and the French found themselves having to raise revenues either to fight a war or to prepare for the outbreak of war throughout the 1700s. John Brewer (1988) has amply documented the tight relationship between the expansion of the British state and the need to collect revenue.

The major conflicts of the eighteenth century, most notably the Seven Years' War (1756–63) and then the American Revolutionary War (1775–83), saw spikes in the British need for income that were really unprecedented in British history. This came on top of an upward trend of revenue collection throughout the 1700s that was already setting European records. Despite having had difficulties implementing income and excise taxes in the seventeenth century, England, then Britain (after the Union with Scotland in 1707), successfully managed to impose new taxes and to collect more revenue at an increasing pace.

One of the central tenets of mercantilism was not simply that trade expanded the capacity to wage war on one's enemies but that halting trade would diminish one's rivals. This was especially the case with France, and post-1689 many agreed with Davenant that "if this Interruption of their Commerce be yet more strictly pursued, it will bring a Ruin upon them, not to be avoided by all their Oeconomy, Courage and Policy (1695, p. 24)." Taxes at home involved rising excises on many items, but notably beer, malt, spirits, sugar, and related products for the production of alcoholic beverages. At the same time, custom duties complemented these taxes by providing some measure of protection for local industry and serving as a means of privileging one or another favored group.

Although most of the mercantilists, from Mun to Davenant to Petty to Steuart, were quite sophisticated in their linking of trade policy and strategic policy, they were prone to a common error that an export surplus (deficit) consisted of the sole gain (loss) from trade.[1] This misperception was so systematic that Adam Smith and his followers made it a focus of their attack on the mercantilists.[2]

One should not be tempted to believe that there was a tight theoretical model underlying policy. The essence of the mercantile view can be summed up by the simple idea that the needs of the state were synonymous with the needs of the nation. Certain writers mistakenly saw this as implying that trade surpluses were economically desirable because they promoted the inflow of specie, and these views have received the brunt of technical criticism in the economic literature. But these theoretical debates distract us from seeing that much of the mercantile policy was a pragmatic reaction to a world situation in which the need for defense combined with the more predatory desire to control larger portions of the globe; this subordinated almost all policy to the goals of thwarting ones' enemies and expanding the collection of various taxes at home.

Understanding why the great nations of Europe behaved in a mercantilist fashion is not the same as saying that such a policy was necessarily desirable. Indeed, it is sometimes suggested even today, with little evidence in support, that Britain prospered because of her mercantile policy.

Many writers have confused the success of Britain in developing colonies as a function of the mercantile policy with the success of the mercantile policy itself (cf. Morgan, 2002, p. 183). This is a common fallacy in the analysis of protectionism. It is undoubtedly the case that protecting and supporting some sectors may lead to the growth and prosperity of certain areas of the country or of particular economic sectors. But, absent any information about the global general equilibrium effects of the policy, one cannot conclude that the nation as a whole benefited. Indeed, when one factors in the deadweight inefficiencies of high taxation and large government with the costs of administering and defending the colonial empire, it is likely on both theoretical and empirical grounds that such large-scale expansion was on net, costly to the nation (the most detailed calculation of the economic burden of empire is still Davis and Huttenback, 1986).

Typical is the claim that absent imperial outreach Britain would not necessarily have spent these resources on productive activity. But this is a distraction. The argument for the inefficiency of mercantilism and the colonies does not depend on some hypothetical about perfect markets and global competition. So long as there were reasonable alternatives that would have resulted in less waste, there was a clear loss from mercantile policies. The only way in which mercantilism would have made sense is if the size of the spillover effects from these policies somehow outweighed their static costs. While it is easy to see why political pressures and the desire for international prestige would have pushed states to pursue these policies, it is hard to justify the expansion of empire or spending on the Navy as having contributed to, let alone serving as, a decisive factor in the development of the British economy.

Modern day research, such as that of Ormrod (2003), helps us understand the international context and the motivations of states such as Britain or the Netherlands in their quest for influence and power. It also provides us with good historical accounts of the extent to which states regulated their economies for the benefit of their political aims—a useful complement to modern theories of political economy. But the fact bears repeating that seeing some economic sectors prosper as a result of government intervention—whether directly through price controls, subsidies, or patronage, or indirectly through protection—does not in any way make the case for the efficiency or desirability of those policies. Absent a theoretically sound economic argument about the ways in which empire promoted overall economic development, accompanied by appropriate empirical evidence, the economists' presumption that such intervention is globally inefficient should be seen as decisive. At best it might be argued that the nature of political incentives was such that no more efficient policy was feasible. But that is simply an observation about the ways in which politics constrained productive behavior; in which case it becomes even more interesting to ask how Britain developed *despite* such inefficient interventions.

Periods of war were especially important because they reinforced the strong pressures to either eliminate or restrict imports from rival nations such as France. War encouraged both sides to think of commercial policy regarding trade and the encouragement of manufactures in terms of promoting a mindset that saw trade as a clear zero-sum game.

This also explains the growing importance that Portugal played in English trade as the English increased their presence and influence in Portugal beginning in the late 1600s. Anxious to find other outlets for their manufactures, the English took advantage of their privileged position in Portugal to promote bilateral trade agreements that would guarantee a market for English goods and develop substitutes for French imports such as wine or linens. The presence of English factories in Portugal— which were actually small areas controlled by the English on Portuguese soil for the production and processing of goods to be re-exported—was an important focus of bilateral policy.

The Methuen Treaty of 1703 between England and Portugal granted English goods, notably wool and cotton cloth, permanent access to the Portuguese market in exchange for guarantees of lower tariffs on Portuguese wines and spirits that would always be no higher than two-thirds the level of duties on other nations' wines and brandies. Though signed when England was still at war with France, the main provisions were maintained and even strengthened after the War of Spanish Succession had ended.

However, the desire to expand trade by encouraging exports at the expense of imports led to policies that even contemporaries viewed as contradictory before the coming of Adam Smith and the free traders. Most prominent of these were the Corn Laws that beginning in 1689 provided bounties to English exporters of grain. The act of 1689 provided bounties to be paid by the commissioner of commerce to exporters of wheat, rye, and malt while these goods were being taxed when imported from abroad or when consumed domestically (Barnes, 1961, p. 11). Other measures were designed to maintain the price of grain at a steady level domestically for the benefit of the consumer.

It is curious that despite the fact that little was accomplished with respect to the stability of prices and that the bounties on grain seemed to go against the desire of the Crown to encourage manufacturing, little was heard in the way of complaint regarding the bounties until the 1750s. At that point questions began to arise about the desirability of a policy that seemed to encourage the loss of grain for home consumption and which seemed to thwart the rising power of manufacturing by encouraging agriculture over industry and by hampering the imports of agricultural goods from nations that might be reciprocal buyers of English manufactures. This was probably less significant when Britain saw rising agricultural productivity and lower prices, as had been the case in the first half of the eighteenth century. But as the century drew to a close, Britain moved away from self-sufficiency in agriculture and increasingly came to depend on imports to feed the growing population. This was especially true of the urban areas such as London, which showed unusual growth and expansion.

Given the success and prominence of the British navy, it is no surprise that a crucial focus of mercantile policy was the expansion of empire, the struggle to deny territorial outposts to British rivals like the French, and the protection and promotion of trade most especially within the empire. Moreover, once interest groups benefited from a specific colony, protected trade, or similar colonial relationship, continued rent-seeking would have caused both merchants and statesmen to argue for the virtues of continued intervention (much as politicians today misleadingly argue that most government projects "create" jobs or protect industry). With well over a million pounds sterling of colonial trade passing through London at the end of the seventeenth century, there were a lot of rents to fight over. But it must be remembered that much of this trade was made possible by destroying or distorting other sources of trade, such as the bilateral exchange between Britain and France. Hence, the high levels of colonial trade are not evidence of the benefits derived by the English economy from this trade.[3]

As is commonly known the views of mercantile philosophers, with their focus on the importance of specie and the preference for exports over imports, began to be challenged on a regular basis in the eighteenth century. Schumpeter spoke for many writers before and since in noting that this transformation seemed to be part of a more general change in ideology: "Free-trade conviction began to spread as part of a general laissez-faire code. With the bourgeois public, the operative impulse was simply surfeit with bureaucratic overadministration . . . free trade was increasingly considered as a part of the autonomy of the individual, which was held to imply a 'natural right' to trade as he planned" (Shumpeter, 1954, p. 371).

The mature expression of this criticism came with Adam Smith's *Wealth of Nations*. This book, which is usually treated as the foundational work in economics and the central work of political economy of the Scottish Enlightenment, starts from the observation that all voluntary trade is mutually beneficial and proceeds to argue that competition for trade allows for specialization that increases the net output of society. The result is a system in which people pursuing their own self-interest still manage to promote the common good.

Smith spoke for all future free traders when he condemned the ideas behind the mercantile system, especially its equivalence of specie and wealth or of the preference for positive trade surpluses. He mentioned both the detailed restrictions on trade, especially vis-à-vis France, as well as the particularity of the Methuen Treaty with Portugal. He reserved special scorn for the various Corn Laws. Book IV, Chapter 5 is given over especially to the criticism of bounties of all kinds, and in particular those provided to farmers for their exports of grain. In this he was at odds with those such as Arthur Young (1770) who maintained that low prices in agriculture were a result of the proper functioning of the Corn Laws while simultaneously claiming that the bounties only served to regularize and not to raise the prices thereof.

Interestingly enough there was also pressure to change the laws because of the increased concern that Britain would not have enough grain and would lose out by encouraging exports. It is not yet clear which forces prevailed, but in 1773 a new Corn Law was passed that served as a compromise that drew the approbation of both supporters and opponents of the Corn Laws. Scholars have noted that 1773 may have simply seen the regularization of benefits at the average levels that were actually enjoyed during the preceding century and hence were not a drastic change in the regulatory regime (Barnes, 1961, p. 44). Smith did not approve of the continued bounties but was in favor of the lowered duty (or more precisely the lowered threshold for paying the lower duty rate) as well as the reduction in the bounty price. As he stated at the end of the chapter on bounties, "we may perhaps say of it what was said of the laws of Solon, that, though not the best in itself, it is the best which the interests, prejudices, and temper of the times would admit of " (Smith, 1776, Book IV, Chapter 5, p. 543).

Smith is especially important because his comments about the Corn Laws played an important role in subsequent debates in the nineteenth century about their reform. What is especially interesting is the tendency to overlook Smith's remarks on restrictions on the importations of wine—which he often used as an example of mercantilism—when discussing the influence of his work on British "free trade" in the nineteenth century. Smith however had been quick to note how unusual were the higher duties on French wines than those of other nations, most especially Portugal. In many cases tariffs on French goods were effectively a form of prohibition.[4] Smith went on to note that the French had similar restrictions on British exports, although he admitted that he was not well acquainted with the specifics as such.

It seems that in the spirit of an increasingly liberal consensus and of a desire to make peace with France, the Eden Treaty of 1786 was signed as a bilateral agreement between France and Britain. While not nearly as far-reaching a document as the Anglo-French Treaty that would be signed in 1860, what is notable about the Eden Treaty is that it already began to make some provision for lightening the burden on French wine and spirits albeit without returning to the open trade of the seventeenth century. It was hoped by many of its supporters that the treaty would serve as a precursor to a more extensive agreement later on.

Those who had hoped for the restoration of normal commercial relations with France, however, were to be disappointed by the upheaval of the French Revolution. Between the Revolution itself, the Directorate, and the Terror, quickly followed by Napoleon and the Napoleonic Wars, Britain and France were to find themselves at odds with one other for another quarter century from 1789 to 1815, a full century after the lengthy outbreak of hostilities that had crippled bilateral trade from 1689 to 1715. There was little time for the Treaty to take full effect and any positive transformation of British commercial policy toward France would have to wait until the middle of the 1800s.

The quarter century from the beginning of the French Revolution to the end of the war with Napoleon did more than destroy all hopes for improved trade relations between the leading European nations. This period may have contributed to a split in policy directions that would play a critical role in domestic policy changes throughout the nineteenth century. Whereas France paid lip service to property rights, but systematically diminished their reliability through confiscations, a disastrous inflation, the coming of the Terror, the shift to dictatorship and then Empire, a foolish experiment with the creation of a continental bloc that excluded the British (cf. Crouzet, 1987) and of course, the direct and indirect harms of a long and disastrous war, the British seemed to be making progress toward a more liberal society despite their mercantilist restrictions.

It is significant that the end of the nineteenth century saw the confluence of a liberal move toward freer trade in all areas of domestic and international commerce, as well as fiscal pressures to change the ways in which the state related to the economy. Sometimes the transformation is presented as a straightforward intellectual transformation where Britain is mercantilist in the eighteenth century and a free marketer in the nineteenth. But this ignores the strong pressures from existing interest groups. This is not the same as the Marxist view that sees the changes in policy as evidence of a class struggle. Rather, changes in the elites' views of the economy interacted with deeper structural changes in technology and the underlying pattern of political relations. The latter placed limits on what could be accomplished by thinkers and politicians, but there is no doubt that the switch in favor of liberal trade was real even if the reason for the widespread support of what may be called the Smithian view is not fully known.[5] It is especially significant that, even though the Napoleonic Wars led to an expansion in the size and role of the state, the British government did not use the war as a pretext for the kind of regulatory stretch that characterized many other wartime regimes. Britain continued to support a very liberal and bourgeois view of property rights, which led to a very modern, almost twentieth-century style of financing and conducting a large-scale war.

It should be noted that the greatest folly of this period undoubtedly belonged to the French, in particular Napoleon's idea of destroying Britain by depriving her of trade. The so-called Continental Blockade was an attempt to create a European trading area that would facilitate trade within the continent of Europe while excluding England from the benefits she had derived from commerce. As it stands, it is unclear whether the French had in fact suffered more from these restrictions than the British, inasmuch as limiting trade with the British Isles restricted contact with British inventors at a time when they were revolutionizing the industries of textiles, iron and steel, power generation, and other areas of manufacturing during the period that historians have retrospectively dubbed, the Industrial Revolution. It is noteworthy that even in the midst of the Continental Blockade both Britain and France agreed to a limited exception that permitted a small trade in fine wines to continue under special licensing against a backdrop of otherwise fully interrupted commerce.[6]

The end of the Napoleonic Wars in 1815 has proved to be a turning point in hindsight. The period from 1815 until the beginning of World War I was unusual for its relatively high degree of peace. Compared to the more extensive wars of the eighteenth century, the smaller and sporadic conflicts of the nineteenth century did little to perturb the lives of the majority of people in Western Europe and complemented a century in which the fruits of the Industrial Revolution spread throughout the continent. From the mid-nineteenth century, even ordinary workers were increasingly able to observe a steady rise in their wages and standard of living (cf. Burnette and Mokyr, 1995), and Europe was marked by an unprecedented coincidence of rising population totals and improved per-capita incomes.

An important shift in tax policy came with the ending of the Napoleonic Wars. Whereas the British had successfully enacted a temporary income tax to fund the war, opposition pressure was sufficiently strong that attempts by the government to extend the tax in 1815–16 were summarily defeated (Douglas, 1999, p. 44). At first there was a move to simply lower the tax rate, but when that was defeated the tax itself was quickly abolished. The Malt Tax, an important wartime measure, was also removed to the delight of agricultural interests. The government had to seek recourse in the money market to fund the budget. But the equilibrium in Parliament, and Britain in general, was moving away from farm interests.

The rapid shift of Britain's economic center of gravity from agriculture to industry led to pressures to move away from policies that favored farmers to those that were compatible with the wishes of manufacturing. These broad trends were also matched by the rise of a liberal ideology derived from Adam Smith and his successors that focused on the virtues of more open trade and fewer regulations at home and abroad. The coincidence of changes in the underlying economic interests, as well as transformations in the ideas that guided many members of the ruling classes, paved the way for the debates that eventually led to the repeal of the various agricultural subsidies on export and import duties on grain that were generally referred to as the Corn Laws. A tax on imports was imposed on corn in 1815, if prices fell below a certain level. Later as prices rose the law was modified so that a sliding scale was implemented after 1828, with duties at different levels designed to be highest when agricultural prices were low.

A huge literature has emerged on the repeal of the Corn Laws, and the interested reader should consult some of the specialist works for the details of the transformation that led to the budgets of 1842 and later (e.g. Hilton, 1989). The essential point is that a coalition of free trade liberals led by the Anti-Corn League had begun to promote free trade through a process that focused first on the abolition of the Corn Laws, and then sought to push for complete free trade by abolishing all other duties and prohibitions.

Beginning in 1842 Peel began to reduce taxes on hundreds of items while proposing new income taxes that would remove some of the pressure from customs for revenue. By 1846 a plan to abolish the Corn Laws and most other taxes on imports was pushed through Parliament. However, most of these duties did not play a large factor in overall revenue, and many of the critical tariffs on items such as wine, brandy, coffee, tea, sugar, and rum remained essentially unchanged or were slightly modified. Despite the insistence that these tariffs were simply revenue duties designed to match domestic excises, they were set much higher than domestic excises on beer, for example. In fact, these tariffs effectively prohibited the cheapest class of wines from entering Britain, a method that did not maximize revenue from customs. As shown later, this was necessary to protect the government's ability to tax domestic brewing (cf. Nye, 1993).

A change in government did not do much to reverse the trend toward liberalizing policy under constraints. And Prime Minister William Gladstone's first budget in 1853 resulted in further tariff reductions—again, mostly on items of limited weight in the trade totals—and modifications in domestic taxes. During this time Britain had become the world leader in textile manufacture and had begun to see the fruits of the Industrial Revolution. Free traders pushed for freer trade in manufactures worldwide but could not make headway with either the French or the Spanish because of British intransigence over their wine tariffs. Eventually the government of Napoleon III in France was able to reach an agreement with Britain in 1860 that caused Britain to modify her tariffs dramatically, including those on wine, in exchange for France lowering her duties while removing all prohibitions on British products.

The Unbearable Lightness of Drink: Assessing the Effects of British Tariffs on French Wine

> [W]e have laid on such an enormous amount of duty that
> nothing but wines of the very strongest character, the effect of
> which could be suddenly felt in the head, were ever thought
> worth purchasing. When a man had to pay 6d. or 9d. for a
> glass of wine containing a few thimblefuls, he wanted
> something which would affect his head for his money; he would
> not buy the fine, natural, and comparatively weak wines of
> France, though every other country in the world but England
> has regarded French wines as the best wines in the world. The
> English taste had been adulterated, and our people, or those
> who could afford it, have preferred the narcotic and
> inflammatory mixture which is called port, or even sherry.
> —*Richard Cobden, Rochdale Speech, June 26, 1861*
> *(Bright and Rogers, 1908)*

WINE was for many centuries one of the two or three most important sources of export revenue for France and was the most important cash crop throughout the seventeenth, eighteenth, and nineteenth centuries. France's domination of the world market in wine extended back into the fifteenth and sixteenth centuries, and many of its leading products could point to a much older history. However, wine, a highly popular and visible commodity, was also an easy target of foreign taxation. Its sales to other nations were often at the mercy of the changing political winds. By the seventeenth century French wines were securely established as a major British import, and claret, or red Bordeaux, was the drink of choice in the court of Charles II. This happy situation for the French was not to last. A "temporary" tax on wine in 1670 was extended and then renewed permanently. Concerns over imports of French wine that had loomed large since the fifteenth century impelled the British to gradually raise tariffs on French products, while still preserving France's role as the major supplier of wine to the world.

Attempts have been made to determine the volume of wine imports in England prior to the seventeenth century. Various wine historians have tried to calculate imports of British wine from France by focusing on

TABLE 3.1
Total Wine Exports from Bordeaux

	Tuns	Imp. Gallons
At peak 1303–37	83,165	17,464,650
During mid-century crises 1337–56	14,282	2,999,220
During govt of Black Prince (1356/69)	30,000	6,300,000
During crises of 1366–69	11,400	2,394,000
During difficulties of 1440–53	11,000	2,310,000

Source: Francis (1972) based on Higounet (1962).

Note: These are the earliest figures from Bordeaux converting at 1 tun = 252 old gallons (5 imp gal = 6 old gal). No complete English import figures exist, but it is said that half of the exports went to England during the occupation of Aquitaine while in the later Middle Ages about 30,000–40,000 tuns were exported annually. Exports declined during the Hundred Years War reaching a low of 3000 tuns when England lost Aquitaine(1453). Subsequently, exports increased to 5000–6000 tuns in 1475 and 8000–10000 tuns in 1476–79.

direct trade with Bordeaux, the largest wine exporting region of France. For the period prior to the mid-1600s the data are not very precise, but the rough figures that exist indicate a much larger wine trade in some years of the fifteenth and sixteenth centuries than that of a typical year in the late 1600s.

Tables 3.1 and 3.2 include data taken from A. D. Francis's history of the wine trade (1972) based on published work of M. K. James (1951–52) and Charles Higounet (1962). For ease of reading, all of Francis's figures of old tuns have been converted into British imperial gallons. While many of these numbers are somewhat suspect the range is such as to indicate that 3.5 to 4 million gallons a year was not unusual for the fifteenth and sixteenth centuries. Further, if André Simon's work (1909) is to be accepted, imports from Bordeaux alone may have reached a high of 6 to 10 million gallons in some years of the late 1560s, with averages around 5 million.

These estimates are roughly twice or even three times the figures given for *total* imports of wine from all sources given by the customs office for 1675, when systematic official estimates first became available. If one considers the qualitative change in the consumption of wine as well as the cumulative effects of rising seventeenth-century tariffs, the impressively large imports of British wine on the eve of war with Louis XIV were themselves below what they might have been had free trade prevailed between Britain and France.

And yet the British continued to drink large amounts of wine a century before the Industrial Revolution and the accompanying rise of the middle class. Considering what is known about the extent to which the

TABLE 3.2
Henry VIII's Reign—Average British Imports by Type
(First Half of Sixteenth Century).

	Tuns	Imp. Gallons
Non-sweet wines		
A.	6,959	1,461,390
B.	1,604	336,840
Sweet wines		
A.	14	2,940
B.	103	21,630
Malmseys		
A.	687	144,270
B.	435	91,350
Totals		
Average for half century	9,800	2,058,000
for 1509	4,194	880,740
for 1521	17,518	3,678,780
for 1542	15,494	3,253,740

Source: Francis, 1972
Note: A = imports (tuns) in English ships; B = in foreign ships.

population would grow over the next century and a half and the degree to which modern economic growth would begin to set in, British wine consumption can be seen as having been in its infancy. Indeed, the *vignerons* of Bordeaux and elsewhere in France, though ignorant of the extent to which Britain would emerge as a major economic force in the next century or two, looked forward to a prosperous and ever expanding trade with the British.

But changes in the international political situation saw Britain tilt toward Portugal, and this preference was translated into tariff policy that favored Portuguese products. The British had long been interested in developing a wine market in Portugal to offset Britain's perceived dependence on imports from France.

The cessation of hostilities at the end of the War of Spanish Succession did not lead to business as usual with France. In 1713 Parliament rejected most favored nation articles in the commercial treaty with France, while maintaining the Methuen Treaty with Portugal. Although French wines (especially the *vin ordinaire*) tended to be lighter (in alcoholic content) on average than the Spanish or Portuguese wines and were of lower value by volume, the French wineries had to pay substantially higher duties per gallon than did the Spanish or Portuguese. French brandy, most likely a competitor with port and sherry, was taxed at a still higher rate.[1] Most important of all, the imposition of tariffs on a volumetric basis meant much higher effective ad valorem duties on cheap wines relative to the best wines. In effect, this kept virtually all of the cheaper and more common wines out of the British market until the 1860s when, thanks to the Anglo-French Treaty of Commerce, the duties were lowered and applied on the basis of alcoholic strength.

Although precise information on wine prices that is carefully broken down by quality at the wholesale and retail level is not possible to come by, Simon (1909) put together a table of wine prices that allow us to see how the price of typical French wine—both the *vin ordinaire* and the more desirable claret—compared to the more alcoholic sherries (or sack) of Spain. Generally speaking, the lighter products of France were cheaper on a volumetric basis than the Spanish products. For ordinary beverages, which excludes the really fine claret, champagnes, or burgundies, there was usually a rough correspondence between price and alcohol content, making all necessary allowance for fashion and perceived quality by national origin. Nonetheless it seems clear the ordinary clarets were generally priced about 60 to 75 percent of the price of the sack/sherry/muscadel per gallon, and the more nebulous category of "French wine" (which might or might not have included some claret) was more typically about half or less of the price of sack.

Thus any fixed custom duty levied on a volumetric basis would lower the quantity demanded of all wines and spirits affected and would change the relative quantities demanded of the two products. This clearly shifts consumption away from the nominally cheaper product to the costlier, which though still costlier in absolute terms, would now have declined in relative price. This is a straightforward consequence of the elementary Law of Demand. The net result was to virtually prohibit the import of the cheaper classes of French wine. The tariff would have been discriminatory for the French wines relative to all competing beverages— whether the aforementioned sack and later Portuguese equivalents, or the homegrown beers, whiskies, and gins, which would have had to pay no customs duties.

The virtually prohibitive character of the fixed volumetric tariffs can be seen from the fact that even measures that equalized tariffs by volume on wine from all foreign countries in 1831 did little to change imports of French products. This resulted from Spanish/Portuguese wines having much stronger alcohol content and costing three times as much as the very cheapest French wines known to have been imported, making the duties relatively less important ad valorem. Only the adjustments resulting from the 1860 Treaty of Commerce began to approximate ad valorem rates a little better by establishing alcohol content as the principal basis for setting the tariff duties.

In addition to the problems of the discriminatory and prohibitive tariff that persisted until the mid-nineteenth century, French imports were constantly suppressed as domestic excises were manipulated to grant beer a reasonable margin of protection. Throughout this whole period (1700–1860) it was mostly the highest quality and highest priced French wines and spirits that continued to be imported (such as the best Bordeaux claret). Demand for these products remained strong, especially as wealth at the top of the income distribution increased, but the tariff was also less binding since it was lower on a percentage basis.

Indeed, much of the development of high-quality, high-priced claret was a response to the fixed, volume tariffs on French wine. Throughout the eighteenth century the French pushed to produce and export higher quality, higher priced wines for sale to the British. Developments that encouraged high quality and demanded long cellaring became more desirable relative to the cheap, quick-drinking wines that could not sell when burdened with heavy duties. Yet, for all the innovation and effort to push the high end of the market, even these wines entered at substantially lower levels for most of the 1700s than had been typical of the mid-1600s.

It is instructive that in reviewing the history of the British wine tariffs the authors of the Parliamentary inquiry into the history of customs and tariffs published in 1898 noted: "In the present day, when the duty is levied according to alcoholic strength, it strikes the enquirer as curious that until 1831 French wine, which is alcoholically amongst the lightest of wines, should have been saddled with the highest duty of any description" (Great Britain, 1898, p. 141). Most of these duties were imposed over the course of the eighteenth century to extend and increase the already serious duties on French wines that were in place during the reign of Charles II. Furthermore, William III, George II, and George III imposed new duties on French wines—which were not imposed at all or, if so, at a much lower level on competing imports from Spain and Portugal—essentially eliminating trade in all but the elite of French wines. Many of these tariffs did little to raise total revenues; rather, they facilitated protection of local spirits and countered French attempts to circumvent the volume tariffs by creating higher quality wines with a greater capacity for lengthy storage.

These duties extended British efforts from the mid-1600s onward to shift their imports of wine from France to Spain and Portugal. This tendency had already been noted in the late 1600s. Initially (during the war periods of 1689–1713) this meant that some French wines entered Britain listed as the products of Spain or Portugal. Indeed, the early 1700s is the period when the trade data are most suspect, because of the likelihood of French wines being smuggled into Spain and Portugal to be re-exported and relabeled as local product. But the long duration of the prohibitions led to renewed efforts to increase production of Portuguese wines, and the 1703 Methuen Treaty caused commercial production in Portugal destined for export to Britain to be focused almost solely on wines and spirits. The British aided and encouraged their allies on the Iberian Peninsula to develop viable substitutes for the superior products of their political enemy and economic rival, sending representatives to educate and in some instances engage in viticultural espionage for them. Wine makers in Portugal and Spain took cuttings from Bordeaux, and British partners and even government consuls pushed for the development of wines whose character more closely approached that of the French than the typical fortified products. Christian Huetz de Lemps cites Casaux du Hallay, deputy from the Nantes Conseil de Commerce, who noted:

> [The English] have long urged the peoples of these countries [Spain and Portugal] through their consuls and emissaries to plant vines everywhere; and since the climate, being hotter than that of France, produces wines which are not suitable to the palate, they have established and sent to these regions gourmets to harvest less mature grapes, and, in making wine before the regular harvest, produced wines that were not as strong; the youngish grapes correcting the natural liquor produced and thus resulting in wines that approached the taste of those made in France. (Huetz de Lemps, 1975, p. 118)

Nevertheless, the attempt to produce Portuguese wine that mirrored the products of the Gironde had little success throughout the eighteenth century, and the tariff policy chosen by the British only reinforced the tendency to switch away from claret; the common people moved to beer for lighter drinking and the upper classes redefined their taste for the best Bordeaux and the finer Ports.

All the efforts to promote production in the Iberian Peninsula did not change the fact that France retained an edge in producing higher quality wines. The French had an absolute advantage in the production of wines that could be stored for half a dozen years or so throughout the eighteenth century. Their main competitor in the world market, Spain, did not yet have the technology to produce high quality, long-lasting wines. According to Huetz de Lemps (1975) the earliest recorded attempts to create wines in the Bordelais style (i.e. suitable for cellaring) did not commence until 1787, and this met with little initial success. At that time Spanish wines could not even survive the year-long trip to the new

TABLE 3.3
British Wine Imports for Selected Years

	Tuns	Imp. Gallons
1675		
French	7495.0	1,573,950
Portuguese	20.0	4,200
Spanish	4012.0	842,520
Italian	30.0	6,300
German	539.0	113,190
Total	12,096	2,540,160
1677[a]		
French	9789.0	2,055,690
Portuguese	177.0	37,170
Spanish	5272.0	1,107,120
Italian	104.0	21,840
German	808.0	169,680
Total	16150.0	3,391,500
1679–1685[b]		
French	0.5	105
Portuguese	5833.0	1,224,930
Spanish	5781.0	1,214,010
Italian	112.0	23,520
German	2748.0	577,080
Total	14474.5	3,039,645

Source: Francis, 1972
Note: Large swings from year to year with Spanish reaching 8,420 and 11,286 in 1680 and 1684 and Portuguese 13,861, 16,772, and 12,186 tuns in the years 1682, 1683, 1685 though only 1000–2000 tuns in last four years.
[a]Before Prohibition of French wines
[b]Average during Prohibition

world that was needed for transatlantic trade. Spanish and Portuguese wines tended to be mixed with stronger brandies to help preserve them when shipped to Britain. Again, the high duties imposed per bottle guaranteed that the only wines entering Britain from France were mostly the clarets of the highest quality.

Thus, the French wines were kept out of the British market during a period of rapid growth in income and population.[2] The French wine merchants benefited little from the increases in demand that accompanied the revolutions in agriculture and industry and from Britain's fourfold increase in population over a century and a half. Just as importantly, cheap

TABLE 3.4
British Wine Imports from the Principal Places of Origin

Averages for the Years 1686–89	old tuns	imperial gallons	fraction of total
French	13,401	2,814,210	71.6%
Portuguese	434	91,140	2.3%
Spanish	3,914	821,940	20.9%
Italian	159	33,390	0.8%
German	796	167,160	4.3%
Total	18,704	3,927,840	100%

Note: During the war from 1690–96, no French wines imported except 770 tuns at the very start.

TABLE 3.5
British Wine Imports during the Years of War and Prohibition

Averages for the Years 1690–96	old tuns	imperial gallons	fraction of total
French	0	0	0%
Portuguese	5,491	1,153,110	42.4%
Spanish	6,253	1,313,130	48.3%
Italian	61	12,810	0.5%
German	839	176,190	6.5%
Total	12,954	2,720,340	100%

Source: Francis, 1972

TABLE 3.6
British Wine Imports in Old Tuns

	France	Portugal	Madeira	Spain	Other	Total
Year						
1713	2,458	5,861	112	4,116	3,360	15,907
1714	1,196	8,652	308	5,605	2,872	18,633
1715	1,261	10,334	387	6,768	2,967	21,717
1716	1,568	8,923	179	4,718	3,417	18,805
Ten-year averages						
1717–26	1,297	12,066	195	7,458	1,480	22,496
1727–36	845	12,211	380	8,467	1,029	22,932
1737–46	374	12,330	542	3,305	481	17,032
1747–56	490	10,321	607	3,867	384	15,669
1757–66	541	11,221	754	3,555	493	16,564
1767–76	491	11,849	952	3,554	319	17,165
1777–86	436	11,300	548	2,434	196	14,914

Source: Francis, 1972

TABLE 3.7
British Wine Imports in Imperial Gallons

	France	Portugal	Madeira	Spanish	Other	Total
Year						
1713	516,180	1,230,810	23,520	864,360	705,600	3,340,470
1714	251,160	1,816,920	64,680	1,177,050	603,120	3,912,930
1715	264,810	2,170,140	81,270	1,421,280	623,070	4,560,570
1716	329,280	1,873,830	37,590	990,780	717,570	3,949,050
Ten-year averages						
1717–26	272,370	2,533,860	40,950	1,566,180	310,800	4,724,160
1727–36	177,450	2,564,310	79,800	1,778,070	216,090	4,815,720
1737–46	78,540	2,589,300	113,820	694,050	101,010	3,576,720
1747–56	102,900	2,167,410	127,470	812,070	80,640	3,290,490
1757–66	113,610	2,356,410	158,340	746,550	103,530	3,478,440
1767–76	103,110	2,488,290	199,920	746,340	66,990	3,604,650
1777–86	91,560	2,373,000	115,080	511,140	41,160	3,131,940

Source: Francis, 1972

TABLE 3.8
Share of British Wine Imports by Place of Origin

	France	Portugal	Madeira	Spain	Other	Total
Year						
1713	0.155	0.368	0.007	0.259	0.211	1.00
1714	0.064	0.464	0.017	0.301	0.154	1.00
1715	0.058	0.476	0.018	0.312	0.137	1.00
1716	0.083	0.475	0.010	0.251	0.182	1.00
Ten-year averages						
1717–26	0.058	0.536	0.009	0.332	0.066	1.00
1727–36	0.037	0.532	0.017	0.369	0.045	1.00
1737–46	0.022	0.724	0.032	0.194	0.028	1.00
1747–56	0.031	0.659	0.039	0.247	0.025	1.00
1757–66	0.033	0.677	0.046	0.215	0.030	1.00
1767–76	0.029	0.690	0.055	0.207	0.019	1.00
1777–86	0.029	0.758	0.037	0.163	0.013	1.00

Source: Francis, 1972

French wines were unavailable at the very moment in history when mass consumer tastes were formed, establishing the peculiar British national taste so evident in the nineteenth century—beer and gin drinking at the low end of the scale and sherry, port, and expensive claret at the higher income levels. Even after nineteenth-century trade reform the duty and taxes on wine and liquor still kept the French from offering the British public any table wines cheap enough to be fully competitive with beer (Briggs, 1985, p. 65: "Nor was there any wine as cheap as beer—at 2½ d per pint" [quoted from Minutes of Evidence of the Select Committee on Wine Duties, 1879]). Although wine tariffs were supposed to have been set equal to domestic excises on beer, British trade statistics show that excises on beer were adjusted (and even abolished for part of the late nineteenth century) and remained roughly 50 to 60 percent lower on an ad valorem basis than average tariffs on wine.

To some extent these numbers may exaggerate the effects of the prohibitions in the early part of the 1700s because a great deal of French wine was smuggled in the first decade or two. But the strict impositions of volumetric duties at least removed the problem of underreporting of value common to other items. Furthermore, as British interests in Portugal and Spain began to develop viable wine production in quantity, there was less of a desire or willingness to import or smuggle the cheapest wines that were the greatest potential source of competition for British beverage interests. However, this was offset by the fact that smuggling almost certainly was focused on the more expensive wines because they were easier to conceal (relative to their value), and the tariff had been designed in such a way as to make its burden least onerous on those very same wines, eliminating much smuggling.

PARALLELS IN DISTILLING: THE RISE AND FALL OF THE GIN AGE

A related but different dynamic involved changes in the market for stronger alcoholic beverages. Distilling in its simplest forms was common throughout Britain in the seventeenth century as a form of home brew. However, professional distilling began to emerge as an important force in the early 1600s. Moreover, rum was being introduced from the colonial possessions. Nonetheless the market for professionally produced spirits was repressed by the coming of excise taxes on all local liquor beginning in 1643. Initially foreign spirits from wine or cider were untaxed, though the situation rapidly changed so that domestic liquors paid a tax of eight pence per gallon while the top rate on foreign brandy and spirits was as high as a shilling per gallon (Harper, 1997, pp. 73–74).

This did little more than slow the growth in demand for spirits. What was more interesting is that foreign produce was of sufficiently high quality and local spirits sufficiently poor that demand for the former continued to outstrip the latter, with some estimates in the 1680s showing between 527,000 and 700,000 gallons produced at home versus 1.5

million imported from France alone (p. 78). Rum had been considered such poor fare that it was described as "a mean spirit that no Planter of any Note ... will deign to drink" (p. 73, citing John Oldmixon, 1741), yet it was still preferred to the English spirits.

It is only with the mix of prohibitions and the coming of war in 1689 that the local distillers received the protection they needed to thrive and expand. As with wine the war saw the spirits industry flourish and the end of war saw prohibitive import duties designed to keep out foreign liquor and to punish France relative to Spain and Portugal, while granting protection to colonial and domestic interests. The industry also received a boost in 1729 when confiscated wines (due to smuggling or spoilage) were allowed to be made into spirits (Harper, 1997, p. 104). Unlike beer, however, there was not as much industry concentration, which led to an expansion that was initially unchecked and difficult to regulate.

Some estimates (see Coleman, 1977) claimed as much as a ten-fold increase from 1684 to 1750 in production of distilled liquor. Taxation of this product led to increases in revenue at first, but by the early 1700s production of spirits climbed without a corresponding increase in revenue. Heavy taxation of malt led to shifts in the production of spirits from unmalted grain (Harper, 1999, p. 135). And a 1729 law to increase taxation and impose licensing seems to have been widely evaded, leading to repeal in 1733. This rise in production hit a peak of 8.2 million gallons of spirits subject to official taxation in 1743 (Mitchell, 1988, pp. 401–11), with much more in clandestine production. This period of expanded liquor consumption and the complaints about public drunkenness is often called the "Gin Age."

The Gin Age provoked the rise of the temperance movement with its broadsides against alcoholism and public intoxication. But it also aroused the concern of the more established distilleries and the beer brewers who were under more stringent controls. This eventually led in 1751 to the statute 24 George II c. 40 (The Tippling Act), which simultaneously increased taxation on spirits and above all limited the locations where liquor could be produced and sold. Poor harvests in the 1750s also led to short-term prohibitions on the production of liquor from grain so that spirit production fell from 6.3 million gallons in 1750 to 3.1 million in 1757 to a measly 863 gallons (official statistics) in 1758 and zero in 1759. Distilleries had rapidly gone out of business or were demolished.

Eventually complaints about this and the return of good harvests led to a relaxation of the ban on corn distilling. But the continuance of high taxation and very strict regulation meant that only twelve of the hundreds of distilleries that had been shuttered were reestablished under much tighter government supervision at the wholesale and retail levels, and official production would hover between 2 and 2.5 million gallons from 1760 to the 1780s and would not recover its 1743 peak for at least a century (Harper, 1999, p. 182; Mitchell, 1988).

The history of distilling seems to roughly match the pattern established with wine and beer. An initial period of high imports and poor local product, followed by war and urbanization, which lead to the closing of foreign markets and the rise of professional domestic production. Eventually this expansion of the industry is accompanied by expansive peacetime controls to limit foreign (i.e. French) imports, while local industry is seen as a means of expanding government revenue and regulatory control.

CHAPTER 4

The Beginnings: Trade and the Struggle for European Power in the Late 1600s

> Britain though is not at heart, nor in fact, a wine-producing, nor even—yet—truly a wine-drinking country. Governments have constantly fenced the trade round with obstacles and burdens; above all, taxation has made wine exaggeratedly dearer than it need be.
>
> —*John Arlott in Briggs, 1985, p. 3*

> Except for the brief period from 1786 to 1793, . . . the keys to commercial relations between France and Great Britain were war, political hostility, and economic rivalry.
>
> —*Judith Williams, 1972, p. 186*

THAT the British drink beer and the French drink wine is a truism that has held for nearly three centuries. To the extent that any wines were consumed in Great Britain two hundred years ago, it seems to have been confined to the more heavily fortified ports and sherries of Portugal and Spain or to the occasional glass of fine claret from Bordeaux. This pattern was so prevalent, throughout a period of rising British incomes and dominance by the French of total world production of wine and spirits, that the assumed disparity between British consumption habits and those of the rest of the world due to differences in taste might be forgiven. Yet specialist historians have long known that this was not so. Economics and politics had more to do with shaping these "tastes" than any cultural preference or natural endowment. Up until the end of the seventeenth century the British drank substantial amounts of wine, mostly French, and only changes in trade policy resulting from war and protection over several decades produced the marked shifts in drinking habits that were to be identified with the British peoples in subsequent centuries.

In the last decades of the seventeenth century the monarchs of Britain and France had a good deal more to be concerned with than the buying and selling of alcoholic beverages. Nevertheless, this was the age of the "mercantile system" that Adam Smith (1776) and many others were to decry as indicative of the mistaken notions about the economy that typified the era. Central to the mercantile system of these two countries was the control of international trade flows. Commerce, like production, was not to be viewed simply as a means of enhancing the wealth of the nation's individuals but was integral to the management of the state and to the expansion of state power. In the eyes of the authorities favorable trade created the state, and the state had to dictate the conditions of trade.

Since wine formed the greatest part of Britain's large trade deficit with France, it was a major source of concern to the English government and local merchants. Throughout the seventeenth century British protectionists had decried the size of the nation's trade deficit with France, and the French crown was zealous in protecting her putative dominance over Britain in international trade. Trade policy was at the very heart of both Crowns' concerns over the appropriate form and direction to be taken by the newly emerging state apparatus. The rise of the modern nation-state, with its expanded bureaucracy and large-scale centralized tax operations designed to finance the new administration, came with the view that the economic welfare of the nation was freely intermingled with its political health (cf. Brewer, 1988).

England of course did not embark on absolutist rule as did the French under Louis XIII and XIV. The Civil War left decisive power neither in the hands of Parliament nor the King. James II achieved stability through a royal apparatus supported by a strong standing army, the whole of which was dependent in financial and economic matters on the will of Parliament. Such a financial arrangement prevented the Crown from undertaking unrestrained campaigns with attendant need for large revenues. Almost paradoxically this made it substantially easier for the English state to raise funds over the long term than the French.[1]

But however much the rise of Britain in the eighteenth and nineteenth centuries has been associated with the rise of the modern liberal state and the economic successes of the Industrial Revolution, economic policy in the seventeenth century was overwhelmingly mercantilist. It is important to remind ourselves that seventeenth- and eighteenth-century English statesmen did not hold ideas about economic policy very far removed from those of their French equivalents. If there was no fully consistent and coherent theory of mercantilism, as Adam Smith came to define that philosophy in his condemnation of the mercantile system a century later, the English actually charged with developing policy and administering the budget had very similar ideas to those of Jean Baptiste Colbert and his officials in France. Undoubtedly the circumstances differed, especially considering the constraints under which they operated; even so, the economic principles that seem to have guided them were cut from the same cloth.

In the end British statesmen remained concerned about trade and, much like political leaders in most times and places, considered deficits to be bad for the economy and surpluses to be unambiguously good.[2] It will thus surprise no one to observe that the British were particularly exercised over the state of their trade with France in the seventeenth century. As France was both Britain's closest neighbor and most important rival, it was a source of great concern that most of the merchandise that made up the trade between Britain and France, both for re-export and for final home consumption, moved in the direction from France to Britain rather than vice versa.

Descriptions of trade flows in the seventeenth century indicate clearly that Britain had a large merchandise trade deficit, most of which could be attributed to French imports. British and French preoccupations with strategic policy concerns over narrowly defined economic welfare were somewhat justified given these circumstances. The constant need to support large and growing military establishments explains at least part of the bullionist tendencies of the major European powers. The availability of specie was seen as a necessary condition for states to perform their most urgent concern, prosecuting expensive wars.

Warfare was especially costly and indecisive at the end of the seventeenth century. The Nine Years War and the War of Spanish Succession left England (later Britain) and France in almost perpetual conflict for the quarter-century from 1689 to 1715. This quarter-century clarified the strategic positions of the two nations while making neither dominant. Instead it left their respective governments burdened with debt that would only increase throughout the eighteenth century.

Britain probably gained most from the conflicts. While France had little to show territorially for their part in the struggle, Britain obtained a strong foothold in the Spanish and Portuguese markets, in some respects virtually colonizing foreign trade in the latter country (Bonney, 1995, p. 321). The Methuen Treaty of 1703 provided the British with secure access to Portuguese markets while assuring the Portuguese of favorable trading status vis-à-vis the French. This would have long-term repercussions for the evolution of the wine trade into Britain.

This behavior was consistent with the strong British preference for destroying the enemy's trade rather than simply defeating them on the battlefield. For instance, in comparing the policies of Britain and Holland during the period from 1689 to 1697 (Nine Years War or War of the League of Augsburg), G. N. Clark notes the British preference for the encouragement of privateering against France:

> [T]he English, though equally inconsistent, tended on the whole to work against it. Less commercial and more predatory, they believed that

an enemy's freedom of commerce so prolongs his power of resistance that no countervailing advantage can justify the permitting of it. . . . During the second half of the century, while the Dutch were signing treaties for "Free ships, free goods," the English were trying to lengthen the list of contraband and to maintain the right of searching neutral vessels. (Clark, 1923, p. 5)

That trade was central to the disputes between France and Britain is not really in doubt. What is surprising is the extent to which the astonishingly rapid change in France's role in British trade has gone unnoticed. Although France would always remain an important trading partner of Britain, it would never again have the kind of dominance it held in British trade during the seventeenth century. This swift change in fortunes, particularly concerning its effect on exporters of wine, had more to do with war and politics than any structural shifts in the British or French economies.

The relative neglect of these issues by economic historians has been odd given the quantitative importance of the wine trade in the French economy and the weight of British wine tariffs in total customs receipts.[3] Perhaps some of this neglect arises because most of the published series on British trade and national income do not go back before 1700 (cf. Mitchell, 1988). By 1700 trade with France was virtually nonexistent because of the state of war between the two nations, and the process of restricting trade in wine, spirits, and other deficit-inducing imports was in full swing. Nonetheless, enough trade data exists from the seventeenth century to indicate how important France had been to British trade and how changed the landscape of international commerce had become by the eighteenth century.

France was Britain's largest trading partner throughout the seventeenth century except for the periods when they were at war. David Macpherson indicates that as late as 1675, when wine tariffs were already set at a level approximately 50 percent of pre-tax retail price of wine, about 1.5 to 1.7 million pounds of British imports were from France (out of a total of 4 to 4.5 million pounds sterling) with nearly a third of all French imports wine and spirits (Macpherson, 1805).

Data in C.G.A. Clay's discussion of seventeenth-century British trade paints a similar picture. For the period before 1699, Clay's data was drawn mostly from trade coming into London. Table 4.1 shows that wine was the largest share of British imports, representing nearly a fifth of all imports by value early in the century. From 1699 to 1701 wine still averaged about 10 percent of London's imports. For most of the century at least two-thirds of wine trade was with France, indicating that as much as 12 or 13 percent of all imports came in the form of French wines.

TABLE 4.1
Imports of Foodstuffs, etcetera, in the Seventeenth Century (Pounds Sterling)

	London				England
	1622	avg. 1634–40	avg. 1663–69	avg. 1699–1701	avg. 1699–1701
Wines	275,000	274,000	144,000	467,000	546,000
Pepper	87,000	48,000	80,000	103,000	103,000
Sugar	82,000	106,000	292,000	526,000	630,000
Fruits	80,000	145,000	196,000	135,000	174,000
Tobacco	55,000	171,000	70,000	161,000	249,000
Spices	32,000	35,000	34,000	24,000	27,000
Others	54,000	52,000	129,000	167,000	240,000
TOTAL	665,000	831,000	945,000	1,583,000	1,969,000

Source: Clay, 1984, p. 156

Other information on the size of British trade with France before 1689 is also to be found in this extended passage:

> The ingenious author of a treatise, entitled the British merchant, and many other writers, loudly and justly complain of the too much encouragement given to the consumption of French wines and brandies, silks, linens, hats, etc. He observes, that, though a duty of 4d a quart was this year [1668] laid upon French wines, which raised their retail price from 8d to 1s, we still took off prodigious quantities of them, and of almost every other species of French merchandise, while the French were continually diminishing their consumption of English manufactures and merchandize by new and high impositions, obstructions, and at length prohibitions: insomuch that the general balance of the trade of England for this same year was most grievously to our loss, viz.

> Imported into England from all the world   £4,196,139 17 0
> Exported   2,063,274 19 0
> The imports exceed the exports, the sum of   £2,132,864 18 0

> This great national loss was owing to our having a full trade with France. That full trade being afterwards prohibited, the general balance in 1699, was got to so far in our favour as £1,147,660:10:9. Total gained by us, from having no trade with France in the year 1699, £3,280,525:8:9, which balance, in the year 1703, was increased to £2,117,523:3:10½. Total gained by us, from our having no trade with France in the year 1703, £4,250,388:1:10½. A most interesting consideration (Macpherson, 1805, vol. 2, p. 534).

In 1675 Macpherson reports that imports from France into England amounted to some £1,500,000, while English exports to the French were no more than £170,000. Macpherson calculates that in 1683 the French were suffering an annual loss in revenue of £200,000 from wines and £80,000 from brandies, which could no longer be exported to Britain (taking into account the fact that exports would have been lower anyway, owing to the "great improvement of our own distillery and to the much increased taste for plantation rum") (p. 574). This is roughly 15 percent of what Macpherson suggests would have been the value of French exports (about £1,880,000) to England (p. 610). He also calculates not having to import some £1,702,000 worth of goods from Holland as well. In both cases, he reckons these to be net gains to the British through the trade balance.

The Nine Years War and the subsequent War of Spanish Succession cut off all trade with France and greatly reduced the supply of wine, spirits, assorted manufactures, and numerous luxury products. Inasmuch as trade in alcoholic beverages constituted a large fraction of British imports in the seventeenth century, British consumers turned to a variety of substitutes for these products. Domestically, beer producers began to benefit from the complete lack of cheap wine. Whiskey, gin, and rum distillers also benefited from the curtailment of the imports of French spirits. But beer and whiskey are quite imperfect substitutes for red wine from Bordeaux. To satisfy this unquenched British demand, importers looked to other countries for wine. This led the British to increase their imports from Spain, the only serious competitor in world wine markets faced by the French, and more curiously from Portugal, which had not hitherto been a major exporter of wine and spirits.

Lower tariffs on Spanish and Portugeuse wines allowed for this transfer of wine supply. Because of the complicated way in which these tariffs were calculated (so that it mattered whether the imports had been placed on French or British ships and which ports they had passed through), no simple table can offer the different configurations. Nonetheless, the basic rate on French wines had been raised to £53. 1s. a tun compared to a raise of £22. 12s. and £23. 8s. a tun for Portuguese and Spanish wines. Though these preferences were maintained and increased after the Methuen Treaty of 1703, it is noteworthy that the general pattern of preferential duties for Portugal was already in place prior to the treaty so that by 1704 the duties for wines from France, Portugal, and Spain were respectively £57. 6s., £26. 13s. and £27. 9s a tun (Fisher, 1971, p. 27).

Given this preference for Portugal, a country with no established wine industry, the peculiar relation between Britain and Portugal in the seventeenth and early eighteenth centuries is deserving of greater elaboration. In many ways the British influence on Portugal was sufficiently great that one might almost speak of parts of Portugal having been colonized by Britain. The British began to extract extremely favorable treatment from the Portuguese with the Treaty of 1654.

The history of Anglo-Portuguese commercial relations has been well told by Violet Shillington and Beatrice Chapman, who observed that with the Treaty of 1654,

> the English were to import what they pleased to Portugal, and trade as they choose, unthwarted by monopolists, and not bound to a set price. The general clause that English merchants should be as well treated as those of any other nation, was crystallised into various very definite stipulations, embodying the privileges that had been granted them from time to time.
>
> ... Special Articles (3,20,21) also asserted the English right to employ brokers under the same regulations as the Portuguese, to wear arms, to live where they chose, and to pay no dues but to the king or the chamber at Lisbon. (Shillington and Chapman, 1907, pp. 199–200)

As trade with Portugal grew, wine imports from the Portuguese grew as well. Inasmuch as Britain had a more favorable trade balance with Portugal, British mercantilists began to note that Portuguese wine might conceivably take the place of French imports, particularly from Bordeaux, that they felt were not counterbalanced by equivalently large imports of British manufactures. Thus, the British tried in the early 1700s to involve Portugal in the War of Spanish Succession both for political and commercial reasons. Politically they hoped to offset what they feared was the imminent alliance of France and Spain. This fear encompassed concern over the importance of Portugal's harbors, especially given the treaty with France and Spain in 1701 indicating a realignment away from Britain. The closing of the ports to English ships led to Methuen's negotiations to return Portugal to the Alliance, with the conclusion of the 1703 commercial treaty that bears Methuen's name as a large side benefit (Sideri, 1970, pp. 40–41).

The Methuen Treaty guaranteed favorable treatment of Portuguese products in exchange for the free importation of British textiles and manufactures.[4] Portuguese wines were to pay a duty assessed *by volume* that would never exceed two-thirds of that to be paid by the French. The imposition of a volume—rather than an ad valorem tariff—would play an important role in the discrimination against French products. However, so long as Portugal received preferential treatment, England was not prevented from unilaterally raising the overall wine duties as it saw fit.[5] This would lead to a general repression of British demand for foreign wine throughout the eighteenth century.

It is easy to overemphasize the particular prejudices of the day and undervalue the role of political economy in explaining the policies that were ultimately selected and, more importantly, sustained. The importance of strategic considerations and the desire for a mercantile system colored the general view of policy, but protection in foreign trade managed to coexist quite well with a move toward greater liberalization in domestic trade. A general tendency toward export promotion will give one only the vaguest notion of which goods should be promoted and how.

Even the most distinguished scholars of eighteenth-century Britain have at times understated the role of narrow commercial interest in discussing the evolution of British trade policy. For example, observing how constant was the rivalry between Britain and France, Paul Langford claimed that: "[I]nherited prejudice was perhaps as instrumental as anything in preventing attempts to modify such a deep-seated rivalry. Perhaps this was why, when Britain and France made peace in 1713, Bolingbroke's ambitious plan for a commercial rapprochement was rejected; perhaps too, it explains the reluctance of the Whigs, when they became advocates of alliance with France, between 1716 and 1731, to revive it" (Langford, 1989, p. 176).

Yet the very example that Langford provides demonstrates how unsatisfactory "inherited prejudice" is as an explanation for the protectionist policies adopted after 1713. Despite the preference for an alliance with France during the Whiggish 1716 to 1731 period, tariffs on French wines remained high and even increased. The most consistent explanation that also takes into account the favorable policies toward Portugal is that the interest groups that had sprung up to benefit from the strict prohibitions on French imports from 1689 to 1713 now sought to protect those rents through the maintenance of favorable legislation.[6]

Langford also makes the claim that "the customs duty, which, despite its fiscal consequence to government, was increasingly seen [in the eighteenth century] as a means of protectionism rather than a revenue-raising device" (p. 175). But this statement imposes an unnecessary dichotomy between protection and revenue-generating tariffs and overlooks both the actual magnitude of the customs duty and its relationship with the excise. Large revenue streams were generated by the tariffs in place and grew as a share of total income during this period. More importantly, protective tariffs and domestic excises were an integrated system that were used as a method to protect client groups such as domestic cloth and beverage producers. These producers could then be taxed at a higher rate in exchange for continued protection from foreign competition. As John Brewer (1988) and Patrick O'Brien (1988) have noted, the rise of the modern state owed its growth precisely to this capacity of the government to extract greater and greater revenues from the populace through customs and excises. As with much political economy, our task is less to explain the idiosyncratic specifics of a policy's origin than to explicate the longer-term consequences of a policy's survival, persistence, and overall effects on the populace at large.

The resumption of trade that followed the end of hostilities with France was of considerable interest to many different groups both in and out of government, and the prospect of renewed commerce with a prosperous France caused an outpouring of opinion on the proper course of policy. This is reflected in the numerous pamphlets, petitions, and analytical volumes published in 1713 for the sole of purpose of influencing the Parliamentary debate about Anglo-French trade.

As the War of Spanish Succession progressed following the passage of the Methuen Treaty, British merchants and brewers who benefited from the restricted trade with France and expanded trade with Portugal began to agitate against any improvement in trade relations with the French. The crisis came to a head in 1713 when a bill was introduced into Parliament for the purpose of returning to a commercial arrangement that would approximate the status quo ante. The arguments made in favor of maintaining preferences for Portugal and Spain were the same ones that had been made time and again throughout the early 1700s.

In 1709 pamphlets were published showing *Reasons Humbly Offer'd by the Portugal, Italian, and Spanish Merchants against Importing French Wines, in Return for Tobacco*, (Anonymous, 1709). These emphasized the quid pro quo with Portugal by arguing that "a liberty to Import French Wines, may cause another prohibition of Cloath in Portugal . . . and that by reason of a large Importation of Wines thence, since which vast quantities of Cloath hath been Exported thither, to the great support of many Families, which must have been ruined, if that Trade had not been opened" (p. 1). This is virtually the same as the arguments made in 1713:

> The *Portugal* Trade furnishes us with some dying Commodities; and the *Italian* Trade with *Raw Silk*, to imploy our poor industrious Weavers of *London, Norwich, Canterbury*, &c.
>
> All these Trades have as constantly increased every Year, as we have increas'd the Demand for their Wines; by which means the Navigation and Seamen of this Kingdom have been greatly encourag'd, especially to the *Mediterranean*; . . . But small Ships, with an easy Charge of Men, can fetch Wines from *France*; which will discourage the bringing in other Wines, and have this further bad effect, that the greatest part of those Ships must lie and rot, or come home dead freighted: The charge

whereof will fall on those British Commodities they carry out, which rendring them dear will lessen their Exportation; as will also the Incapacity the *Spaniards*, *Portuguese*, and *Italians* will be in to pay for them. For no Nation (no not the Spanish itself with all their Mines) can take off the Commodities of another Nation, unless they likewise take the greatest part of theirs. (Anonymous, 1713d, pp. 2–3)

The core of the protectionist arguments centered on the debt owed by the British to the Spanish and Portuguese for their support of Britain. Or, as the aforementioned pamphlet argues, "the Nations, that favour us most, ought to be most favour'd by us" (p. 1). Whereas Portugal and Spain took in a significant quantity of British manufactures, particularly from the textile industry, in exchange for any wines or foods furnished to British consumers, France sold more wines while finding little need to import British manufactures in return. Acting in favor of France would both destroy good relations with Portugal and ruin British trade through the sales of French linens and woolens.

Pamphlets with titles such as *The Consequences of a Law for Reducing the Dutys upon French Wines, Brandy, Silks and Linen, to those of other Nations* and *The Trade with France, Italy, Spain, and Portugal Considered*, sought to make the case of the imminent loss that would be suffered by the British Crown and her people should trade be reestablished in a manner favorable or even neutral toward the French, as had been typical in the third quarter of the seventeenth century. Although it was widely acknowledged that the French were to lower their tariffs substantially further than the British in the proposed treaty, fear of French trading prowess was enough to make such an arrangement unacceptable to many groups lobbying for attention.[7] Some pamphleteers interspersed strategic with economic considerations.[8] Still others made clear the interaction between trade policy and the strategic negotiations with Portugal and France, calling particular attention to the latter's prohibitions on many British textiles.[9]

Ultimately the British were less concerned with Portuguese demand per se than they were with the Portuguese and Spanish colonies. Inasmuch as half of export growth in the first four decades of the eighteenth century could be attributed to trade with these empires, there was some justification for that view. The French were not seen as a suitable partner partly out of political interests but mainly because France, by virtue of the diversity of her production and the assistance given to her luxury industry by tariff protection, was rightly discounted as an outlet for British products.

Richard Bonney has further argued that the importance of world competition caused Britain to stress the deployment of powerful armies and navies. In this view Britain's cultivation of Iberian partnership was a means of facilitating the development of the British navy through long-distance colonial trade (1995, p. 322).

The actions of these lobbyists proved fruitful in policy formation. The attempt by the Crown to reestablish normal ties with the French on the basis of commercial treaties negotiated in 1713 was strongly rejected by Parliament in June of that year. This rejection also marked the first time that the newly collected statistics on British trade entered the political debate in a substantial way and served as a basis for the mercantilists' published statements of economic doctrine (Clark and Franks, 1938, p. 18).

All this activity was accompanied by and simultaneously induced a vast expansion in the duties of the customs administration. While the 1660 act on tonnage and poundage listed only three classes of duties on wine, poundage, and wool, the next few decades saw a veritable explosion in the range of goods taxed and the complexity of the rules regarding imports and duties. In noting this change, M. J. Braddick gave as an example that "a merchant importing 20 reams of French paper . . . paid revenue under thirteen different headings" (1996, p. 58). All this is in addition to the variety of direct restrictions on trade (such as embargoes), which changed regularly with war and policy swings.

Braddick's discussion of this shift in regime through a history of the customs administration places too much emphasis on changes in administrative structure as the "cause" of the complex customs rules. By focusing primarily on the supply side of the equation, he neglects the increasing demand for revenue and protection that was facilitated by supply side changes, not so much in the administration, but in the political balance for and against freer trade.

He (along with other historians) have often erred in thinking that "wine imports . . . were not in competition with domestic production" (p. 121).[10] Though the full economic effects of the tariff are treated in subsequent chapters and the appendix, it is worth noting that contemporaries were certainly aware of the ways in which the wine trade had and might affect their livelihoods. The variety of petitions from brewers and distillers reacting to the possibility of normal trade with France—especially on wine—in 1713 and specifically pointing to competition with local substitutes, refutes the claim that there was nothing to protect and makes clear that an important and influential constituency was certainly aware of these linkages.

The utter and complete devastation of what had been a fine and steady trade with France was welcomed by many. It did receive its share of criticism, notably from the founders of classical liberalism. One of the best-known critiques is to be found in David Hume's essay, "Of the Balance of Trade," in which he charged:

Our jealousy and our hatred of FRANCE are without bounds; and the former sentiment, at least, must be acknowledged reasonable and well-grounded. These passions have occasioned innumerable barriers and obstructions upon commerce, where we are accused of being commonly the aggressors. But what have we gained by the bargain? We lost the FRENCH market for our woollen manufactures, and transferred the commerce of wine to SPAIN and PORTUGAL, where we buy worse liquor at a higher price. There are few EnglishMEN who would not think their country absolutely ruined, were FRENCH wines sold in England so cheap and in such abundance as to supplant, in some measure, all ale, and home-brewed liquors: But would we lay aside prejudice, it would not be difficult to prove, that nothing could be more innocent, perhaps advantageous. Each new acre of vineyard planted in FRANCE, in order to supply England with wine, would make it requisite for the FRENCH to take the produce of an English acre, sown in wheat or barley, in order to subsist themselves; and it is evident, that we should thereby get command of the better commodity. (Hume, 1777, essay V paragraph 16)[11]

The rise in tariffs in the eighteenth century primarily benefited those industries, such as ale and gin, that were in competition with French wines and brandy, but it also had protective effects on domestic production of silk, cotton, linen, and white paper (Clay, 1984, p. 213). Although these items were not to have that much weight in fiscal and other deliberations in the eighteenth century, the protection of textiles was, of course, integral to agreements like the Methuen Treaty with Portugal, which was an explicit exchange of openness to British exports of cloth in exchange for the relatively privileged access to the British market of the Portuguese wine industry.

It is also of interest that the one branch of textiles that emerged at the heart of the British Industrial Revolution—cotton—played an insignificant role in these policy shifts. Indeed, the woolen and linen industries were meant to be the prime beneficiaries of protectionist legislation, leaving us open to interesting speculations about the stagnant nature of protected industries and the growth of innovation in new, and often politically unimportant (at first) sectors of the economy.

THE VIEW FROM FRANCE

The French had long been cognizant of the important role that the leading powers of Britain and Holland played in the French export trade. As T. Malvezin noted in his history of Bordeaux, Minister Colbert had a number of misgivings in his construction of a trade system in the mid-1600s (Malvezin, 1892, VIII, p. 268). He wished to raise tariffs on imports to the point where any serious competition with French products was eliminated. Such tariffs should not serve to provoke retaliatory duties on French products according to M. de Souzy. Though Colbert thought it was possible to thread the needle and avoid extreme reactions, many of his correspondents registered their concerns in this matter.

In a letter dated August 8, 1669, M. de Souzy wrote to Colbert to warn him not to do anything that would oblige foreign nations to find the means to do without France's wines.[12] The advice was apparently ignored, perhaps for good reason. At least in the short run (prior to the Nine Years War, begun in 1689) the rise in British tariffs was not so high as to prevent the French from serving as the dominant supplier of wine and spirits to the English. For instance, writing in 1670 with respect to the Dutch response to new tariffs on French wine, Colbert stated his belief that the newer English duties were unlikely to endure because it was impossible for the English to cease drinking French wine.[13]

Colbert had felt that he had succeeded in steadily raising the duties on certain critical categories of imports from Britain without provoking what in his view was a lasting reaction from the British. This proved to be an enormous error in the long run. Items excluded from France were never and could not have loomed large in French trade throughout the seventeenth or eighteenth century, while the eventual exclusion of French wine was to have substantial and lasting consequences.[14]

Why were the French not overly concerned with British trade policy to the point of encouraging a trade war—that was ultimately more damaging to them than to the British? First, international trade was always a relatively small share of the French economy. The French economy was large and highly diversified with a wide range of goods produced. It is not a surprise that trade policy was viewed in terms of its political relevance more than for its macroeconomic effects. Second, even physiocratic theory placed little importance on trade. For the physiocrats agriculture was the true, sole source of a nation's wealth and was the appropriate focus of economic attention. This was consistent with the view even of the eighteenth-century trade liberalizers, who saw British trade as secondary to the problem of promoting freer trade both internally and externally.

Internal tariffs were a much greater concern than external protection. The problems of domestic transportation combined with the vagaries of internal customs often made Paris and the west of France less accessible to the southern and eastern countryside than England was to Bordeaux. These internal tolls and the problems with coordinating them arose from the general problem of revenue extraction faced by the French Crown in the seventeenth century. Colbert's reforms meant to address these problems but did not do much in the end to either simplify or remove internal barriers to trade. Thus, the trade issue was of secondary importance.

Even the various negotiations over the Eden Treaty of 1786 with Britain were often linked to potential support for the single-duty project in France that would replace all internal tariffs. For both reformers and physiocrats the move to open French ports to British goods only made sense if inland duties were abolished or reorganized so as to replace the complicated system with a uniform, easily imposed excise. The harm caused by external British and French tariffs seemed minor compared to the damage to French industry resulting from the cumbersome inland duties that had the effect of partitioning the nation into virtually autarkic regions (cf. Bosher, 1964).

Bordeaux was the primary loser from the tariffs because the southwest exporters had been the major purveyors of French wine to the international markets. Not only was England their major export market, but the Bordelais could not easily find domestic outlets for their product. Interregional trade in France was hampered by a mass of internal tariffs, taxes, and regulations on the one hand and a poorly developed transportation network that limited both physical movement and communication on the other. Only the larger producers, who had developed a close relationship with a variety of middlemen, could even hope to sell their wines in Paris (Brennan, 1997, pp. 275–76). Though Thomas Brennan was speaking primarily of Burgundy, one can take as universal the observation that "power in the wine trade exhibited the classic forms of commercial capitalism, based on control not of production but of the market" (p. 277).

Bordeaux did its best to make up for the deficiency by the development and promotion of higher quality wines for sale to the British market. Their brandies, which one might think of as most likely to match the port and sherry imports because of their strength, were also excluded because brandies and spirits from France were taxed at a different rate from wine, while port and sherry were treated as wines. Their only option was the encouragement of production for the luxury market in both wine and brandy. The fixed tariff would mean that the higher the price of the good, the less the burden of the tariff would be felt. Absent a market for cheaper product, the producers had no choice but to deal with wine as a luxury product. All incentives were such as to force them to promote their products at the highest end and neglect any possibilities in building a mass market.

Historical accounts have noted that the early 1700s were a period of increasing production of cheaper and poorer quality wines, especially in many of the regions around Paris. Fears by the government of this so-called "overproduction" led to the Arret of 1731, a prohibition on further conversion of grain lands to vineyards. Nevertheless, the law was widely disobeyed (Brennan, 1997, p. 244).

The spread of cheaper wines at a time when the top merchants and properties were focusing on the luxury end of the market is perfectly consistent with the greater difficulties that France was encountering in international trade, especially with Britain and Holland. While the lower effective demand for French wines and the fixed tariffs led to attempts to promote luxury wines, the loss of an international market for cheaper, midlevel product meant increasing pressures at home even in the face of normal increases in productivity and increased production. Having nowhere to go, the rising supply of cheaper wines would be consumed locally and, consequently, depress prices throughout France as the small-scale production of such wines spread. Little incentive existed for the best houses to organize and profit from lower quality wines because of the costly national trading conditions as well as the truncated international market. The result was a virtual two-tier market, with the best wines traded by powerful brokers with access to the national and, especially, Parisian markets, and a large but disorganized set of small producers selling mainly to local or regional markets.

Nonetheless the vintners hopes for a return to better days never quite went away. When the Eden Treaty of 1786 was first negotiated, wine was an important component of the negotiations, and it was hoped that over time this would lead to more dramatic tariff reductions. All hopes were dashed when the French Revolution ended all trade between the two countries and prevented the resumption of normal trade relations. Only at the end of the Napoleonic Wars did France return to the trading status quo of the eighteenth century. Real reform with a substantial impact on the trade balance between the two countries was not made until the 1860 Anglo-French Treaty of Commerce.

Even the good fortune brought in the mid-nineteenth century by the 1860 treaty was not unblemished. The centuries' long misfortune in Britain on the French wine industry was only compounded in the 1860s by the arrival of pestilence in the form of oidium, a blight that presaged the more famous phylloxera outbreak of the 1880s. Still, trade reform made the Second Empire a happy and prosperous time for the French wine producers, especially the Bordelais, as it allowed them to look forward to the reconquest of France's most important export market. Oidium did limit the French supply response to more open markets. The later scourge of phylloxera eventually retarded French inroads into the British market in the 1880s. This occurred just as France had begun to regain its market share in British imports (about 40% in 1880) and levels of consumption (3 to 4 million imperial gallons of wine from France per year in the late 1870s and early 1880s) that would have been expected given France's position in world wine production, her pretariff market share, and contemporary British income levels.

The eighteenth century began with Portugal and Spain replacing France as the primary supplier of wine to the English and tariffs on wine and spirits at much higher levels than in the previous century. The English deficit with France had largely disappeared. English capital entered into Portugal as merchants, shippers, and marketers of wine inextricably linked the Portuguese economy to England's. This two-way arrangement made a mockery of subsequent characterizations by Ricardo of trade representing simple comparative advantage.

CHAPTER 5

Counterfactuals or What If?

To know what truly would have happened to British drinking habits had French wines continued to be welcome at the British table, is of course impossible. However, the variety of calculations proposed will serve to dramatize the implicit changes in observed British tastes. One does not have to suppose a world in which British drank mostly wine to the exclusion of beer. One merely has to postulate a world in which beer was the dominant drink of the population at large while wine played a much larger role in the nation's intake of beverages than was actually observed. All this presumes that tastes are exogenously given, and relative prices shift consumption levels at the margin. Moreover, if the taste for beer and wine is partially endogenously determined, the effects of the tariff might have been greater still. To the extent that a nation's tastes for any goods are acquired through a dynamic learning process, with characteristics of increasing returns to scale, any counterfactual calculations will only underestimate the effects on British consumption of wine of nearly two centuries of war, tariffs, and the variety of subsidies and various encouragements extended to the producers of substitutes to French products.

Before engaging in a counterfactual exercise, let us first establish that there was reason to believe that British imports of French wines were sensitive to tariffs levied and that substitution possibilities existed. This applies both among French wines and those of Portugal and Spain and between wine and other beverages such as beer or, even at a further remove, tea. Economists know that the technical idea of substitution merely involves any situation in which consumption of one good is negatively affected by increases in consumption of another. More precisely, the degree to which goods X and Y are substitutes is dependent on the degree to which a proportional rise in the price of good X leads to a proportional increase in the consumption of good Y.

Thus stated the common definition of substitution is not as broad as that of economic substitution. Many are reluctant to credit much substitutability between different classes of wine, let alone between wine and beer, and especially between wine and tea. While it is true that the more dissimilar two goods are, the less likely they are to be good substitutes, direct evidence and conceptually sound reasons for believing that most of the above beverages had non-negligible substitution effects exist for both the short and the long run. Beer and wine are both alcoholic beverages, and both were widely consumed in the seventeenth century. Even today, makers of alcoholic beverages understand that beer and wine represent the one end of the spectrum of alcohol consumption, the other stronger fortified and distilled liquors like whiskey, gin, or brandy.

Wine and beer are also beverages and as such are affected by consumption of other beverages, including water, tea, and coffee. Alan Macfarlane cites David Davies in noting how the increased taxation of malt in the eighteenth century drove many people away from beer and increasingly toward tea (Macfarlane, 1997, p. 132). Furthermore, beer served as a substitute for water, providing calories and vitamins that supplemented or even made up a large portion of the regular diet of the lower classes. Indeed, evidence that water was often unfit for human consumption goes back to Biblical times, if not earlier. It is well known that beer and wine were free of pathogens and were therefore superior sources of both liquid and basic caloric intake. Until the nineteenth century there were no safe sources of drinking water, and until the introduction of tea and coffee in the West, no safe widely available alternatives to alcoholic beverages were to be found (Burnett, 1999).

Depending on what one assumes about the amount of beer consumed from private production, one can estimate that on average between one and two pints a day were consumed by the late 1600s by each person in Britain, or approximately 4 to 8 gallons of beer per month per capita. Data on wine imports from earlier in the century suggest that despite high but not prohibitive duties, as much as one gallon of wine a month was consumed for every man, woman, and child in England by the mid-1600s. The increased gap in per capita consumption of the two products is an outcome of the tariffs following the War of Spanish Succession. The size of the wine imports, and their importance in a period that preceded the rise of the modern middle class, does not make it implausible that with substantially lower prices, low taxes, no domestic protection, and rising wages, the amount of wine that would have been consumed in the eighteenth and nineteenth centuries would have been much higher and much closer to the beer totals.

The complex interplay of necessity and choice is brilliantly observed in A. D. Francis's discussion of the discomfort experienced by claret's lovers when imports from France were banned at the end of the 1600s. Richard Ames wrote two books, *In Search of Claret* and *A Farewell to Wine,* describing pub-crawling that produced no claret, only port. Ames is quoted as telling a waiter:

> Hold, you prating whelp, no more,
> But fetch a pint of any sort
> Navarre, Galicia, or anything but port. (Francis, 1972, p. 104)

Thus, to the extent that Navarre and Galicia would not have been consumed by Ames with claret readily available, the absence of French wine forced him to substitute other products instead. That port was not an acceptable substitute for Ames was a reflection not just of his tastes but rather of the presence of other, less unfavorable alternatives. An economist would certainly say that to the extent that the consumption of alcoholic beverages interacted with other types of alcohols as well as with other consumables, French wine's availability and price affected consumption of a multitude of items.

Yet Francis, like many other chroniclers of the history of the wine trade, paid scant attention to less obvious substitutions and underestimated the importance of price in both the long and the short run.[1] Attention was placed on the texts left behind, allowing for little discussion of the economics of beverage consumption. Nevertheless, the most central question is not substitution but rather the own-price elasticity of demand for wine. Conventional wisdom suggests that demand for most alcoholic beverages is inelastic, but it turns out that actual estimates of wine elasticities vary greatly depending on the circumstances. A range of elasticities has been estimated in the literature that are affected not just by changing prices but by the very different regulatory regimes surrounding the sales, importation, production, and provision of all alcoholic beverages. Although demand for all alcoholic beverages may be inelastic, demand for a subset of all beverages, French wines for instance, is likely to be moderately elastic.

In the closest direct test of the effects of a change in prices available for historical Britain, per capita consumption of wine increased substantially following the 1860 Anglo-French Treaty of Commerce. British per capita consumption of beer shows a sudden break in its gradual rise around 1860 with a gradual recovery in subsequent years (see figure 5.1). Total imports of French wine rose some 600 percent in the decade following the 1860 treaty. Of course, we have already seen how dramatic the drop in British imports of wine was when comparing the period of prohibitively high British tariffs after 1715 to the more open period before 1689.

Evidence of the tariffs' effects on wine consumption within the category of wines narrowly defined may be assessed by observing how the form of the British tariff affected the composition of imports of wine from France. We do not have any direct quantitative evidence about the amount of high quality wine imported by the British relative to the imports of cheaper wines. All we have are volume totals. But we can infer something about the relative quality of British imports from France by looking at how much wine was imported in bottles versus barrels.

Figure 5.2, detailing the distribution of French wine exports to various

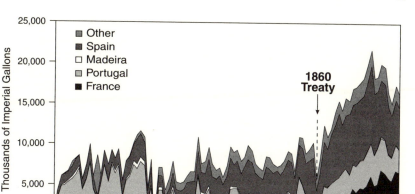

Figure 5.1. British Wine Imports 1785–1881 (Great Britain, 1898, pp. 155–57).

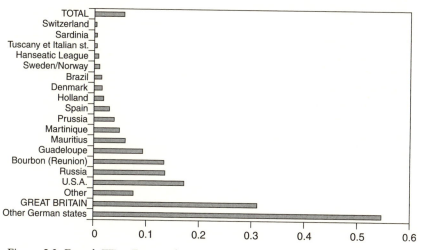

Figure 5.2. French Wine Exports by Destination 1828 (France, Archives Nationale, [1828?]).

countries and categorized by the ration of wine volume imported in bottles to wine imported in barrels, is striking for the contrast between the high tariff states, such as Britain and the Netherlands, and the rest of the world. Where most countries with more favorable treatment of French imports brought in substantially more French wine in barrels than in bottles at ratios of 12:1 or 15:1, the British were importing only three times as much wine in barrels as in bottles. Since bottled wine tended to be the highest quality, highest cost products (given the difficulty of shipping wine in bottles, the risks from breakage, and the general costs of bottling wine), these figures confirm the general impression given by all observers that the British trade was primarily centered on the higher quality product of Bordeaux, such as claret, or the finest examples of wine from Burgundy. This also accords with the efforts of French wine producers to supply and create higher quality red Bordeaux both to please the discriminating upper-class British palate and to evade the effects of duties that were levied by the British on volume. The better and more expensive the wine, the smaller the percentage effect on price of the tariff.

The issues of substitution also emerge when considering changes in the market for strong liquor. Domestic spirits were favored over imported brandies. The initial rise in the beer excise also led to an internal shift from wine and beer to stronger drinks. In addition to the tariff, official policy had been to promote the consumption and production of domestic spirits and friendly imports in contrast to the products of enemy France. After an Act of Parliament in 1690 granting the freedom to distill corn, another act in 1702 encouraged citizens to consume malted corn "for the better preventing the running of French and Foreign Brandy" (Monckton, 1966, p. 142).

Government exhortation and protectionist wine tariffs produced a suitably patriotic response, with consumption of gin escalating in the early 1700s. Protection of domestic production coupled with growing excises on beer saw an increase in the sale of spirits such as gin, with production of 527,000 gallons in 1684, 2,000,000 in 1700, 5,394,000 in 1735 and 7,160,000 in 1742. It is estimated that at its peak in 1742 the consumption of spirits and strong drink reached a total of 20,000,000 gallons. After this high the government came to place increasing restrictions on the distribution, sale, and purchase of the stronger beverages (p. 143).

COUNTERFACTUALS

Now, let us attempt to estimate how large British imports of French wine might have been in the absence of war and tariffs. It seems best to order calculations by presenting them in a range from the excessively conservative to the more speculative. In all cases the potential change in import levels is large.

The following will be considered sequentially:

1. What would have happened if total British imports of wine were unchanged, and only the shares of imports between France and the others were rearranged to reflect French dominance in the late seventeenth century?

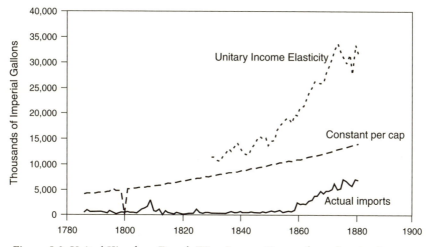

Figure 5.3. United Kingdom-French Wine Import Counterfactuals using Late 1600s Benchmarks.

2. What would have happened if British per capita consumption of wine had remained constant from the period of the late 1600s to the mid-1860s, with French wines predominating in British imports, at the shares they enjoyed in the late seventeenth century?

3. What if the exercise were repeated using the consumption and import levels of the early 1600s as a benchmark?

4. And finally, What would have happened if the distribution of British wine imports remained as it had in the early 1600s, but total wine imports were responsive to changes in income starting from a base in the early seventeenth century? That is, how much more French wine would have been imported if Britain's income elasticity of demand for wine was at least unity?

As is clear from table 5.1, the first two conditions lead to very similar results. Figure 5.3 makes clear that even conservative estimates of how much wine Britain might have imported under a more open trading regime with France would have led to import volumes easily an order of magnitude greater than what was actually observed. Whether assuming constant per capita consumption (i.e., zero income elasticity of demand for wine) or fixed imports with changing composition leads to British imports of French wine in the early to mid-1800s approximately fifteen to twenty times as large as were actually observed. The more reasonable assumption that wine is a normal good with an income elasticity close to one, yields import values some thirty-five to forty times larger than actually observed.[2] This is such a large effect that it seems impossible for unitary income elasticity to be plausible.

TABLE 5.1
Various Calculated French Import Totals

Year	Actual (in percent) in 1000s	Total in 1000s	Assuming No Change in total Imports w/Diff French %s		Assuming 61% increase Avg. Jump. 116%(1850s to 60s) in 1000s	British population in 1000s	Assuming Constant per capita consumption in 1000s
			62% (1675) in 1000s	72% (1686–89) in 1000s			
1677	2,056	3,392	2,103	2,442	3,931	—	—
1686–89	2,814	3,961	2,456	2,852	4,592	—	—
1713	516(15.5)	3,340	2,071	2,405	3,872	6166	2,471
1714	251(6.4)	3,913	2,436	2,817	4,536	6186	2,904
1715	265(5.8)	4,561	2,828	3,284	5,287	6190	3,388
1716	329(8.3)	3,949	2,448	2,843	4,578	6226	2,950
Ten-year averages							
1717–26	272(5.8)	4,724	2,929	3,401	5,476	6338	3,593
1727–36	177(3.7)	4,816	2,986	3,467	5,582	6324	3,655
1737–46	79(2.2)	3,577	2,218	2,575	4,246	6546	2,810
1747–56	103(3.1)	3,290	2,040	2,369	3,814	6849	2,704
1757–66	114(3.3)	3,478	2,157	2,504	4,032	7248	3,025
1767–76	103(2.9)	3,605	2,235	2,595	4,179	7657	3,312
1777–86	92(2.9)	3,132	1,942	2,255	3,631	8360	3,142

Source: Great Britain, 1898, p. 155–157.

Note: British Imports of French Wines under different counterfactual assumptions using 3928/6000, i.e., 1686–89/6000.

But, some modern estimates of British income elasticities of demand for wine hover around 2, which if applicable to the eighteenth and nineteenth century would double yet again the amounts of wine that might have been imported from France (Clements and Selvanathan, 1987). Considered in the context where many estimates of income elasticities of wine are larger than 1, it does not seem unreasonable to take unitary elasticity as a conservative benchmark. What thus seems striking, given the moderate assumptions of income elasticity of demand is the fortyfold increase in French wine consumption that might have come about if Britain had done nothing to discourage alcohol consumption in general, and French wines and spirits in particular.

Wine, Beer, and Money: The Political Economy of Brewing and Eighteenth-Century British Fiscal Policy

ONE of the most significant contributions of the new institutional economics has been the ability to rethink political history in terms of the economic motivations of the state, particularly the revenue needs of the ruler. Beginning with the work of Douglass North and Robert Thomas (1973) and developed further by Margaret Levi, Yoram Barzel, and Mancur Olson,[1] the logic of the emerging state as tax collector or predator has added many new insights to our understanding of the margins at which changes in governance and organization took place as rulers sought to balance their need to maintain power and their desire to extract more revenue.

Levi made this point a central thesis of her historical study of political economy. She focused on seventeenth- and eighteenth-century France and Britain as two of the most illustrative cases. A crucial issue was one of compliance; "war and national defence were the public goods that rulers used to justify taxation" (1988, p. 96). The English move to a representative Parliament produced the preconditions for quasi–voluntary compliance in Britain, a factor missing or weaker on the Continent. The English system had greater "legitimacy" and could raise revenues with less opposition.

The difficulty with this otherwise astute observation is its generality and lack of attention to the specific circumstances surrounding the growth of British tax authority after 1700. Elites dictated fiscal and commercial policy before the Parliament grew strong and wealthy elites, though drawn from a wider cross-section of society, continued to dictate British policy throughout the eighteenth century. Only by understanding how the British conspired to get the elites to permit taxation will one get a clear understanding of how revenues changed so dramatically in the period from the late seventeenth century to the end of the eighteenth.

North and Barry Weingast (1989) and Philip Hoffman and Jean-Laurent Rosenthal (1997) have emphasized that prior to the Glorious Revolution the question of revenue production was dependent on the struggle between the Crown and Parliament. Debate over prerogative and arbitrary overreach on the part of the King placed jurisdictional limits on tax levels. Not until the changes instituted toward the turn of the century did Britain's Crown and Parliament create institutions (such as the Bank of England or the central tax authority) that sustained substantially higher tax levels.

All of this ignores the problems of enforcement and collection even in the presence of Parliamentary sanctions. The ability to raise revenues to dramatic levels in the eighteenth century was closely tied to changes in the base to be taxed, and that in turn facilitated the rise of the new administration. After the fact, it seemed obvious that raising the land taxes further would have been difficult and that shifting to indirect taxes like customs and excises made more sense.

Such a claim (see for example Koehn, 1994) is not as straightforward as it sounds. Consider first the shift to excises that had begun in the seventeenth century with the Restoration and seemed to have proceeded smoothly to the enormous tax receipts of the eighteenth century.

Theoretically, it is not obvious that customs and excises are a superior form of revenue generation. Standard public economics usually indicates that direct taxes on wealth and income are more efficient mechanisms than indirect taxes for generating revenue. This is because direct taxes do not distort the relative prices of goods and services produced. Excises and customs do more harm in theory by distorting market signals leading to misallocation of resources. In a world of near perfect enforcement, indirect taxes would actually generate less revenue than a system built on direct taxes because the economy would have to bear a greater burden in opportunity foregone from inefficient indirect taxes for the same level of revenues as would be derived from a properly enforced direct tax. Thus, the state that relies on indirect taxes would seem to begin with an unavoidable handicap when compared to those able to tax wealth and income directly.

However, this all presupposes perfect enforcement with little or no transaction costs. The argument for indirect taxes is that customs and excises were easier to collect and manage than direct income taxes. For all but a handful of wealthy families it would have been impossible or, at least incredibly costly, to calculate and then collect income tax from the majority of English households. Indirect taxes levied on widely used commodities such as salt or beer could be imposed at the point of production and, as in the case of customs, could be collected easily on imports at British ports of entry. Hence, ease of collection led to the supposed superiority of excises and other indirect taxes from the standpoint of enforcement costs.

Such a simple claim runs up against the difficulty that all countries, including Britain, used a combination of direct and indirect taxes at various points and often did not find it easy to shift the burden onto excises. British direct taxes on land continued to be the largest single source of revenue until well into the eighteenth century. Excises were not so commonplace as would be suggested by claims of their ease of collection and did not often produce the high incomes anticipated by its proponents.

A more microanalytic and perhaps cynical view of British finances would note that after 1700 tax revenues did not rise equally. Excise and customs grew to a much larger share of the budget than in the previous century. Though land taxes and other direct taxes on income and wealth also grew, their share in the budget declined steadily. The direct burden on the landed aristocracy and other landowning elites fell in relative terms, while taxes on items of daily consumption with regressive impacts grew at a rapid pace.

Here too were new puzzles. Though the economic incidence of most of the new taxes undoubtedly fell on the common people, its legal incidence would have fallen on many commercial establishments, both large and small merchants alike. How is it that groups like the brewers and the distillers, who had successfully resisted or evaded the steadily higher taxes in the 1600s, were so easily induced to provide dramatically higher revenues to the state in the 1700s? This is especially puzzling since it occurred in a period when brewers' influence in Parliament was at an all-time high. Furthermore, not all extensions of the excise were similarly accepted. An attempt in the early 1730s to rationalize the system of indirect taxes, through the creation of a single universal excise system that handled both excises and customs, led to the famed excise crisis. The event continues to puzzle historians specializing in this period of British history to this day.

All these issues appear in a different light when the struggle over wine and brandy and its implications for domestic substitutes like beer and gin is taken more seriously. It is only by considering the role of the beverage interests and their probable interaction with the state's growing need for funds to support war that one can come to a full understanding of the dynamics of British fiscal policy.

Britain had made the shift from direct to indirect taxes in the seventeenth century with the abolition of tax farming, the granting of monopolies, the modifications on land taxes, and the rise of excises. However, early attempts beginning in 1643 to impose excises on goods—including meat, butter, beer, soap, salt, leather, and cloth—inspired a great deal of opposition, and even provoked sporadic violence in the 1640s and the 1650s.

It is sometimes suggested that the eighteenth-century tariffs on French wine imposed after the War of Spanish Succession were designed primarily for revenue collection from import duties, but it is obvious that the customs duties were too elevated to maximize income. Any tariff designed to maximize customs revenues would not have excluded the vast majority of cheaper wines. Standard notions of an optimal tax preclude taxes that are so high that they actually reduce the value of total tax revenues by severely depressing (indeed virtually prohibiting in some cases) imports of the taxable good.

The role of the tariff was to facilitate the collection of otherwise impolitic domestic excises by securing the cooperation of protected industry. Although the British wine tariffs were not directly revenue maximizing, they did serve to promote the development of an effective fiscal system that extracted tax revenues from the consumption of alcoholic beverages. By protecting domestic producers of beer and spirits, tariffs on imported wine and brandies made it possible for the state to impose high excises on local beverage production while minimizing resistance to the imposition of high taxes.

The great successes of the eighteenth-century excises were twofold: first, the narrowing of the range of commodities bearing the primary burdens of the excise to alcoholic beverages; second, making the producers of domestic beverages so dependent on protection that cooperation would be enhanced or opposition weakened to increased excises.

In the late seventeenth century tariffs and excises were jointly implemented on imported wines and domestic beer. At this time the high tariffs were not yet very discriminatory; revenues collected were actually quite similar from both excise and customs sources. From May of 1643, beer paid a duty of 2/ a barrel on beer valued at 6/ or over and beer valued under 6/ a barrel paid 6d. These impositions were begun at a time when beer still had to face competition not just from substitutes like wine but also from imported beers, which were not yet prohibited. Eventually, differential tariffs and then outright prohibitions were imposed on beer imports. By this time though, these protections had already come at a price.

A belief had formed in the industry that the end of the Cromwell government would mean the elimination of the beer duty. Unfortunately for English brewers, this would not be the case. A royal proclamation in 1660 further extended the excise (Monckton, 1966, p. 118). The gradual acceptance of the beer excises would lead to its use to finance a variety of government ventures, notably the wars with France. With the regularization of the domestic levies on beer came the joint problem of evasion as well as increased agitation by domestic producers against imports of all sorts. Initial attempts to raise greater amounts of revenue simply through an increase in the rate of excise taxation did not produce the desired results. In 1689 and 1690 the duty on beer was raised so that it was virtually double the initial level of 2/ 6d a barrel for strong beer and 6d. for weak beer. This led to a decrease in the number of common brewers and stagnation in the revenue levels after the initial increase. Eventually, income began to fall. Protecting the industry from foreign competition would be necessary if the taxes were to become viable. The government took advantage of this consolidation in the industry to encourage the oligopoly that dominated brewing in London by a dozen or so firms.

By the mid-1700s the new tariffs on French wine were set to eliminate the majority of French trade with Britain to make possible a shift in the composition of indirect taxes so that the bulk of revenues came from excises and not customs. If considering that the tariffs on Portuguese wine were borne partly by English merchants, shippers, and factors and were designed to favor their products over those of France, these revenues can be viewed as yet one more "domestic" or, at least, "colonial" excise.

The eighteenth century is widely acknowledged as the period of Britain's emergence as a dominant world power. This was accomplished through the expansion of the powers of the state, backed by an unprecedented rise in the central government's tax-collecting abilities. Were the increases in revenue simply a case of British income rising with overall GNP? No. As Peter Mathias and Patrick O'Brien (1976a, 1976b) have demonstrated, not only did total tax receipts rise faster than GNP as British incomes and population rose, but even per capita tax levels rose from about 16 percent in 1700 to 24 percent in 1800 and then to a staggering 36 percent during the war years of 1803 to 1812. This was accompanied by a switch in the form of tax collection that largely abandoned direct taxes as the primary source of revenues in favor of indirect excise taxes collected by an effective, well-functioning professional bureaucracy (cf. Brewer, 1988).

The source of these impositions was not uniform: simple examination of the British budgets indicates that an overwhelming part of the excises was derived from taxes on alcoholic beverages. Table 6.1 is reprinted from O'Brien's (1988) work on British revenue sources in the eighteenth century. The table gives the principal sources of British revenue for the late eighteenth century and covers perhaps 90 percent of the central government's budget. Customs revenues from wine and spirits and domestic excises on beer, spirits, and intermediate products in beverage production total nearly 40 percent. Note that this figure leaves out the large revenues from excises and tariffs on sugar, which was extensively used in the production of alcoholic beverages; their inclusion would bring the total closer to one half of all government revenues.

The growth in eighteenth-century British revenue essentially reflects the growth of the excise. Taxes on land, customs, and the excise each accounted for roughly a million pounds in the first decade of the eigh-

TABLE 6.1
Major British Taxes 1788–1792

	Average Annual Yield 1788–92 (thousands of pounds £)	Type of Tax	Percent Distribution of Taxes	
			Itemized	Aggregate
1 Direct taxes				
Land, windows, etc.	3388	Direct		21.2%
2 Food				
Tea	583	Customs	3.6%	
Salt	999	Customs	6.3%	
Sugar	425	Excise	2.7%	
				12.6%
3 Heat, Light, Fuel	969	Cust & Exc		6.1%
4 Construction materials	648	Cust & Exc		4.1%
5 Clothing, footwear	1010	Cust & Exc		6.3%
6 Soap and Starch	501	Excise		3.1%
7 Alcohol and tobacco				
Beer	1968	Excise	12.3%	
Malt	1838	Excise	11.5%	
Hops	121	Excise	0.8%	
Wine	739	Customs	4.6%	
Foreign Spirits	990	Customs	6.2%	
Domestic Spirits	654	Excise	4.1%	
Tobacco	607	Customs	3.8%	
				43.3%
8 Commercial Services				
Newspapers, etc.	533	Stamp		3.3%
Overall total	£15,973			100.0%

Source: O'Brien (1988, p. 11)

teenth century (varying in a range from about 500,000 to 1,500,000 pounds sterling). By the 1780s, land brought in some 2 to 3 million pounds at the most and customs another 3 million or so, while the excise accounted for upwards of 7 to 8 million pounds sterling. Since roughly 5 millions pounds came from beer, malt, and domestic spirits and another 2 million of the customs revenues derived from wine, spirits, and the taxes on sugar for alcohol, it is safe to say that the story of British

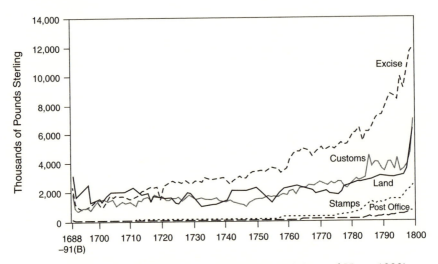

Figure 6.1. British Net Public Revenue 1688–1799 (O'Brien and Hunt, 1993).

tax success in the eighteenth century was predominantly the story of the successful imposition of taxes on alcoholic beverages.

If one examines the relative growth of customs and excises in the records of British central government receipts, the divergence between British receipts from excises and customs is striking. Net receipts from customs and excises are roughly comparable between 1689 and the early 1700s. Customs typically varied from about 8 or 900,000 pounds in the 1690s to about 1.5 million pounds sterling by 1700. Excise revenues are comparable during the same period. From 1703 onwards customs receipts lag behind those of the excise revenue by ever increasing amounts in most years and in all five-year periods. Up until 1711 or 1712 the figures for the two categories are still closely aligned, but with the end of the war revenue from excises is typically 50 to 60 percent greater than those received from import duties. By the 1730s, the time when Walpole first considered replacing all customs duties with excises, the excise brings in twice as much revenue as does customs, averaging 2.9 million pounds versus 1.5 million for customs throughout the 1730s. By the 1780s excises are approaching 8 million pounds and customs 3.5 to 4 million a year.

Taxes on land decline on the average from 1700 to 1740. The only period of increase was in the 1740s and 1750s, but this did not surpass the 1696 peak of 2.5 million pounds sterling until 1781. This pattern is in line with the government's decision to shift the burden of taxation from land to a variety of indirect taxes.[2]

These taxes were fundamentally regressive of course. They confirm the view of Mathias and O'Brien that the relative fall in the importance of direct taxes meant that "the fiscal burden falling upon the principal sources of savings in the economy, and upon those higher-income groups whose capacity to save was highest, declined as national wealth expanded in the course of the century" (1976b, p. 615).

It might be argued that the tax on alcoholic beverages was the natural outgrowth of an excise that was easier to administer and collect. Such a view ignores the fact that an even-handed excise on all alcoholic products would not have been designed to distort production and consumption patterns by favoring the domestic equivalents so strongly as to effectively prohibit the importation of the cheapest classes of French and, to a lesser extent, Spanish wines. Although most countries, including France, had recourse to excises on alcoholic beverages, almost no other state made such extensive use of them as did Britain.

Comparing the role of the salt tax in Britain and France provides a sense of how different the pattern of British taxation was. The British salt excises produced only 4 or 5 percent of government revenues. Meanwhile, the gabelle was responsible for between 25 to 30 percent of French revenues in the mid-eighteenth century (O'Brien, 1988, p. 617).

It is one thing to observe the legal incidence of taxation; it is quite another to be able to demonstrate the actual economic incidence of the tax. Not knowing in much detail what the responsiveness of the different sectors was to the variety of excises and tariffs, one cannot with any degree of certainty establish which groups actually paid the taxes in equilibrium. Nevertheless, the excises were most likely passed on to the great mass of British consumers.

A comparison of the lobbying power of the brewers and English consumers demonstrates how this passing of the tax to the consumers was made possible. At this time English consumers were not in any position to successfully protest the taxes imposed on them. The problem with most excises, as is evidenced by the problems the British had with the beer excise in the seventeenth century, is that resistance to their imposition is likely to be more successfully prosecuted by the producers than by the consumers of the good in question. It is usually only this group that has the organizational capability and the political influence to evade the tax.

It is hard to see how the small-scale, often home-brewed world of seventeenth-century English beer could have provided the level of revenues and easy collection that the eighteenth century witnessed. The advantage of the political system that emerged from the wartime restrictions on trade with France was that the beer excise was easily imposed on a group whose continued profitability was highly dependent on cooperation from the government and coordination on matters of trade policy. Furthermore, technical changes in production contributed to a dramatic rise in the size of the most efficient brewers. From the government's perspective the change in the industrial organization of the brewing industry, especially the trend toward increased concentration in production begun around 1700 and the rise in the scale of production, made it substantially easier to monitor and implement the tax.

Absent such an odd political economy, it is just as likely that the excise would have been more evenly distributed on salt, food, clothing, and the like. This division would have been less discriminatory toward imports, but the government would have had to exert itself to depend more heavily on the direct taxes than was typical of the late 1700s. For instance, in discussing the rise of the British fiscal regime, Brewer makes a point of noting the numerous duties introduced by the Earl of Oxford by 1714 on a variety of products—including "coffee, tea, books, playing cards, calicoes, candles, coal, hackney coaches, linens, leather, paper, parchment, soap, silks and Irish salt"—and the extent to which these duties and imposts tended to remain once they became customary (1988, p. 119). However, with the exception of the duties on tea and coffee—beverages that were potential substitutes for wine and beer—none of the other tariffs were allowed to grow to be a notably large portion of the budget. A world in which Britain had not been in conflict with France would have undoubtedly allowed for a greater willingness to tax items other than wine and spirits, and more likely, a greater recourse to increased taxation on land and wealth than was typical of Britain at the time of the American wars.

The switch from direct to indirect taxes after the War of Spanish Succession was also notable because direct taxes were dominant during the reign of William and Mary. Although it does not seem possible to imagine a British government successfully growing the state through direct taxes on land and wealth in the long run, it should be observed that the shift to excises involved a change in the political treatment of imported goods and the creation of a massive, centrally controlled tax administration that employed thousands of workers whose duty it was to assess and administer the new excises that sprang up from 1714 onward (Brewer, 1988). This shift would then reverse itself in the nineteenth century as tariff revenues began to take up a larger part of the budget. Eventually, all indirect taxes would lose ground to newly imposed direct taxes on income and property in the late nineteenth century.

Seen in the perspective of a grand shift from regulation and direct control to deregulation, centralized collection of multiple excises gives us an opportunity to reconsider another important question in the comparative histories of Britain and France. It has been a staple of economic history to tell the tale of these two countries by contrasting the nature and extent of government control of the economy. Economic historians in particular have emphasized the shift away from regulation toward a more liberal state in Britain than France in the mid- to late eighteenth century. This theme appears in North and Thomas (1973), North and Weingast (1989), Margaret Levi (1988), and Robert Ekelund and Robert Tollison (1981).

Ekelund and Tollison (1981) place emphasis on a rent-seeking explanation for the decline of regulation in England. Competition between the Crown and Parliament led to a reform agenda that decreased the extent of government control of the economy and led to generally less interference in the workings of the market. This explanation, though methodologically consistent in its view of both British and French states as being equally motivated by fiscal concerns, seems inconsistent with the growth of the British state that emerges in work by Patrick O'Brien (1988), Richard Bonney (1995), and Brewer (1988). A story of a weakened Crown, in competition with Parliament, producing a more liberal economy is not entirely consistent with a growing capacity to tax and spend.

A modified analysis that begins from the same rational actor model of the state contained in Ekelund and Tollison, as well as North and Levi, would argue as follows: Britain and France were motivated by similar concerns at the end of the seventeenth century. Both states sought to increase their influence and power, and both developed systems designed to extract revenue while promoting the interests of the state. What was different about Britain from France was that competition between the Crown and Parliament as well as exogenous factors, such as Britain's smaller population, land area, and favorable geography (being an island relatively immune from easy conquest), meant that Britain was able to expand the state while changing the form of intervention in the economy.

My modified perspective on British control would be to argue that the state was willing and able to deregulate the economy precisely because it was able to successfully shift its revenue-generating capacity to the collection of indirect taxes. Britain did not necessarily have less government than France (that is a comparison that would require more difficult calculations than one can undertake given existing information). Rather, the British state was able to shift from interventions that had high costs to the economy at large (Royal monopolies, price and quality regulation, guild restrictions, regional tolls) to interventions that, while hardly first best in the economic sense, were relatively more efficient and less destructive to investment and enterprise than direct regulation.

Because the forces of mercantilism in the form of interest group competition were ever present, the tax system that did emerge was not nearly as efficient as it could have been. It imposed its own set of costs and distortions on the British economy. For example, the attempt to favor various branches of manufacture and production through the complicated tariffs on French products, imposed costs on the British economy that would persist well into the nineteenth century.

In this light the regulation of the British alcohol industry modifies Ekelund and Tollison's comparison between Britain and France. In describing the mercantile system in France, they focused on the French Crown's promotion of monopoly industries as a method of restricting output and providing a convenient mechanism with which to tax the products of those manufactures subject to royal monopoly. Ekelund and Tollison insisted that Louis XIII and Louis XIV "were masters at cartel creation and enforcement" (1981, p. 152), contrasting the French situation with the lack of equivalent monopolies in Britain. Yet, if the British beer industry lacked for an officially sanctioned, royal monopoly on beer, the mechanism by which the industry was permitted to become an oligopoly, the extent to which the British state accommodated moves to monopolize the production and distribution of beer, and the restriction of foreign wine competition created a vast machinery of revenue extraction that would dwarf anything the French managed to implement before the nineteenth century.

The Peculiar Position of the Brewing Industry

Although Brewer (1988) has argued that it is the professionalization of the tax administration that explains the rise in British receipts, the near exclusive focus on alcoholic beverages goes against that argument. The increase in London's population and its development as the center for a new urban proletariat with less opportunity for home brewing seem to have been important developments for the success of the excise. Technological developments resulting in the easy production of beer—primarily porter—in mass quantities led to the increasing concentration of the brewing industry. The coincidence of the war from 1689 to 1713, the rise of London, the concentration of the brewing industry, the stoppage in trade with France, and the rise of a mostly English beverage trade from Portugal allowed a situation in which the government now had a limited number of players to bargain with.

It was both easier to see who benefited from different policies and who would be responsible for payment of excises.[3] In exchange for protection from tariffs the brewing industry would comply with tax payments. It was in the interests of government and the leading brewers to promote oligopoly in beer production through the encouragement of concentration and continued restrictions on entry both at the wholesale and the retail level. The government fixed prices and inspected production of these large brewers on a regular basis.

The ease of collection seems key to understanding the success of the excise. The more scattered the sources of production were, the more troublesome it was to collect the excise. Just as the land tax fell most heavily on the largest holdings, because the state could obtain more income for the least effort, excises that had to be collected from a variety of small producers would quickly run up against diminishing returns as the high costs of dealing with multiple producers would not be offset by the small income from the multitude of sources. Smuggling, fraud, and other forms of evasion would place a heavy burden on authorities seeking to correctly assess, as well as collect, the tax.

The claim that alcoholic beverages were a "natural" revenue source runs counter to the fact that attempts to raise excises brought only limited success in the late 1600s and the early 1700s. Charles Davenant and others were of the opinion that excises were becoming counterproductive as they seemed to be lowering demand to the point where only limited gains were possible at best. This was indeed the situation facing the Crown in the seventeenth century, when continued attempts to raise revenue by raising tax rates could only go so far.

By the standards of the seventeenth century, Britain was moderately successful in raising taxes and revenues in the late 1600s. Yet none of this compares to the astonishing rise in income following the Glorious Revolution that initially took place with only modest increases in the number of taxes and tax rates. It is therefore revenue collection and not the taxes themselves that needs to be the focus of the explanation. To speak of collection is really to speak of the willingness of taxpayers to pay their taxes, without which the government would be in the position of squeezing blood from a stone.

The story presented here permits us to derive fresh insights into the evolution of the eighteenth-century brewing industry, especially in combination with the story told by Peter Mathias (1959). Mathias's great work on the rise of the London beer industry makes three important points relevant to our discussion.

The beer industry, notably the porter breweries, saw an "industrial revolution" in brewing in the early to mid-eighteenth century, which led to a rise in the minimum efficient scale of operations. The changes in technology and organization led to very high levels of concentration in the brewing industry, with only a dozen or fewer firms dominating the market by the end of the eighteenth century. The change in concentration at the wholesale level was associated with the rise of tied houses in the retail market, which led to enhanced state regulation of the entire industry with the cooperation of the brewers themselves. These changes will be examined in more detail because an understanding of the industrial organization of brewing will illustrate how the policy of restricting wine imports came to be sustained by institutional developments at the level of domestic industry.

The revolution in brewing was primarily in the production of porter rather than ale. Porter "seems to have been the first beer technically suited for mass-production at contemporary standards of control, unlike ale which needed 'attemperated fermentation' for stability in large-scale brewing" (Mathias, 1959, p. 13). Porter was the brew of choice because it was capable of being mashed in large quantities while surviving operations in which the release of tannins would cloud and therefore make the mash unacceptable for fine ale. No other grain could survive the many mashings of industrial strength brewing at the time than porter, which made it the natural choice of a growing industry. Perhaps porter would not have displaced ale at the time had there not been such concentration in population in London, which worked to promote both demand and supply. Not only could large-scale production flourish, but home brewing was both more difficult and hence less economical there than in the countryside. Furthermore, the greater opportunities for employment and distraction in the city undoubtedly raised the opportunity cost of attempting to avoid the market product and, of course, war with France destroyed the only other drink with a realistic chance of making inroads into the drinking habits of the small but growing middle class.

Changes in regulation and taxation since 1660 "had been having an effect in concentrating the industry into fewer and larger plants: in particular, Common Brewers had favorable excise allowances" (Mathias, 1959, p. 21). Porter was a relatively undifferentiated product as produced by the most efficient firms, making it much easier to market and sell. The combination of increasing urbanization, the central importance of London, and the successful adoption of porter as a basis for large-scale wholesale production contributed to a situation that moved large numbers of people away from home brewing toward just consuming market products.

Such production and the attendant problems of distribution apparently had enough scale economies to make for a concentrated industry, dominated by a few powerful brewers ("this first generation of industrialists exploited the commercial success of a new product in the main by organizing their establishments deliberately for its large-scale production and distribution," p.63). The number of brewers registered steadily declined from the late 1600s to the early 1800s hovering in a range from 160 to 190 in 1684 to 1708, and falling below 100 in the period up until 1830 (p. 22). As Mathias notes, "the fall in absolute numbers did not coincide with any great increase in absolute quantities. . . . It is this important relative change in relation to the modest aggregate expansion of production which distinguished the industrial revolution of the brewing industry from that of others, such as cotton or iron, which represent the Industrial Revolution" (p. 22).

The third point is of great importance because it underlines the extent to which fiscal and tariff policy did in fact suppress the growth in demand of all alcoholic beverages. Demand for wine and beer as a category usually has a high income elasticity. Despite the growth in income that accompanied the British Industrial Revolution, the increases in total demand for both products were minor until the mid-nineteenth century because taxes and tariffs were so high.

If the industry did not see any substantial growth in demand or output though, why then did they support policies that limited the industry's growth? The answer lies in distinguishing the gains to the industry as a whole from the gains to a restricted industry with monopolistic elements.[4] In a nutshell, control and regulation made possible an oligopoly that derived substantial monopoly profits from the increased concentration in the beer industry. These profits were more easily taxed by the government, and the maintenance of such profits were held hostage to government policy toward international trade in wine and spirits. The regulation and price controls that would have been undesirable in a competitive industry were conducive to the maintenance of a brewing cartel and therefore welcomed by the dominant players.

The brewing industry became larger and more concentrated both in structure and organization in eighteenth-century London. The concentration of power in the hands of the largest brewers is confirmed by the value of these establishments over time. For example, Anchor Brewery was purchased in 1729 for £30,000. It was valued at £78,800 in 1749. This value later rose to £149,200 by 1780, when it was apparently sold cheaply for £135,000. The firm of Benjamin Truman showed similar rises in valuation from £23,340 in 1741 to £225,090 in 1790 (Mathias, 1959, p. 24). In Mathias's words, "Before the mid-eighteenth century, a large porter brewery was as different from the inn brewhouse as the later cotton mill was from a large cottage workshop. As the process continued so the pyramid of production developed ever more steeply sloping sides" (p. 24).

The rise in control of brewing can be seen from table 6.2 of beer output throughout the mid-eighteenth to early nineteenth centuries.

Notice that the total amount of beer brewed was at most 50 percent greater in 1830 than in 1748, despite the rise in income and population that London had experienced. At the same time the share of total output accounted for by the top twelve houses rose from 42 percent to some 85 percent.

TABLE 6.2
Production of Strong Beer in London, 1750–1830 (Figures in 1000
Barrels)

Year	Total Brewed	First Twelve Houses	Percentage of Total
1748	915.5	383.0	41.9
1750	979.5	437.0	43.6
1760	1,114.5	525.5	47.1
1776	1,289.0	707.0	54.8
1780	1,319.5	680.0	52.8
1787	1,251.0	965.0	77.1
1795		978.2	
1800		994.5	
1810		1320.5	
1815	1,768.5	1401.5	77.7
1817	1,532.5	1226.5	80.0
1830	1,441.5	1,200.0	85.0

Source: Mathias, 1959.

Note: Collected originally from excise returns, when available. First twelve houses, MSS. And printed lists at the breweries.

Further evidence of the central government's special relationship between protection of the dominant brewers and the ease with which they could collect excise taxes was seen in the evolution of their attitudes toward restrictions on retailing, especially state support for the notion of the tied house. In the late seventeenth century the government favored unrestricted licensing as the best means to facilitate revenue generation. Yet by the eighteenth century both the government and the leading brewers supported regulation restricting licensing of new pubs and beer houses. Policy that had heretofore been designed to promote revenue through unrestricted retail trade became focused on cautious regulation and protection of the public health. When sixteen licenses were eliminated in Bedfordshire in 1689 the complaint arose from the government that "suppression of Ale Houses is a growing mischief to the Revenue," and encouragement had been given earlier to the Treasury to license on the grounds that, "the more Ale Houses there are the better it is for the Excise" (Mathias, 1959, pp. 125–26).[5]

In contrast, this theme is not taken up at all in the eighteenth century, and there were few concerted complaints from those whose interests lay in the sale of beer against those anxious to control it. Increasingly, arguments emerged as to the need to restrict licensing for the purposes of preserving the public health or to protect the public from fraudulent practices. Whereas previously the government's attitude was clearly "the more, the merrier," the 1700s saw the state involved in fastidious attempts to restrain the uncontrolled spread of retail establishments. From the 1730s on, "surplus" houses were routinely restricted. As the vast majority of retail establishments came to be related to the leading brewers through tie-in sales and franchise arrangements derived from ownership by the large producers, the industry was eager to encourage efforts on the part of the treasury or any other branch of the state to restrain competition in the sale of all alcoholic beverages. In effect the government worked to limit entry into the retail market.

The government support for monopoly practices, and the self-evident increase in the profitability of the large London brewers, actually made for an interesting concordance between the temperance and the free trade movements at the beginning of the nineteenth century. For the first few decades of the 1800s the temperance movement was actually allied to the free traders. For instance, Cobden believed that beer monopolies with their tied houses and the economically inefficient restrictions on the wine trade drove the working classes to hard liquor. While they were not in favor of broader consumption of spirits, those in the movement did feel that wider consumption of wine and lighter beverages would more effectively substitute for rum and whiskey (an argument made equally by lobbyists for the vignerons of Bordeaux).

In describing the logic that united the temperance movement with the free traders, Brian Harrison writes:

> The free licensing argument went something like this: government attempts to regulate the drink trade foster four related evils: high prices, adulteration, smuggling and drunkenness. High taxation and monopoly enable drink manufacturers to make large profits and to adulterate their product at the expense of the poor. Inefficient and corrupt government inspectors do nothing to improve its quality and fail to curb smuggling. Therefore, sweep away medieval sumptuary laws and monopolies, reduce taxes, and institute free competition! This will reduce prices, eliminate adulteration and smuggling, and curb drunkenness—which flourishes only when governments bestow artificial attractions on drink. If drink is made as accessible as bread and cheese, and as cheap as wine in France, it will be taken for granted, drunkenness will fall to the French level and supply will settle down to meet demand. (Harrison, 1971, pp. 64–65)

By the time of the 1860 Anglo-French Treaty a large group of temperance activists, though emerging socially from the same circles as the free traders and other libertarians, came to view prohibition as the only solution to the problem of drunkenness and vice. This they recognized to be a difficult proposition for their colleagues inasmuch as the prohibitionist United Kingdom Alliance was headquartered in Manchester, the spiritual and political center of libertarian free trade.

One important feature of the excise is also worthy of note. Although the duties on imported wines were specific, the various duties on beer and ale varied between strong and small beer, with distinctions derived from differences in the retail price of the products, effectively approximating an ad valorem tariff (Binney, 1958, p. 35). Although the beer excise was a specific one, making the distinctions between strong and small beer permitted a degree of differentiation between beers of different types that was denied to tariffs on lighter French wines—doubly penalized for being cheaper than some of their counterparts in Spain and Portugal to begin with, and then being stuck with a number of discriminatory duties on top of that. As will be shown in the chapter on the nineteenth century, distinguishing between wines of different strengths was an integral component of reforming the wine tariffs, especially in the 1860 Treaty of Commerce.

The Case of Walpole and Failed Excise Reform of 1733

No better clue exists to the peculiar interaction between trade and fiscal policy than the strange case of failed excise reform in the early eighteenth century. Historians have long been puzzled about the Walpole government's spectacular failure to promote tax reform in the form of the Excise Bill of 1733. To summarize Walpole's actions, the administration sought to alleviate the tax on property and continue their success in creating an efficient and effective tax administration by replacing all tariffs on wine and tobacco with excises, which would be collected through government bonded houses in Britain.

In principle the idea was sound and fully in accord with neoclassical economic notions of an optimum domestic tax today. Indeed those economic writers, (for example, Douglass Irwin, 1993), who saw nineteenth-century British tariffs on French wines as simply the counterpart of domestic excises on beer, would agree that the theory of public finance would dictate that the most efficient form of excises would be nondiscriminatory taxes levied equally on all goods without regard to type, quality, or country of origin. No real world taxes have ever matched the theoretical ideal, but a nondiscriminatory set of taxes on beverages used for home consumption would require equalizing local excises and import tariffs (as Irwin, 1993, argues specifically). If that were the main point of the tariffs on French wine, though, there should have been no objection to replacing the complicated, highly discriminatory, and cumbersome system of import duties with uniform excises on wines treated as consumables domestically.

The Walpole government's concern was not primarily with the niceties of the theory of public finance but rather with the practical difficulty of maintaining the current system of import duties that were rife with fraud. Underreporting of imports, complicated duty schedules, troublesome monitoring, and corrupt petty officers made imperative a reform of these important duties. As the historians of this period have noted and puzzled over, there were no serious obstacles to the reform of the wine and tobacco trade. The objections to the current system seemed legitimate, and the government had enjoyed notable success in extending the excise to items such as tea, chocolate, and coffee in the 1720s. The reenactment of the salt duty in 1732—notorious in France in the form of the gabelle—produced very little opposition in Britain, making clear that the extension of the excises to both luxury goods and more common necessities were not inherently unacceptable to the public and were politically feasible under the existing social regime. Yet the 1733 attempt to reform the wine and tobacco duties went down to utter defeat, a puzzle not fully solved by the most notable historians of the incident (Langford, 1989). Paul Langford wrote, "It is against this background that the origins of the excise must be seen. It was a logical extension of the system which Walpole had already employed and found useful, and above all it provided the one apparent means of escape from the financial dilemma in which Walpole found himself" (pp. 34–35).

Although customs duties had been used in conjunction with excises, all of Walpole's earlier initiatives had demonstrated that excises could substitute easily for all duties. Walpole sought to reduce or even eliminate the land tax as much as possible and replace almost all property taxes with an efficient tax administration founded on the collection of excises. The salt tax had been the first really big venture in this regard, but it did not bring in nearly as much revenue as he had hoped for. Walpole realized the need to attempt to deal with alcoholic beverages, which were looming ever larger in the British budget.

The unexpected defeat of the 1733 Excise Bill, and the hostility it generated on the part of the merchants as well as common people, led to the defeat of many members of Parliament in the next general elections. Given the evidence at hand, it is easier to understand why Walpole's elegant and theoretically correct system would be so hard to implement. The customs duties on wine were not simply an inefficient and cumbersome counterpart to the domestic excises on beer and other alcoholic beverages; they were the very reason for the effective maintenance of domestic excises in the first place.

Given the experience of Britain having limited success in collecting the standard excise on beer in the 1600s, it was necessary to issue duties on French imports to protect local brewing interests and to hold a stick with which to threaten them. A shift to a theoretically efficient system of universal excises on all items of consumption would have the unfortunate drawback of being easily converted from a system designed to favor certain products to a uniform system with no built-in protection for domestic production. It is likely that the increased transparency of such a venture would make the uniform excise inevitable. In contrast, the import duties could be negotiated and observed separately from the excises on domestic goods.

Walpole's hopes for the new system give further insight. Ultimately it was his intention that liberalization of trade would be the endpoint of his reforms. With all duties replaced by domestic excises, Walpole wanted to make England a free port both for revenue considerations and for the promotion of her commercial prosperity (Langford, 1989, p. 32). Direct taxation on property and income would be minimized, and the centralization of tax collection would continue.

Yet for the brewers, this is precisely what could not be allowed to happen! Other statesmen, such as Colbert under Louis XIV, had dreamt of a uniform revenue system maintained efficiently by a central government. However, Colbert had been thwarted by the provincial system, the multiplicity of tax regions, and the inherently high transaction costs of monitoring and enforcing such a system in a nation the size of France (at that time with a population several times that of England). Walpole did not appreciate how fortunate the government was in finding a particular customs regime that allowed for the promotion of a tax administration in keeping with the overall goals and desires of the state. While another system could have been devised to generate more revenue, such a system would not, as Walpole found, have conformed to the specific configuration of interests confronting the English government at the time.

Further evidence of the special significance of the taxes on alcoholic beverages can be seen in the following: Tax proposals could only be opposed or petitioned against after they had already been enacted. This was the standard practice throughout the eighteenth century and signaled the acknowledgment of the treasury's monopoly on finance. Though opposed by many, the treasury's prerogative in this regard was challenged on only three occasions—the Excise Crisis, the Gin Act, and the Stamp Act Crisis in 1765 (Brewer, 1988, p. 236).

The final result of all this taxation and regulation is that beer—one of the most basic staples that would be central to British drinking habits for the next two centuries—consumption did not increase dramatically in the eighteenth century. The figures on beer under duty in England and Wales

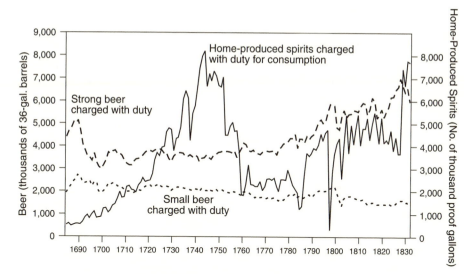

Figure 6.2. Beer and Home-Produced Spirits under Duty in England and Wales, 1684–1830 (Mitchell, 1988).

from 1684 to 1830 show that, except for a brief spurt at the end of the 1600s, there was essentially no substantial change in the total amount of beer produced throughout the 1700s. Only strong beer shows a significant rise in the late eighteenth and early nineteenth century. Considering that this was a period of rapid population growth, this indicates that the per capita consumption of beer (both strong and small) fell quite substantially in the 1700s. The direct beneficiary (as far as sheer quantity goes) of the early taxes and tariffs in beverages seems to have been gin, which was a favorite both for drinking on its own and in combination with beer and other beverages. This run-up is coincident with the so-called Gin Age. It is worth noting that strong measures were eventually taken by the government to depress its production and consumption.

Alcoholic drinks, which have always been among the most income elastic of all goods—with demand usually increasing quite substantially with income—saw a notable drop across the board in per capita consumption throughout the eighteenth century. Domestic production was relatively flat or, at best, showed modest increases while foreign imports were kept at fairly low levels.

One experiment whose outcome was not readily observed was that associated with the Eden Treaty of 1786, which was to begin the process of reopening trade between Britain and France. Although the alcoholic duties were not dramatically changed, the treaty, which really would not have had an effect until 1787 at the earliest, was effectively stillborn. The French Revolution and the Napoleonic Wars meant that another long period of interrupted trade between Britain and France, exactly 100 years after the first bout of trade hostilities in the period 1689–1713, would see to it that reform in the trade between Britain and France would have to wait until the 1860s for substantial progress to be made.

CHAPTER 7

The Political Economy of Nineteenth-Century Trade

WE can now return to the nineteenth century and reconsider the role of Britain as a commercial power and its treatment by historians as the preeminent and pioneering free trader of the period. In returning to the question of British policy in the nineteenth century, we will see how a particular historiographic tradition has arisen and led to a host of theoretical interpretations that hinge on the fact of British leadership—sometimes referred to as British free trade hegemony. In the light of my revisionist view of British trade history an alternate interpretation of this period can be constructed that fully integrates the question of free trade with the rise of the modern state and the importance that is accorded to both revenue collection and to commercial protection.

Let me restate the major claim of the book. Britain was not in any reasonable sense of the term a free trader prior to the Anglo-French Treaty of 1860 and, arguably, not until the last quarter of the nineteenth century. Furthermore, the British problem with shifting to a more liberal trading regime was intimately tied to the domestic struggles concerning the appropriate way to fund the growth of the state.

So we have two very different stories of British trade history in the nineteenth century. Let us review the traditional tale: in the eighteenth century, Britain was an expansive, mercantilist power with a growing state and increased colonial ambitions abroad. But thanks to a movement begun by writers and philosophers like Adam Smith and David Hume, and continued by ideological groups like the Anti-Corn Law League, a struggle broke out in the 1830s that culminated in the repeal of all the major tariffs on foreign agricultural products in 1842. This was the major policy transformation of the century; the world's dominant trading nation chose unilaterally to begin a process of moving to free trade by eliminating almost all of its tariffs on imports. Its advocacy pushed other nations to follow suit, until Germany and France reversed their positions by imposing new duties at the end of the nineteenth century. By the World War I, Britain was virtually alone in holding on to free trade.

My version takes an entirely different view of British policy. In rethinking the history of British trade reform, we will see how existing formulations have relied too much on the myth of British trade leadership and have confused an ideological commitment to policy with the actual, effective policy as implemented by the state. In so doing there has been a misreading of the way in which domestic fiscal and international commercial policy have been linked, even when scholars have bothered to link the two. We will understand how a more narrowly self-interested view of British policy, coupled with a shift in domestic interest-group politics, made use of an elite ideology of freer trade to gradually shift Britain away from trade restriction and protection. But because of the constellation of domestic interests involved, much of the shift toward free trade was initially exaggerated and focused primarily on politically contentious duties that were latecomers to the mercantile policy. The repeal of the Corn Laws, the critical juncture for the shift to free trade as seen by historians, economists, and political scientists, are herein reinterpreted as more important for the politics and ideology of free trade. But deep and genuine liberalization would take several more decades to accomplish and would not come without bilateral negotiations that the more fervent free traders had long rejected as being unnecessary and even detrimental to the cause of unilateral free trade.

MODELS OF THE STATE

There are basically two general classes of models of the state and policy decision making used in political economy. On the one hand, you have cases in which the state is treated as if it is maximizing some utility function, as if it were a single, rational entity. This sometimes leads to the characterization of the state as some sort of welfare-maximizing idealist, and theories that explain political action in terms of the changing beliefs of the leading elites are an important subset of this view. More commonly, this view of the state as unitary actor underlies a variety of realist theories of international relations in which the *state* is maximizing some aspect of *state* influence or power subject to constraints imposed by politics or arbitrary cultural or social imperatives.[1] Britain would be seen as a single actor whose motivations are inferred both from general considerations as well as from the motivations of the leading state actors. In the nineteenth century this focus would naturally place greater emphasis on issues that had a high degree of political salience and that were prominent in the public eye—such as repeal of the Corn Laws—or else on issues where foreign and strategic policy were of greater importance. Arguments about the nature and extent of British free trade that stemmed from concerns about international power—the need to encourage or defend an international trading regime, or the utility of concluding a commercial treaty as an adjunct of other negotiations having to do with war and diplomacy—fall naturally within this modeling tradition.

On the other hand, you have models that have a more domestic focus. These pressure-group stories usually contain some variant of an optimizing struggle between different groups, where the intensity of their interests is a function of their potential gains modified by the transaction costs of organizing (usually involving collective action problems) and the assumptions one makes in aggregating upwards. If one assumes that there are effectively no constraints on collective action, then one ends up with an interest-group story in which the state maximizes the general welfare because those with the most to gain or lose from any policy are able to shape policy at margin.

This type of model, quite common in economics, has typically been employed to understand issues such as the nature and extent of protectionist legislation or government subsidies to industry. The focus is on the state as a mediator between domestics and as an instrument for rent-seeking by those who would exploit the power of the state to make selective transfers. It is fair to say that redistribution is the natural focus of most of these models, although one could also see this as a means of basing claims about state actions on a more microlevel analysis. An important variant sees the state (usually the leadership or the permanent bureaucracy) as a separate actor, with some degree of independent latitude in dealing with the various interest groups, which will consequently have its own interests that may diverge from those of the nation. This is also the case when the ruler or ruling class is sufficiently powerful or authoritarian that it is easy to see how the powers that be can exercise authority with some independence from the demands of the people. Obviously, all states are constrained by domestic politics, and usually it is a matter of degree as to how much independence is appropriate for any given situation.

The more typical historical variant accounts for the greater part of the story. In times of war the logic of the state as individual is paramount and likely to make treating the state as a rational unitary actor reasonable and plausible. In times of peace, and especially when considering economic policy, some version of the collective action/public choice school is relevant. Despite the tendency to sometimes treat the state as a single actor, any analysis that sees commercial policy as having evolved from the interplay between pressure groups desiring protection and a state apparatus that seeks greater revenue will default to an interest-group analysis. The virtue of a history of trade policy that has considered how demand for revenue interacted with the forces of protection, and has policy changeovers that are triggered by the fortunes of war, has the advantage of pinpointing some of the crucial instances in which strategic and individualist considerations override those of the longer-term economic and social forces that economistic analyses tend to emphasize.

Yet, unlike static models, the historian is forced to deal with the shifts introduced by historical change over time. In this environment the assumption that the actors cannot fully internalize or calculate all the expected effects ahead of time is plausible and necessary for realism. Given this introduction of dynamic change, the constant moves from static model to static model create periods of transition that give rise to new or more powerful economic agents. However much specific conditions lead to a particular equilibrium set of behaviors, changes in institutions brought on by changing policy and evolving public institutions, create vested interests that then become significant constraints on subsequent bargaining and political change. Were these effects fully calculable and predictable, then it would be sensible to ignore institutional changes or randomness over time. The presence of new entrenched interests could have been foreseen and taken into account in decision making. Absent such foresight though, the combination of changing rules and the emergence of new interest groups that benefit from the rents created by all these changes leads to unintended consequences that are often thought of as a sort of path-dependent historical system.

BRITAIN AS A FREE TRADE HEGEMON

An important set of models, in the state as rational actor vein, are those realist models usually assembled under the heading of theories of "hegemonic stability." The idea in trade policy is that the maintenance of a free trade zone suffers from a free-rider problem, with nations having an incentive to encourage free trade in others while imposing tariffs individually. This is rational economically only if the nations have some market power; otherwise, unilateral free trade is the optimal policy. However, a view of the state constrained by domestic special interests would make possible a variant wherein the temptation to give in to domestic demands for protection serves as the basis for free riding. In this model a free trade leader is needed to maintain the system, which would otherwise collapse. These ideas—common in the literature on international political economy—are said to have derived from the work of Charles Kindleberger (1978), though he himself was ambivalent about Britain's role as a free trade hegemon, preferring to ascribe British policy to the ideological beliefs of the political authorities.[2]

Many political theorists are of the view that economic growth, especially in the nineteenth century, required both a technological and political leader to promote innovation and to support a regime of liberal trade.

Typical is the claim of Robert Gilpin: "A third feature of these features of extraordinary growth is that they are characterized by a movement toward free trade under the leadership of the hegemonic economy. . . . The repeal of the Corn Laws in 1846 witnessed the British launching of an era of free trade that lasted until the revival of economic nationalism in the 1870s" (1987, pp. 104–5). Though hegemonic theorists are often reluctant to make precise claims about the causal links between hegemony and performance, this claim by one of the pioneers of the field is notable for its explicitness.

This claim is also remarkable for its inconsistency with the chronology derived from the trade statistics. The Corn Law repeal did not lead directly to a free trade era; rather, the period from 1870 to the 1890s was almost certainly a period of more open trade in Britain and Europe than the period from 1846 to 1870. British tariffs did not go below those of France until the 1870s. From this point British tariffs stayed low until the World War I. Moreover, the spurt of nationalism associated with the Meline Tariff does not seem to have led to particularly high average tariffs in France in comparison to those of the 1860s and 1870s. These levels were certainly below those common in Britain and France in the late 1840s. Apparently hegemony did little for the expansion of free trade except perhaps in providing a rhetorical label for the mid-nineteenth century.

Understanding the true nature of British trade policy has special importance in evaluating claims about British influence in the nineteenth century. Despite the lack of an empirical basis for the theory, Britain has been elevated as the leader in foreign trade and even free trade during this period. For an example of this type of claim, Gilpin maintains that "using primarily the instruments of free trade and foreign investment in the political-strategic framework, Great Britain was able in effect to restructure the international economy and to exercise great influence over the course of international affairs" (1971).

This argument conflates two very different things. The evident benefits Britain derived from world trade are presumed to coincide with successful British manipulation of the conditions of world trade in its favor. The former is easy to accept, the latter is inaccurate, unless one wants to define "influence" so broadly and vaguely as to rob the notion of hegemony or leadership of any analytical significance.

Gilpin's argument incorrectly assesses the true power of a world trade leader. To be the leading partner in world trade does not mean you have any real influence on trading patterns. Nor does it imply that you successfully control and dominate this trade. In economics this is the fallacy of automatically conflating a large share of the market with monopoly power.

In the same article Gilpin spoke of British power disappearing or erod-
ing at the end of the nineteenth century. But since Britain had only a limited role in promoting international free trade in the first half of the century, and was unable to halt the rise of protectionist barriers on the part
of France and Germany at the end when British trade was at its freest,
can one really say that the existence of the liberal trading regime of the
nineteenth century owed much to British unilateralism? The answer is
obvious. This in turn makes a mockery of claims that Britain "shaped"
world trade to benefit itself especially.

It would be fairer to argue that a liberal trading regime was created
when Britain acquiesced to a trade treaty with France, a treaty the unilateral free traders never wanted, and when the European trading network started to unravel as France and Germany—two of the pioneers in
signing trade agreements with Britain and other nations—began to pull
back from free trade. Being an efficient exporter of manufactured goods,
the rise of a liberal trading network was bound to intensify British specialization in manufactures. One could just as well argue that the network was created for trading partners in need of both new products and
industrial knowledge from Britain, instead of arguing the reverse. This
would place the importers of British goods in the leadership role of foreign trade. By no means would it be accurate to claim that Britain "fash-
ioned an industrial division of labor" (Gilpin, 1971). The historical
record by no means provides evidence of deliberate action on Britain's
part to justify such a claim.

THE CORN LAW REPEAL

Because of its importance in the historiography of British trade policy,
no work on nineteenth-century trade policy is complete without at least
an attempt to summarize some of the key results of the literature. An
earlier chapter dealt extensively with the question of British openness
and the extent to which it was genuinely a free trader. This section will
briefly review the political economy of the repeal to ask how this change,
in the light of a revisionist interpretation of tariff history, might be understood.

For commercial historians the central question in the nineteenth century was, "Why did Britain unilaterally move to free trade and How did
repeal of the Corn Laws come about?" (Schonhardt-Bailey, 1997, p. 1).
These questions presuppose that repeal of the Corn Laws really did lead
to free trade. And that assumption frames all issues in the analysis of the
political economy of Victorian Britain. But then, what if Britain was not
the free trader it claimed to be?

The repeal of the Corn Laws was undoubtedly the watershed event in the intellectual history of nineteenth-century commercial policy. But it is important to distinguish between the importance of the event for the ideology or promotion of free trade and its actual impact on commercial policy.

Existing historiography has tended to treat the two as identical, assuming mostly without proof that repeal of the Corn Laws opened the gates to unilateral free trade on the part of Britain. It is not surprising therefore that analysis has focused on the specific conditions surrounding the repeal and treated the process of repeal as equivalent to the onset of free trade in Britain, then Europe.

Consequently, two strands of reasoning have emerged. As Iain McLean has noted (2002, p. 133), this has either been treated as the ideological triumph of the Manchester school, or as the beginning of British international hegemony in the nineteenth century. Yet McLean notes that according to Peel himself the Manchester explanation is inaccurate unless one postulates a sort of false-consciousness on his part. The latter explanation is bound up with questions of what constitutes British hegemony and how lowering tariffs unilaterally may or may not have contributed to its establishment.

It is in the latter case that the approach taken in the present work becomes especially appropriate. When speaking of de facto British dominance of European trade through a liberal trading regime, it is imperative to ask whether or not Britain was in fact a free trader. If the evidence presented about the maintenance of British tariffs is to be taken seriously, the answer is evidently a resounding No. Moreover, since British attempts to liberalize trade after the Corn Law repeal did little to move the other European powers before 1860, regardless of what one thinks about British success in liberalizing her own trade, it seems hard to believe that a theory relying on British dominance as anchoring a European trading system would be considered as a viable explanation.

The Corn Laws had also been complicated by the mix of tariffs on imported grain and export subsidies or controls depending on the relative price of grain and its perceived surplus or shortage.[3] It is not often noted that duties on products such as grain, which were produced by the importing nation and were exported in years of unusual abundance, are usually less harmful to the nation than those on items produced at a cost that is nowhere near competitive. Put another way, the closer the domestic substitutes are to the imported good, the less binding the tariffs are likely to be. It is however the case that those tariffs, precisely because of their direct, observable impact on local products, are also likely to be the center of political attention.

In that sense the struggle to repeal or maintain the Corn Laws is classic in the sense that it combined narrow political maneuvering between various special-interest groups with broader concerns about the appropriate extent of government and questions about the proper degree of interference with international trade. The presence of a large group of men, actively promoting the doctrines of Smith and Ricardo, made for a coherent intellectual debate that mobilized the elites' views of economic theory against much older concerns about the importance of supporting and maintaining the agricultural sector as a critical component of national production—a debate that persists to this day in most industrialized countries. At the same time the shift in British production, which moved decisively in favor of manufacturing and heavy industry in the nineteenth century, undermined the relative power of the farmers in the economy, even as they nearly united as an interest group. It is also the case that the activities of the Anti-Corn Law League made the interests of the consumers in cheap bread an important issue in the substantive debates, even if there was no truly effective lobby for the mass of consumers in Britain.

But at the end of the day, lowering the tariffs on grain only began the process of liberalization. It did not break through the mercantilist hold over the tariffs on wine. It led to the removal of hundreds of duties that were largely ineffective or irrelevant to the overall trade of Great Britain. And as noted in an earlier chapter the removal of British agricultural tariffs was largely matched with much less fanfare by the French at roughly the same time.

The mistaken identity between Corn Law repeal and a move to nearly pure free trade has bedeviled even the more rigorous economic literature on the subject. Both Deirdre N. McCloskey (1980) and Douglas A. Irwin (1988) analyze the welfare effects of British tariff reduction by considering the effects of the policy shift on national income. Both addressed the paradox of a country whose market power actually justified—on purely economic grounds—a positive, optimal tariff, choosing to forego income by moving to free trade. McCloskey did a simple back-of-the-envelope calculation to show that the loss was likely small. Irwin did a somewhat more sophisticated analysis, which suffered from the problem that the model assumed that Britain was a competitive actor to begin with, and imposed an ad hoc adjustment in the case that Britain possessed market power. Both were forced to deal with the conclusion that the nation lost from this exchange, by noting that the models in economics were purely static and did not take into account the dynamic effects of the transformation. Yet the dynamic effects were not really explored in depth and there was no acknowledgment that Britain in fact had very little success in promoting freer trade in the 1840s and 1850s in response to British actions.

Most important of all—as Dakhlia and Nye demonstrated (see the appendix for a detailed analysis) in an economic model in which the issue of British market power is treated explicitly and the actual tariffs of both Britain and France are compared—Britain did not in fact lose even in the short run from moving to freer trade. Its tariffs were still sufficiently high that in the period just after the Corn Law repeal, and before the 1860 Treaty of Commerce, Britain still had more to gain from a removal of all remaining tariffs. In a hypothetical comparison with France, it becomes clear (Dakhlia and Nye, 2004 and appendix) that Britain stood to gain more than did France, which means that tariffs were effectively much more binding on the British economy than they were on the French.

A renewed examination of British policy suggests that no contorted explanations need be given for British behavior. If one looks at the overall pattern of trade in the nineteenth century, one can easily see that British tariffs tended to be high in the first half of the century when British market power was probably at its maximum. Conversely, as the century unfolded and Britain lost its commanding lead due to industrial catch-up on the part of the leading European powers, the nation moved to an approximation of free trade when any tariffs were likely to have been damaging to her economic well-being. Thus, for this policy a realist and group interest story would coincide. Britain would seem to have been singularly fortunate in the 1890s to have had a political balance that favored trade policy that was genuinely efficient for the whole economy.

If this focus on trade policy as indicative of strategic considerations in international policy is abandoned it makes sense to descend to the level of domestic interests. Tariff policy is responsive to the changing fortunes of the different domestic groups contending for influence. This set of explanations, sometimes called Endogenous Tariff Theory (ETT), derives from the public choice literature and its related strands in political economy. The major addition to the view of the state as purely a pawn of special interests is to see the state as an independent actor in and of itself. This assumption allows the state bureaucratic machinery and the persons who benefit from it to have an independent existence apart from the domestic interest groups that selected them. While mediating between contending agents, the state bureaucracy has a vested interest in self-preservation and therefore desires—all else being equal—to expand its range of influence and to preserve the means necessary for the intervention of the state, particularly through a large and growing revenue stream.

In that vein, the claims presented in this work take on added significance. For example, the Corn Law repeal remains an important political event. One can study its genesis for any variety of reasons independent of theories of international political economy. It is especially interesting to reconsider the role of "cheap bread" in motivating support for the various incarnations of the law and how the lack of a corresponding argument for wine—which by then was seen as a pure luxury—may have hindered prospects for an earlier agreement between France and Britain in the 1840s and 1850s (Dunham, 1930, p. 282).[4]

However, given the considerations discussed above, it is undoubtedly the case that the Corn Law repeal loses its special claim on our attention as the pivotal event in the history of trade in the nineteenth century. This is not simply a matter of opinion but rather a judgment based on the range of empirical evidence at hand. The British free trade movement in the nineteenth century should instead be acknowledged for its role in the history of ideas more than for its success in inducing liberal policy throughout Europe.

THE EVOLUTION OF BEVERAGE AND FISCAL INTERESTS: THE BEER ACT

Conforming to the standard account of British free trade can cause us to overlook any number of interesting side cases that do not easily fit into the standard accounts. An excellent example is the Beer Act of 1830.

The enormous changes wrought by rapid increases in population, widespread economic growth, the end of Napoleonic Wars, and the Industrial Revolution dramatically changed the dynamic of relationships between the major political actors in Great Britain. These events laid the foundation for legislative acts that would free up the beer industry and weaken, if not totally remove, protection for beer vis-à-vis wine. This transformation involves a consideration of the interrelationships between the need to maintain the tariffs and excises for revenue versus the declining power of agriculture relative to industry and food production relative to manufacturing. Three political acts spanning the middle of the nineteenth century are of crucial importance, despite almost never having been linked together in the historical literature. These are the Beer Act of 1830, the Corn Law repeal of the 1840s, and the Anglo-French Commercial Treaty of 1860.

The Beer Act of 1830 is rarely mentioned in the literature on free trade and is often completely ignored in discussions of Corn Law repeal (cf. Hilton, 1989). The pressures leading to the act are indicative of the conflicts engendered by the promotion of oligopoly in brewing in the eighteenth century, and the odd interaction between monopoly brewing and high domestic duties on beer production. Consumption of beer had been static throughout the eighteenth century despite rising income and population. Undoubtedly some of this was offset by private brewing, especially in the countryside. Nevertheless, the importance of London in total population and the rise of an industrial proletariat meant that any such unlicensed production did little to alleviate the plight of the average working man. The situation was exacerbated after 1813 by the fall in retail prices, while duties remained at their high level (Gourvish and Wilson, 1994, p. 9). Unsurprisingly beer consumption continued to stagnate in the early 1800s, and high population growth meant a decline in per-capita consumption.

These problems undoubtedly contributed to the renewed scrutiny into the monopolistic practices surrounding the licensing of beer production and sales. Despite the fact that retail establishments such as inns and taverns were authorized in annual sessions since 1729, it was not until 1817 that the Select Committee on the Police of the Metropolis drew official government attention to the ways in which the arbitrary control of licensing led to monopoly profits in the sale of beer (Great Britain, 1817, VII). The outrage over such practices seems more indicative of the changes in the influence of consumer demands—especially from London's working class—and perhaps the changing ideology of political leaders for whom the ideas of Smith and Ricardo began to acquire prominence. Yet most of the changes brought on by this scrutiny and the Beer Act itself did little to alleviate the actual plight of the consumer and in fact merely provided relief to beer producers.

While this might be seen as a perverse outcome of policy "designed" to help the consumer, those who are well-versed in the literature on public choice and the influence of special interests will not be surprised at the outcome. Malt duties were reduced by 40 percent in 1816, contributing to the profitability of producers (Gourvish and Wilson, 1994, p. 9). The 1830 Act repealed duties on strong beer and cider while allowing the right to sell beer for a modest fee subject to a limited number of regulations (p. 14).

Unsurprisingly this did not address monopoly production of beer nor undermine the well-established system of tied houses set up by the large brewers over the century that had preceded the act. It did little to alleviate the plight of consumers. Prices did not fall substantially, and beer house producers who were supposed to be the source of new competition accounted for no more than 10 percent of production by 1860 (p. 19). The rise of new retail establishments did not lower prices or reduce monopoly profits because the new sellers basically obtained all or most of their beer from the large breweries, who continued to flourish. The various reductions in duties on beer or malt might have weakened the influence of the brewers on policy insofar as their contribution to the overall revenues of the kingdom would have declined. By lowering duties on beer the government chose to focus on adjusting tariffs in consideration of the tradeoffs between protection and revenue that were integral to the impact of the 1860 Treaty.

REVENUE AND THE BUDGET IN THE MID-NINETEENTH CENTURY: FROM PROTECTION TO STABILITY

Other issues of relevance involve the way that revenue concerns interacted with protectionist and mercantilist sentiment as the power of beverage interests waned throughout the century. That the wine tariffs were implemented initially for purely protectionist reasons did not prevent them from becoming integral to the public finance, as the revenues from duties and excises on all alcohol-related items increased. The problem for nineteenth-century leaders was how to reform the protectionist side of the ledger while preserving the revenues that the state had come to rely upon.

Concerns about the budget were major considerations that delayed the ability of Britain to conclude trade treaties with France and other nations in the first half of the 1800s. Given the importance of these concerns it is useful to consider how the revenue actually changed with the major tax changes of the 1860s, and then compare that with official expectations regarding the effect of the 1860 Treaty and associated tax adjustments that followed. Conveniently *The Economist* reproduced a table based on government statistics in 1865, indicating the expected shortfall from the reductions in the duties on wine, spirits, hops, et cetera.

Taking into account the few taxes that were added or raised in the early 1860s, the budget was predicted to lose a net amount of over 16 million pounds over the first years from 1861 to 1866 after the Anglo-French treaty was brokered by Cobden and Chevalier. A look at the official receipts of both customs and excise shows that revenues were remarkably constant over the period of the 1850s and 1860s; revenues show only a noticeable but still modest drop at the end of the 1860s. In general, customs receipts stayed within a narrow band of about 22 to 24 million pounds sterling annually from 1840 until 1870. This is consistent with our more elaborate computable general equilibrium calculations, showing that in general the British trade policy was more or less revenue maximizing.

The wine tariffs allowed for the greatest change because of their protectionist design, but the government was not going to remove those distortions completely without compensating or adjusting the impositions on the domestic brewing and distilling industries. The results seem self-evident, and we see remarkable stability in the overall receipts-partly re-

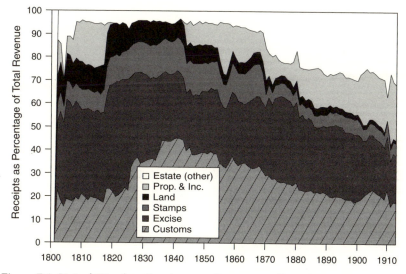

Figure 7.1. United Kingdom Receipts as a Percentage of Total Revenue, 1802–1913 (calculated from Mitchell, 1988).

flecting the supply-side benefits of removing distortions that did little to promote the common good and generated little in terms of net revenue. Lower average tariffs on wine combined with the change in the calculation based on alcohol levels meant that total receipts were not so different; British imports of French wine showed a 600 percent increase in the 1860s with smaller, though significant gains, for other wines and spirits as well. Cheaper beverages and those with less alcohol appear to have been imported in substantially greater volumes.

The general picture of British revenue fortunes is virtually the reverse of what is observed in the eighteenth century. In an earlier chapter it was argued that the shift in British interests, which allowed for increased customs and excise taxes, spared the Walpole government from putting direct pressure on landowners. The late nineteenth century—when British trade was freest—saw a marked shift in the composition of taxes toward the newer income and estate taxes.

Figure 7.1 shows how the composition of British taxes changed throughout the period from 1802 to 1913. Customs revenues declined substantially as a share of the total, after reaching a peak in the early 1840s. Excise share also declined somewhat from the first half of the nineteenth century to 1913. In contrast income, property, and estate taxes accounted for roughly half of all government revenue on the eve of World War I. Though direct land taxes remained a small part of the total

TABLE 7.1
Particulars of the Amounts of Taxes Repealed or Reduced and Imposed

Head of Revenue	Year	Taxes Repealed or Reduced		Taxes Imposed		Net Estimated Reduction of Taxation
		Estimated Annual Relief	Particulars	Estimated Annual Produce	Particulars	
Customs	1860–61	2,840,931	Duties repealed, under the French treaty On butter, cheese, eggs, oranges, etc., rice, tallow, silk manufactures, gloves, and sundry other articles. Duties reduced on wine, spirits, wood and timber, currants, raisins, and sundry other Articles	577,904	British Colonial spirits, charges on bills of lading	
	1861–62	279,558	Duties on books, paper repealed. Duties On wine and hops reduced.	15,000	Chicory	
	1862–63	98,671	Hop duty repealed			
	1863–64	1,896,319	Duties reduced on tea (1s 5 d to 1s per lb) and tobacco. Charges on bills of lading, repealed.	6,811	Chicory	
	1864–65	1,744,384	Duty on sugar, molasses &c. reduced			
	1865–66	2,300,000	Duty on tea reduced from 1s to 6d per lb.			
	In 6 years	9,159,863		599,715		8,560,148
Excise	1860–61	105,000	Hop duty reduced	1,090,000	Spirits and chicory, licenses to refreshment house keepers	

Category	Year	Reductions	Reduction description	Increases	Increase description	Net
	1861–62	1,350,000	Paper duty repealed	5,000	Chicory and licenses	
	1862–63	250,000	Hop duty repealed	232,000	Brewers' licenses	
	1863–64			24,000	Stage carriages, beer retailers Licenses, etc.	
	1864–65	15,000	Tea licenses reduced	9,000	Duty on sugar used in brewing and on chicory increased	
	1865–66					
	In 6 years	1,720,000		1,360,000		360,000
Stamps	1860–61			163,000	Stamp duties on various instruments, etc.	
	1861–62			60,000		
	1862–63	5,000	Fire insurance duty reduced	20,500		
	1864–65	255,000	Ditto			
	1865–66	520,090				
	In 6 years	780,000		243,500		
Income Tax	1860–61	1,060,000		1,060,000	Tax increased 9d and 6.5d to 10d and 7d.	
	1861–62	2,750,000	Tax reduced to 9d and 6d			
	1862–63	1,230,000	Ditto to 7d.			
	1864–65	2,600,000	Ditto to 6d.			
	1865–66		Ditto to 4d.			
	In 6 years	7,640,000		1,060,000		6,580,000
Totals	6 yrs inclusive	19,299,863		3,263,215		16,036,648

Source: The Economist, June 24, 1865. p. 751.

and even declined, it is clear that the shift away from protection meant that Britain had to rely on direct taxes on income and wealth as the basis for increased revenues in the late nineteenth century. Notice that since these are percentages, tax revenues from excise and customs also increased in absolute terms as total revenues increased. But most of the increase had to come from the newer direct taxes, which quickly came to match or outstrip revenues from the old staples of customs and excise. This is consistent with our view that Britain would have been forced to raise taxes on land and property in the eighteenth century, or find another source of income, if it had not raised revenue successfully through higher, more easily collectible customs and excises. The change in the composition of revenues in the nineteenth century may be said to have begun with the decline in British tariffs, beginning with the repeal of the Corn Laws. But the truly large shifts in composition due to increased property and estate receipts came in the last quarter of the nineteenth century—after the 1860 Treaty and after the spread of bilateral free trade agreements with most of Europe before 1870.

The overall success of the English policies, in the face of budget fears, arguably makes the 1860s the true starting point for British free trade in the nineteenth century. The April 22, 1865 edition of *The Economist* argued: "There can be no doubt that the present Financial Administration has been a remarkable one. Certainly it has taken off a great number of taxes, and certainly we have still a very flourishing revenue. Frenchmen, accustomed to a chronic deficit, cannot comprehend that the taking off taxes should be compatible with, nay should produce an augmenting revenue" (p. 462). These remarks and the two decades of debate about the budget that preceded the 1860 Treaty make clear that revenue generation and the tariff were related. Nevertheless, the government was well aware that revenue considerations hampered Britain from attaining a fully free trade status. They knew that prior to 1860 their duties on French wine were not entirely consistent with the principles of free trade, but they still justified them on the grounds that they were necessary for the maintenance of revenue. They understood that reform of the wine tariffs would encourage reciprocal moves on the part of the French, as did in fact occur in 1860, and would make that part of the general tariff more in line with the free trade principles they had been espousing.

The 1860 Treaty had called into play pressures to repeal the Malt Tax—for which the tariff reforms must receive some of the blame. Here it is clear that all involved understood that the losses were potentially quite large and the Malt Tax was seen in opposition to the taxes on land or property. Thus, in the very same issue of the *Economist* cited above there was a communication on the Malt Tax, which claimed:

21. As no rational person can suppose that the Exchequer can bear a loss of six millions without the imposition of fresh taxes, which must be of a general nature, falling upon farmers as well as others, . . . it follows that if their petitions against the malt tax were to meet with complete success, the only gains to them would consist in a very slight fall in the price of beer, purchased by the imposition of some other tax, which, under the circumstances, could hardly be other than augmented Property Tax. (*The Economist*, April 22, 1865, p. 469).

As noted in a previous chapter this was the bargain that permitted the land taxes to be spared in the eighteenth century. Absent the excises on alcoholic beverages of all sorts, land and property taxes would have had to have been raised substantially to generate the levels of income enjoyed by the British state after the Glorious Revolution. Yet it is not clear that, despite the creation of a central tax authority, the state would have been able to overcome the political opposition that would have formed against such a rise in property taxes. It also would not have been guaranteed that the yields would in fact have produced the desired revenues.

It should be noted that those writers who have tended to see the British tax system on beer and wine as having no protective effect and merely as revenue taxes would be forced to concede that in theory the property tax would have been the more neutral and more economically efficient tax. Focusing purely on the issue of efficiency, though, is deceptive. It is the very nature of the beast that the excises and duties were sustainable because of their protective as well as their fiscal nature. A genuinely neutral tax, contrary to the arguments of Irwin (1993), would need to have been placed on all goods to have been a truly neutral imposition.

As it stood, a repeal of one of the major excises on beer eventually passed in 1881.

A Revised History of British Trade Policy and the Role of France

How do we summarize this modified history of Britain's international policy stance? In this retelling, little changes concerning the motivations and pressures faced by the British for the repeal of the Corn Laws in the 1840s. An anti-Corn Law movement—consisting of a coalition of ideological free traders, advocates of cheap bread for the masses, and industrialists eager to improve conditions for a industrial working class that was of increasing importance in the great urban centers—still serves as the force that impelled Parliament to eliminate most tariffs and restrictions on the import of foreign grain. This triggered a desire to eliminate the overwhelming majority of tariffs and duties on manufactured products of all sorts and began a process that lowered average British tariffs with regularity for the next few decades.

However, concern over the budgetary repercussions of lowered tariffs on wine—which were tied not simply to the potentially large direct loss of revenue—and the need for compensatory relaxation of taxes on domestic products, made the government reluctant to eliminate or substantially change the various tariffs on alcoholic beverages and on inputs, such as sugar, that were critical to the production of alcohol. Since alcoholic beverages such as wine were seen increasingly as luxury products—indeed more so than even in previous centuries—there was no equivalent to the pressure for "cheap bread" that would have permitted a larger mass movement in favor of lower wine and spirits duties. Undoubtedly there was also residual concern about favoring France, which was still seen as an important rival to Britain. Certainly no one would have foreseen at the end of the Napoleonic Wars that Britain would never again be involved in a full-scale conflict against the French, and it would not have been surprising had foreign policy considerations had a residual impact on questions of trade policy.

Nonetheless, the intellectual movement towards freer trade was strong and led the British to advocate both unilateral tariff reduction in all of Europe and to consider the possibility of bilateral trade agreements with France and Spain. Despite the strength of this movement, British intransigence over the wine tariffs meant that all approaches to these latter two countries would be rebuffed in the 1840s. Ironically and possibly unknown to world leaders at the time, France had a more open trading regime than did Britain both before and after repeal of the Corn Laws. France had undertaken parallel reductions in agricultural duties that can be seen in hindsight as entirely independent of the British decisions. No doubt much of this had to do with both the spread of classical liberal ideas throughout Europe, as well as the more concrete reality that in the two pioneering industrial countries the power of industry and manufacturing was increasing and that cheaper grain was an important demand of those seeking to promote the enlargement of the industrial workforce.

Changes in the 1850s opened up renewed opportunities for freer trade in both France and Britain. In Britain the rise in property taxes and a renewed income tax removed some of the pressure for revenue in the short run that might have been endangered by reductions in the wine tariff (see figure 7.1 for the shares of different categories in the budget of the United Kingdom).

On the Continent the French had undergone a number of important transformations. Most important was the installation of Louis Napoleon to head France, first as president for life and then as self-proclaimed Emperor Napoleon III. If there is a role to be ascribed to the power of ideas, it is to Napoleon III that one might turn as a likely suspect. Influenced by his years of exile in Britain, Napoleon III was an enthusiastic economic liberal as well as a clever politician. In his two-decade reign he did more than any single French leader in the nineteenth century to promote industrialization, encourage economic growth, and reform trade policy.

In business Napoleon III deregulated the limited liability corporation that would allow France to match many of the corporate innovations that were increasingly commonplace in Britain by mid-century. Through the Crédit Mobilier and other institutions, investment banking was encouraged and allowed to flourish. The French railroad system successfully aided in the breakdown of the autonomous nature of many regions of France and contributed to a truly united domestic market. Macroeconomically it is now agreed that the 1850s were the turning point from which average wages for the working classes turned consistently upward and continued to rise throughout the rest of the century.

Most important for the purposes of this work was his ardent promotion of freer trade both at home and abroad. Napoleon III understood that it was unlikely that a frontal campaign for "free trade" would work in France despite the agitation of free traders such as Frédéric Bastiat from the 1830s on. The government of the Second Empire (begun in 1852) established the Conseil Superieur du Commerce for advice on trade policy. Despite the preponderance of avowed protectionists on the council, Napoleon III was able to promote more liberal trade by a series of continual "modifications" and rationalizations of the trading regime throughout the 1850s (Dunham, 1930, pp. 19–27). Careful reading of the various *enquetes* issued to the departmental chambers of commerce throughout the 1850s also shows that Napoleon's government had been making inquiries into the benefits of reform by asking different industry leaders for their views regarding the benefits of modifying the existing tariff structure. Although as many groups and regions favored more protection as those who wished for lower duties, these surveys would be important as sources of information for the government in identifying more precisely the groups that would oppose reform (cf. Nye, 1991a).

An important role was also played by Michel Chevalier of the Council of State. Whereas in Britain the ardent free trader Richard Cobden had helped to bring about the repeal of the Corn Laws, Cobden's attitude that unilateral tariff reduction was necessary and sufficient for policy reform meant that little actually was accomplished by way of encouraging tariff reductions in other countries (Dunham, 1930, p. 40). In contrast, Chevalier worked steadily for freer trade within the Council of State and by proposing trade treaties with Britain. An attempt to negotiate a treaty that was never made public was undertaken by Chevalier in 1856, but this was rebuffed by the British as were earlier negotiations in the 1840s (p. 47). These preparations did pave the way for the negotiations that eventually led to the signing of the famed Anglo-French Treaty of Commerce in 1860 that removed all French prohibitions on English manufactures. On the British side, the treaty both lowered the duties on French wines substantially and changed the basis for determining the level of the duty from volume to alcohol content. For cheaper products a tariff based on alcoholic strength removed some of the prejudicial favoritism that had been built in against the lighter wines of France in favor of the heavier products of Portugal and Spain.

It is sad that when a treaty was finally negotiated in 1860 Chevalier's name was not associated with it and it was commonly referred to as the "Cobden Treaty," despite the fact that Cobden had long thought of treaties as inferior means of promoting trade. Part of the historical neglect comes from the private and hence unknowable nature of Chevalier's exact communications with the Emperor, but more likely from what Dunham so eloquently notes:

> Chevalier never took an important part officially in the negotiations. He never held the rank of plenipotentiary and did not sign the treaty, and he attended the few formal meetings of the plenipotentiaries only as a technical adviser to the British negotiators. Finally, the Treaty of 1860 was signed for France through an act of autocratic power in violation of public opinion and in defiance of the well-known views of the majorities in both houses of the French Parliament. . . . Thus, while Cobden became once more a national hero in England, Chevalier received little praise and much abuse in France. (p. 59)

France seems to have become more genuinely free than Britain because it involved less fanfare and worked against a backdrop of ideological opposition. However, the power of the Emperor was such that executive decisions could be made in signing a treaty that did not require Parliamentary approval. Also, by never claiming to be aiming for free trade, Napoleon III avoided a direct confrontation with ideological forces that he was sure not to defeat. Napoleon III also cleverly authorized special government loans to many of the industry groups—especially in textiles—that were likely to be affected by the 1860 Treaty. This did more than undercut the likely political opposition that the treaty would have faced after being announced to the French public in January of 1860. The Emperor almost literally paid off those most likely to lose from the treaty. This is unusual because economists often speak of the benefits of free trade by discussing the possibility that the winners from trade liberalization might compensate the losers. In practice however, these so-called "side payments" are almost never made and hence policy changes that may be better for a nation in aggregate are often avoided whenever the losing parties are better able to organize to stop a change whose costs they will have to bear. Were side payments more common in practice it is likely that welfare-improving reforms would be more easily promoted.

The 1860 Treaty was significant because this single event arguably launched free trade throughout Europe. Concerned that they would be left out of a trading arrangement between the two leading economic powers, most of the other nations in Europe rapidly signed trade agreements with either Britain or France. Because the 1860 Treaty was a most-favored nation treaty, which meant that any subsequent tariff reductions would be shared by all parties to prior agreements, bilateral agreements between either Britain or France and any other nation effectively created an enlarging trading bloc that covered virtually the whole of Europe in little more than a decade.

Thus the hegemonic story is virtually turned on its head. The British were unable to exercise leadership when it counted. Ideological free traders made no headway by arguing for unilateral free trade. It was the theoretically impure trade treaty with the French that had earlier been rejected by the British but eventually accepted that triggered the wave of tariff reductions throughout the Continent. This strategic bargain is very different from the notion of a free trade regime held together by a leader who willingly absorbs the static costs from foregoing the monopoly benefits of limited tariffs in order to reap the dynamic gains of a large trading area. As has been already established (also, see the appendix), Britain's tariffs were in fact still high enough that they did not lose even in the short run from moving to freer trade. It was domestic considerations that dictated whether and which tariffs would be lowered or eliminated, and no leadership was involved.

The greatest test of the theory would come in the late nineteenth century. By this time the British did have the freest trade policy in all of Europe and could be said to have exercised leadership. But when France and Germany chose to go against free trade by imposing new import duties in the 1890s—effectively damaging, perhaps even crippling the European free trade regime—Britain did not succeed in getting them to change their minds. As a so-called hegemon Britain did little to induce Europe to move to freer trade when European free trade was getting started and when it was the dominant player it did little to stop other critical players from defecting towards the end.[5]

CHAPTER 8

Trade and Taxes in Retrospect: Were British Fiscal Exceptionalism and Economic Success Linked?

THE view that the mercantilist, state-oriented England of the eighteenth century transformed itself overnight into the liberal, free market Great Britain of the nineteenth century was never entirely plausible. Political economy is most always marked by gradual rather than revolutionary transformations. Political historians often overvalue the role of ideas in contrast to the more invisible, but longer-term forces of economics and politics. Nonetheless, it is undoubtedly the case that the United Kingdom had probably the most open economy—at both the international and domestic levels—of any nation in the West on the eve of World War I. So how should one think of the transformation of Britain from mercantilism to liberalism?

There has recently been a revival of an old argument about the rationality, indeed efficacy, of British mercantile policy by Patrick O'Brien, who links British fiscal expansion in the eighteenth century to spending on national defense as a necessary condition for British economic development (cf. O'Brien, 2002 and 2006; see also discussion by Mokyr, 2003 and 2005). This revisits an important scholarly debate that goes back to the proper interrelation between power and wealth in mercantile thought, that involved such economic luminaries as Eli Heckscher, (1935), Joseph Schumpeter (1954), and Jacob Viner (1948).

Attempts to rehabilitate British mercantilism have usually pointed to the following as rationales for policies that regulated commerce unduly or that interfered with trade and commerce to an unseemly degree:

1) *Protection was good because it stimulated production through the encouragement of manufactures.*

This is the most easily dismissed of the alternatives. If any textiles were protected prior to industrialization it was certainly the woolens that were in greatest competition with products from the Continent. Cotton was the upstart industry and low-end product that arose in the interstices of protection and regulation in the eighteenth century. No contemporaries would have pegged it as the industry that would serve as the most advanced standard bearer of industrial transformation and rapid innovation. The industry benefited from entrepreneurial risk-taking, technical invention, and benign neglect that characterized newer businesses, in which ways of production, organization, and political relations were not yet set and hence needed no defending.

Of course, it is even harder to argue that the broader system of tariffs and taxes on agricultural products and on alcoholic beverages or colonial goods did much to enhance British industry. If anything, it made brewing and distilling more profitable than otherwise. But it is hard to see how this promoted economic development and easy to imagine that by keeping workers in inefficient industries protection impeded the necessary transformations that standard economic liberalism would promote.

2) *Britain needed revenue—tariffs and excise taxes were the means to an end.*

Here we are a little closer to the truth or a plausible facsimile thereof. If we postulate that the provision of public goods is a necessary precursor to successful development and that such provision needs to be funded, we would seem to be on firmer ground. But it is still not clear that the method of financing through rent-creation and protection was good policy or that the funds were primarily spent on projects that were clearly in the public interest.

As the excise revolt or crisis of the 1730s demonstrated, a policy designed to enhance the efficiency of tax collection—the creation of a general excise to replace eventually the welter of inefficient customs and excises then in place—was roundly rebuffed. And a policy based on sound, nondistortionary methods of public finance was not necessarily feasible in the eighteenth century. Only the more complicated policies—with their high and attendant deadweight losses and encouragement of rent-seeking—seem to have been viable. It remains an exercise for a future scholar to show that benefits significantly outweighed the obvious costs.

A more sophisticated variant of 2) is most favored by modern scholars (O'Brien, 2002)—that Britain could not do without some sort of mercantilist policy to achieve its more liberal ends. Therefore,

3) *Tariffs and taxes, and the mercantilist system that generated and supported them, were a rational response to a world in which commerce and economic growth were only possible if Britain secured her borders, protected her sea-going trade, and otherwise saw to the support of her Allies and the maintenance of a far-flung trade regime.*

This is the most promising line of argument for any who would argue for the soundness of eighteenth-century British policy. But even here (as O'Brien, 2006 readily acknowledges) it is too easy to fall into the trap that whatever happened was for the best. To say that actual policy was based on broader societal forces is one thing. To argue that it was inevitable is another. And to argue that it was inevitable and that there was no less costly alternative is a stronger claim still. It may be that the necessary functions of government—including the defense of the nation and the creation of a modern civil service—would not have been possible without the compromises that actually emerged in the period.

But one must then view the rise of a bureaucratic state and the explosion in fiscal spending and taxation that we observed as a cost of paying for necessities of government. You could take this position, but you would still need to prove it. Did the spending on national defense primarily benefit the security of British trade or was it also, if not largely, an exercise in power that did not pay for itself? Did the benefits of state expansion outweigh the costs such a system engendered? Or was it inevitable that a ruling class filled with liberal ideology, but constrained by the weight of real-world entanglements would oversell the extent of British liberalization? Were the opportunity costs of increased regulation, heavy taxes, official rent-seeking, and restricted trade so large as to disqualify their efficacy, or can a case be made that they not only promoted British development but were the only viable set of policies that could have promoted development in that particular time and place?

The positive case for British policy is a plausible one but it remains unproven. And it would be an overstatement to say that the preponderance of evidence favors the supporters of British mercantile restrictions. Indeed, given the obvious efficiency costs of the Hanoverian expansion, promoters of the necessitarian view have a high hurdle to overcome in seeking to justify ex post the virtue of high taxes, retail and wholesale monopolies, and the distortions induced by restrictive trade practices.

Ultimately, the best case to be made for mercantile policy is a weak one: The creation of a large and fiscally voracious state bureaucracy did not impede Britain's transformation into the first modern industrial economy. But it still remains to be determined whether Britain grew because of, or in spite of, mercantilist policy. And perhaps we will never know for certain if an alternate set of policies—more liberal, more conducive to long-term growth, and more consistent with Smithian theory—was feasible or not. But we need to pose the question in the right way and we must begin from more accurate premises if we are ever going to understand the true nature of the West's attainment of modern economic growth.

To begin with one should always bear in mind that the mercantile system that Adam Smith criticized in Britain and France was never a coherent, universally applied ideology. Very often it was an ex post generalization or rationalization of existing political economic systems.

The more accurate characterization is that England—then Britain—emerged at the end of the seventeenth century as having survived a century of revolution and war with a disorganized administrative apparatus, a divided government, and a continuing need for revenue both to fend off British rivals and to assist in imperial expansion overseas. Somehow the impecunious England of the early seventeenth century managed to create a centralized, professional civil service in the eighteenth century that successfully oversaw an unprecedented expansion of the state. Taxes and more importantly tax revenues rose to unheard of heights when all the while the economy grew and flourished. This allowed Britain to overcome her rivals abroad without destroying the economy at home.

There were any number of reasons for this. The one most favored by economic historians is some variant of the views propounded by North and Weingast (1989). In a century that saw England try to wrestle with the problems of the appropriate limits of the state and the virtues of protecting private property, a crucial event was the Glorious Revolution. The coming of William III and the compromise that was reached when Parliament limited the arbitrary power of the King and kept for itself the power to tax, actually led to a system in which it was both easier for the state to promote economic activity and to tax the nation as the needs of state dictated. In addition the establishment of the Bank of England helped to institutionalize a formal market for government debt that would aid both by lowering the transactions costs of borrowing and by increasing the transparency of state financing. The creation of a centralized, professional fiscal system for the collection of domestic taxes helped to replace the decentralized and difficult-to-monitor system of tax-farming that had been more characteristic of the early seventeenth century and that was still commonplace in France.

But this version of the story has not made clear that these changes must have come with a variety of continuing costs to the economy and society overall. Scholars looking at political transformations have not put enough emphasis on the shift from retail corruption to a more centralized, Parliamentary influence that accompanied the centralization of tax collecting authority in the new professional civil service. Throughout the early eighteenth century the various systems of local patronage and retail corruption, especially at the judicial level, were replaced by influence-peddling and patronage at a much higher level of authority. Walpole's government was especially adept at representing the interests of the landed classes in limiting the taxation of wealth and income while raising the taxes on excises. But these excises required that entry be restricted and regulation increased on those products that were to be the focus of tax collection.

Trade policy was subservient to the needs of running the state and of geopolitical ends. The government wanted to punish its enemies and reward its friends. The evidence shows Britain's policies functioned within the constraints of the political interest groups that existed in the early eighteenth century. The importance of big brewers in Parliament, the rivalry with France, the rise of industry in the growing urban center of London, and the dominance of aristocrats controlling agricultural land who resisted paying more taxes, were all taken into account in achieving the financial goals of the government.

The changes in the economy that accompanied the Industrial Revolution and started to shift the center of gravity from agriculture and land to manufacturing and industry in the late 1700s and early 1800s also coincided with the rise of a liberal economic ideology that promoted the importance of growth and development through increased commerce. This led to political pressures that favored freer trade and a more laissez-faire economy. But even though many of the changes in economic thought and philosophy played a significant and independent role (this is not a brief for vulgar economism) any shifts in economic policy were bound to come up against the twin forces of entrenched interests and the new dependence on revenue from a fiscal system that had involved a careful balancing of economic and political interests over the preceding century. Where once the tariffs were primarily about punishing the French and rewarding the Portuguese, they became integral to a system in which domestic excises could be collected only with acquiescence of Big Brewing. Obtaining their cooperation meant restricting all possible substitutes, especially cheap wine and brandy from France.

This meant that reforming the various alcohol taxes that were longstanding—which involved more questions of strategic (foreign relations) import than did other trading restrictions and which did not have the benefit of the popular support that was symbolized by the "cheap bread" movement during the repeal of the Corn Laws—was bound to serve as a brake on liberalizing interests or policies. It is also worth noting that despite a liberal economic theory that gave no preference to one industry over another—as is the default position of modern neoclassical theory—most contemporaries did tend to view manufacturing and industry as more important than food processing. They viewed demand for wine, beer, spirits, cocoa, tea, coffee, and sugar as luxuries that were of secondary importance for the growth of the economy. But it is not in fact obvious that any one sector was significantly more important than another for overall economic growth.[1] The costs incurred by inefficiencies and restrictions in these markets exerted an important influence on the economy and welfare of the British people throughout the nineteenth century. This has tended to be overlooked by historiography that has focused on the "leading sectors," such as textiles, or on the vast traditional economy of grain production.

David Stasavage (2003) has made an argument that is an interesting complement to the North/Weingast view in his work on fiscal power and political competition in the eighteenth century. For Stasavage it is the peculiar mix of checks and balances and not financial innovation that made fiscal success possible, thus expanding on the North/Weingast thesis. But the central claim is his view that divided government and Whig/Tory balances in Parliament are said to explain successful or unsuccessful periods of revenue collection for the government, based upon a statistical analysis from the eighteenth century.

The problem is that Stasavage's models are about relative changes in the ability to borrow or collect government revenue, which swing up or down depending on circumstances. But the crucial point about British revenue is not the ups and downs of the state's functions throughout the eighteenth century. What needs to be explained is the *one-time* shift upwards in total income starting at the very end of the seventeenth century, that leads to a mostly uninterrupted secular rise with much smaller variation from year to year or decade to decade. Nothing in his model really addresses this one-time shift. In that sense one is left either with the North/Weingast story—which is more gradualist than they seem to think—or the Brewer story about the rise of the new fiscal administration. While they can be seen as complementary theses, North/Weingast treat the separation of powers as virtually a sufficient explanation of eighteenth-century fiscal success. In contrast, Brewer often seems to see the administrative changes as if they were the crucial technical change: that made for increased state income.

But the claims for the effectiveness of a new administrative structure are too deterministic technologically and organizationally. They imply that all Britain had to do even earlier was to set up an appropriate central tax authority. The state's problems in earlier periods did not stem from the ability of the government to either raise tax rates or to impose new taxes.[2] The problem was that given the failures of enforcement faced by the Crown in the seventeenth century it was just as likely that rising tax rates would have led to modest gains in revenue, at best or, at worst, declines in the total. Hence the real issue to be explained is not how Britain managed to change the rates imposed or even the items being taxed, but how they were able to do it so that they could count on collecting much more in total than they ever had before. And that change comes only from the early 1700s, and only comes about with a sudden focus on revenues derived from wine, beer, malt, hops, and sugar—all tied to alcoholic beverages. It ignores the fundamentally political nature of the change. Only a fundamental change in the relationships between the main political interests, including the makers and importers of alcoholic beverages, could possibly have led to such a dramatic and unanticipated change in the state's capacity to extract revenue. If not for that it is likely one would have seen a long struggle with a brewing industry—and indeed, much domestic industry—that in the seventeenth century had already shown an ability to resist rising taxation and would have led to greater pressures on the landed interests to accept higher taxes on land and farming in general. Recall Charles Davenant's observations (1695, pp. 46–47) that excises from beer and ale had fallen from 1689 to 1693 due to increased rates of taxation and that this was already promoting a shift to private home brewing. Under such arrangements, further increases in rates could not possibly have led to substantial revenue gains without political realignment and organizational shifts to large-scale oligopoly.

The pressures were finessed by the British in the eighteenth century and threatened to spill over into other issues of political economy, as they did in other nations of Europe, most notably in France, where the question of how to allocate taxation in a world of changing technology and institutions was at the core of the crises that eventually led to the French Revolution. The interesting question that cannot be answered yet is how binding the constraints on the land tax were. Was Parliament fundamentally unable to raise taxes on land and property in the eighteenth century, or did those limits seem more inflexible and insurmountable given how much easier it was to shift the burden to customs and excise?

By the nineteenth century the completed transformation of power from agriculture to new manufacturing and industry (i.e., the "high tech" sectors of textiles, coal, iron, and steel) would shift the ability of farming and other traditional production to dominate politics. But the inertia of the fiscal structure that relied upon a compromise between a protectionist foreign tariff and a pliant industry response to domestic excises would serve as a drag on the political and ideological movements towards freer trade at all levels. There can be little doubt whatsoever that the British policy of tariff reform in the 1800s proceeded through first lowering tariffs mostly on items competing with her exports, generally goods on which she had a comparative advantage or in the case of the Corn Laws involved taxation of items that the textile and heavy industries viewed as "critical" to the needs of their workers. In contrast, the strategic and long-standing tariffs on imported comestibles and beverages were not lowered until the 1860 Treaty.

Defending the 1860 Anglo-French Treaty from those free traders critical of these exclusive arrangements, John Bright wrote to the President of the Manchester Chamber of Commerce: "All that England has done in this case has been to carry out in practice, towards all the world, in respect of some remaining items of our tariff, that principle of free trade which we have so loudly professed and which we had previously applied to our important articles of production" (Howe, 1997, p. 93).

There is no doubt that the British thought of themselves as having created a regime of free trade, and free trade ideologues thought of the remaining tariffs as being of minimal importance. Conversely the French willingness to eliminate prohibitions on some products, including some British textiles, was considered of great political significance, a virtual repudiation of French protection, despite the fact that the overall trade regime was quite liberal and the prohibited items would never constitute a major part of trade. The enormous amount of historical work done on nineteenth-century British trade policy leaves no doubt as to the importance these changes made in British politics, and there is no doubt that advocates of free trade viewed England after repeal of the Corn Laws as having the most liberal commercial policy in the entire world—which eventually was true by the end of the nineteenth century.

But the very unanimity of the view, both among contemporaries and subsequent scholars of trade history, about the unilateral and nearly universal character of Britain's ostensible move to free trade points to the danger of judging the importance of an economic policy by its political or public salience. One is so overwhelmed by the breadth of the historical consensus about British policy transformation that it is tempting to redefine contradictory evidence (such as the unequivocally restrictive tax on alcoholic and nonalcoholic beverages) as somehow consistent with a wider view of "liberal" policy despite its noncorrespondence with standard Ricardian notions of pure free trade.

It is worthwhile saying something about the role of methodology and economic reasoning in all this. Since the early 1960s economic historians have proved best when using economic theory and statistics to clarify important debates that cannot be settled by textual evidence alone. Political economy is at its core a technical subject, requiring a certain degree of technical analysis, and economic phenomena were to a great extent amenable to quantification and measurement. Moreover, because of the nature of market competition, contemporaries are not in fact the most reliable witnesses as to the nature of a particular economic phenomenon. Conscious, purposive action is an essential component of the social sciences, but conscious, accurate knowledge and understanding of one's actions is not a prerequisite for the proper working of the economy. As such the standard tools of the historian are often inadequate to describe, let alone analyze, changes in the economy over time and space. Knowing that one group opposed price rises here or that a state wished for open trade there did not in any way guarantee that what transpired had anything to do with their wishes or even with their perceptions of events. Policy sincerely designed to accomplish one thing could easily have resulted in the opposite. The fact that people are well-informed about events that directly affect them does not imply that people are equally well-informed about macroeconomic and political phenomena that also affect them. In fact, the opposite is usually the case. Absent good theory and careful measurement, contemporary observers were often *less* reliable witnesses to the economy of their day than modern-day scholars making effective use of retroactive tools of discovery.

So in a very important sense the standard, economic vision of the world seems vindicated by this research—the overarching question of whether or not Britain was a free trader is to be settled by recourse to statistical estimation. But it is uninteresting if chronicling the changes in attitudes to trade is not tied to the deeper debates about policy and to more modern concerns about the proper understanding of dynamic forces in history.

There is an interesting discussion in the historical literature that focuses on both the narrative of British administration as well as the ideology of the dominant political actors, which questions whether or not an age of laissez-faire ever existed in the nineteenth century (cf. Paul, 1980). But interestingly enough most point to the late nineteenth century as the period when Britain moved farther away from the direction of laissez faire by extending state intervention on a variety of margins. This increased intervention in the domestic economy parallels the clearcut decline in trade barriers throughout the century. Thus the willingness to tolerate an unusually open international commerce was somewhat offset by renewed and increased domestic interference in the economy.

Perhaps the most perceptive view of this comes from H. Scott Gordon (1971). Gordon distinguishes between the support for free trade and the belief in laissez-faire. In his view the former was commonplace, but the latter never an important philosophy of government. What is clear is not the degree to which the central politicians were or were not consistent in their ideological views, but the extent to which actual legislation was primarily driven by case-specific considerations. Even here the problem of characterizing actual British policy, as opposed to simply describing various intellectual positions, is not as simple a task as counting up pieces of legislation or seeing how often certain statements were made. In the end what should be clear is the fact that only a quantitative estimate of the relative impact of various tariffs can give us an accurate portrayal of the true state of economic policy. For similar reasons, absent any systematic weighting of the impact of various interventions in domestic production, there is no way to make a really persuasive claim as to whether or not the decline in external trade barriers was only slightly or greatly offset by changes at home. It is not even clear that the list that writers such as

David Roberts (1960) have worked up, of the various commissions and committees established by mid-century, constituted a substantive change in economic policy, plausible as such an account may sound.

At the same time a strong case is made that shows the limitations of economic and cliometric research in understanding economic and political phenomena over time. There are not and will likely never be precise dynamic economic models that will allow us to predict accurately or even to analyze economic phenomena over time. There are no real equivalents in economics to the equations of motion in the physical sciences, and most of the dynamic models in the literature are much more qualitative metaphors than precise economic engineering. The most interesting features of this historical case study might only be subject to ad hoc modeling, if at all, and would more likely deceive us with a false precision. The important changes in the shape of the British state, the effects on French and British relations, the changes in consumption and production patterns, the effects on government revenue, and the growth of administration were either completely unforeseen or at best dimly glimpsed by contemporaries during the struggles between England and France after the Glorious Revolution and at the end of the reign of Louis XIV in the early 1700s.

On the one hand broad technical, economic, and demographic forces shaped the contours of political economy. These include changes in the brewing industry's technology as well as the rise of London's population. Changes in the composition of national income—particularly the mix between industry and agriculture—played an important role, especially the increased importance of textiles and heavy industry and the role that cheaper grain and raw materials played in encouraging freer trade in the nineteenth century. Longer-term strategic considerations centered on the century and a half of conflict between Britain and France served as a permanent frame on foreign and commercial policy.

On the other hand specific historical events were critical contingencies. Of particular interest were the wars from 1689 to 1713, the poor timing of the Eden Treaty in 1786 vis-à-vis the French Revolution in 1789, and then the Napoleonic Wars cutting off normal trade once more for the quarter century until 1815. Finally, the highly specific and particular circumstances of a relatively autocratic France presided over by an economically liberal emperor made possible a critical trade treaty with Britain in 1860 that had eluded previous governments.

Combining history and economics in the analysis of the politics not only creates a richer story than could be derived independently, but also provides a more rigorous standard against which to judge the critical saliency of political decisions that may all, in hindsight, seem important and unique but which obviously were not of equal importance in the longer term. But one is left with a new set of questions about the role of the state that wait to be answered. Most of important of these will be measuring and estimating the true impact of fiscal expansion on the British economy of the eighteenth century.

Modeling the Effects of British and French Tariffs on National Income[1]

THIS appendix provides a detailed statistical analysis of the welfare effects of the British and French tariffs in the mid-nineteenth century that should make amply evident the fact that Britain had a less open trade policy in practice than did France. For a variety of reasons, simple comparisons of average tariff levels, as mentioned in the body of the text, may be misleading. Though allowances have been made for these problems within the text, it is useful to see what a more complicated and rigorous analysis might add to our understanding of the situation. Noneconomists may be surprised to learn that there still exists no universal measure of trade liberalism, despite the variety of accounts suggesting that country X is freer than country Y or that policy regime A is more protectionist than regime B. Most comparisons of trade freedom are based on very crude measures or very limited accounts of trade distortions. Beyond determining whether or not Britain was a free trader at this time, this work also provides a more applicable method for comparing trade liberalism between countries, even though it cannot be used as a universal measure in this regard.

The work presented in this section is inspired by the ideas of James Anderson and J. Peter Neary (1996). These authors first proposed that one measure of trade liberalism with some claim to generality would involve asking what single tax rate on all imported commodities would have the equivalent welfare effect on the nation to the existing mix of tariffs and quotas on imports. Nevertheless, their approach is not perfect. It is highly dependent on a number of assumptions, as Kevin O'Rourke (1997) noted when using a variant of the Anderson/Neary measure to address the issues raised by Nye (1991b).

But there is also a particular problem in dealing with nineteenth-century Britain. Being the dominant player in international trade, it is likely that measures that treat Britain as a perfectly competitive country with no market power are misguided. This complicates both the calculation itself and its interpretation.

As will be made clear in this appendix, Dakhlia and Nye (2004), from which this appendix was derived, was the first piece to deal explicitly with British market power in the context of a model of trade restrictiveness. Using such a model, it is not possible to create a unique tariff rate that accounts for the degree of restrictiveness as proposed by Anderson/Neary. Given this difficulty, we chose to modify their approach by focusing directly on the welfare effects of the tariff regime itself. To simplify a bit, we ask how much would the welfare of France and Britain be improved in the mid-nineteenth century if all trade barriers were dropped. Presumably the bigger the gain, the bigger the distortion effectively imposed by the trade barriers actually in place.

If a nation has no market power in world trade, any positive tariff lowers welfare. Complication enters when a country with some degree of monopoly power might actually benefit from a positive tariff. This is referred to in the trade literature as the choice of the optimal tariff. If Britain did have a positive optimal tariff and her tariffs were at or below this level, dropping the tariff to zero would actually lower British welfare. One of our innovations in the model is to permit Britain to have greater market power than France, thus mitigating the likelihood that the tariffs were harmful. Nonetheless, despite this bias in favor of Britain, the high welfare costs of the actual regime in place—in comparison to that of France—indicate that the British duties were so high that they were clearly suboptimal. Hence, a drop to zero tariffs would have provided Britain with more of a gain than the equivalent action for France. In our view, this is a fairly good indication that Britain's trade regime was not very free, especially in comparison to that of her supposedly less liberal rival.

Previous work regarding Britain's stance as the world leader in free trade has noted the seeming inconsistency with Britain's standing as dominant trader. As the leader in world trade, Britain probably had substantial market power and, if so, would have gained more in the short run by maintaining a positive optimal tariff. McCloskey first drew attention to this problem in a noted essay published some two and a half decades ago (1980). Using purely hypothetical elasticity parameters and speculating as to the values of the most significant variables, McCloskey concluded that if the optimal British tariffs were positive, Britain did pay a price for moving to free trade. However, the price was small in static terms, and whatever welfare losses incurred were undoubtedly offset by the dynamic gains from moving to freer trade. About a decade after McCloskey's work, Irwin (1988) made much the same point with a simple model that sought to measure the welfare change associated with Britain's trade reductions. He too concluded that in going to free trade, Britain was moving away from the optimal tariff and that the nation had therefore suffered a loss in utility on the basis of static calculations. He conceded that his calculations seemed "to confirm the judgment that adverse terms of trade shifts would outweigh efficiency gains from a British tariff reduction" (p. 1158), but he repeated McCloskey's claim that these were static calculations that ignored the dynamic effects of free trade. In particular, Irwin ignored the demonstration effect of British tariff reduction in terms of spurring other nations to move to free trade.

There are serious difficulties with the calculations on which these claims have been based. By looking at the gains to Britain and France derived from abandoning all tariffs in a rigorous, computable general equilibrium model that allows for the possibility of market power, we can determine how binding those tariffs were and how significant they were in distorting the trade patterns of both nations. The size of British welfare losses is found to be large enough that it is clear whose commercial regime deviated more significantly from both the ideal of free trade and the surplus maximizing, economically efficient ideal. This point is made stronger by comparing the welfare losses to those from France because, unlike previous estimates, we systematically factor in British market power in a model designed to allow for positive optimal tariffs.

MEASURING PROTECTION

Traditional tariff indices have usually focused on one of three measures: (1) the nominal level of tariffs per class of goods, (2) weighted measures of average tariffs defined as total revenues divided by total value of imports (and various modifications to this basic idea), or (3) measures of effective protection on an item-by-item basis, where nominal tariff levels are corrected for tariffs on inputs used in production of these goods. All three methods suffer from a variety of theoretical and empirical problems. The first measure ignores the relative importance of a good in total trade; the second has serious problems with respect to trade weights, given the problem that a nearly prohibitive tariff might add little to the revenues received; and the third is problematic when used to create an overall index and suffers because effective protection measures ignore the costs of tariff restrictions to the consumer.

The most widely cited recent attempt to create a more universal tariff measure is the Trade Restrictiveness Index (TRI) first promoted by Anderson and Neary (1994) and adopted by O'Rourke (1997) in his own contribution to the debate on whether nineteenth-century France, rather than Britain, was the freer trader. The TRI—which is calculated within a computable general equilibrium (CGE) framework—is the first theoretically sound index for comparing trade liberalism. Unlike earlier methods, the TRI is directly derived from an economic objective, in this case, welfare maximization.

By explicitly modeling tariffs and trade in a general equilibrium framework, O'Rourke quantified and thereby clarified the terms of the debate. He demonstrated that the outcome of the debate hinges on the functional forms and calibration of preferences and technology; in particular, he showed that the degree of substitutability between beer and imported alcoholic beverages turned out to have a remarkable impact on the welfare effects of British tariffs. The question, thus, is no longer whether or not beer and wine are substitutes (and thus whether tariffs on wine should be included in a tariff index), but rather for what range of elasticities of substitution between both types of alcohol France would indeed have been the freer trader.

Unfortunately, in order to compute a country's TRI in the style of Anderson/Neary and O'Rourke, one must ignore the issue of market power and assume a small country whose decisions have no effect on world trade. As shown in the appendix, a large country's TRI will be either ambiguous or not defined at all (see also Dakhlia and Temimi, forthcoming). Since the small-country assumption is evidently not ideal when studying how a country that loomed large in international commerce might have benefited from a positive economic tariff and its subsequent reduction, the TRI-based measure must be abandoned. In doing so, though, we must be careful not to toss out the baby with the bath water. In order to create the appropriate means to compare France and Englands' trade, we preserve the CGE framework, since it offers an unusually rich context in which to interpret our sparse data. While we cannot derive an index, the framework still allows us to track welfare effects of protectionism. Specifically, we track the national welfare effects of a progressive counterfactual tariff reduction down to zero. This suffices for our purposes, since we merely wish to know whether British tariffs were higher or lower than those suggested by static welfare maximization.

The Model: Background

Our approach follows Anderson/Neary and O'Rourke by modeling the economy in a general equilibrium framework. The general equilibrium framework provides a particularly appropriate tool for performing comparative statics exercises in trade. It is also very useful for studying the static effects of policy changes and their impact on trade flows, allocation of goods, and welfare effects on consumers, since the interdependence among the various markets is at the heart of the measurement problem. A tariff imposed on wine, for example, will affect both the demand for wine and the demand for beer and other goods. A partial equilibrium approach would only capture bits and pieces of a tariff's intricate effects.

A model should be sufficiently rich to shield itself from the R. W. Fogel (1967) critique and leave room for the data to matter. The downside of a rich and flexible model, of course, is that it may be too complex to allow for simple, closed-form solutions and comparative statics: Thus, the need for a computational approach. Moreover, the beauty of a computable general equilibrium approach lies in its direct focus on the welfare or utility of the representative consumer, thereby avoiding awkward approximations typical of partial equilibrium welfare analysis.

As in Anderson/Neary, we assume that region i has a representative consumer who values a large variety of imports as well as a generic, nontraded, domestic product. This specification conforms to the available records, which are rich on import and export data but scarce on nontraded commodities. Region i's consumer is endowed with nontraded inputs and receives all tariff revenue. Furthermore, she consumes her entire production of the nontraded good, while none of the exportables are consumed at home. As in O'Rourke, a two-level nested CES (constant elasticity of substitution) utility function allows us to specify different elasticities of substitution within bundles of goods and among different bundles. The malleability of nested CES offers an attractive compromise between realism on the one hand and computational expediency on the other. The first utility level combines comparable consumption goods into bundles. For instance, wine and brandy, which can be considered close substitutes, belong to the same bundle generically called alcohol. The second utility level then combines the various bundles, for example, alcohol and textiles. The assumed preference structures for Britain and France are represented by figures A.1 and A.2.

Our model differs from Anderson/Neary and O'Rourke in two essential ways. First, our world economy consists of three finitely sized regions—Britain, France, and the "rest of the world"—instead of a single, price-taking country that faces an infinitely large "rest of the world." While this forces us to drop the TRI as a convenient measure of protection, it also relaxes the assumption of a zero optimal tariff vector, thus acknowledging the issue of market power raised by McCloskey and Irwin. Second, in addition to imported intermediate goods and a mobile, nontraded input, we include capital as a third type of input and assume that it is sector-specific. This is a reasonable assumption, given a brewery cannot be transformed into a steel mill. Our specific-factors model (Jones, 1971 and Samuelson, 1971) stands in contrast to the one-factor model that is usually derived from basic Ricardian theory. As a consequence, falling tariffs can increase capital incomes in some sectors at the expense of others. Moreover, there are decreasing returns to labor. Imported inputs, capital, and labor enter a nested CES production function.

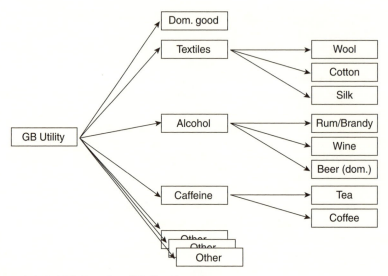

Figure A.1. British Two-Level Utility Function.

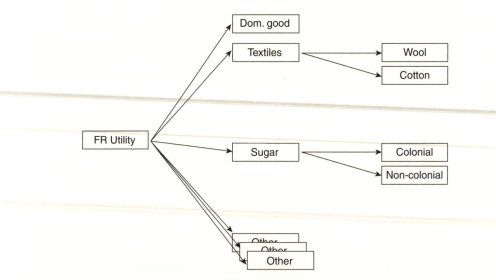

Figure A.2. French Two-Level Utility Function.

Output supply and input demand functions are derived from profit maximization.

From the Tableau Décennal du Commerce we know what France exported to, and what it imported from, Britain. It also provides us with France's tariffs on imports. McCloskey (1980) provides British and French total import volumes and tariffs. British and French import and export figures with the "rest of the world" are thus computed as the difference between both data sets. Tables A.1 and A.2 show French and English import figures and tariff rates for the most important commodities traded in the years 1841 and 1854 respectively. Also noted is that, by the mid-nineteenth century, British tariffs were evenly imposed on most countries and preference for Portugal's wines had ended.

Given the data's imperfections and incompleteness, trade among the three regions requires balancing. We do so by introducing an artificial commodity produced in France or in Britain (or, if necessary, in both) and exported to the "rest of the world." Given the lack of data on domestic production and consumption, we are left to assume that each region produces a generic nonexportable good for domestic consumption. A region's expenditures on this generic domestic good are assumed to equal GDP plus intermediate imports, including tariff revenues, minus exports. Finally, we assume that the rest of the world produces and consumes the same goods as Britain and France and in proportional amounts. In our standard baseline calibration, we let Britain and France make up half the world's economy and, thus, purposely bias their market power upwards.[2]

In empirical work it is often assumed that final demand is elastic while intermediate demand is inelastic. James Anderson's (1995) calibration, just to cite an example, specified elasticities of substitutions of 0.7 among input bundles and 2.0 among bundles of consumption goods. We made the same numerical assumption for our base case. Within bundles, we typically chose 3.0 among textiles, 5.0 between tea and coffee, 5.0 among various alcohols, and 8.0 between foreign and colonial sugar. While these assumptions strike us as reasonable, we also ran our simulations over a wide range of alternative elasticities assumptions, between 0.1 and 2.0 among input bundles and between 0.5 and 4.0 among final consumption goods. We found that our results are rather robust to alternative specifications in the higher elasticity range.

A final caveat: despite the quantitative—or, rather, numerical—nature of our simulations, we feel that their qualitative implications deserve most of the attention and interpretation. The shape of curves and their positions relative to other curves are more significant than are their absolute magnitudes.

TABLE A.1
Import/Export Data for 1841

British Imports	From France	From RoW	Tariff
Wool Fab.	6.95		
Cotton Fab.	2.70	270.50	96.0%
Coffee		45.32	67.0%
Sugar		318.50	6.5%
Cereals	7.91	204.90	113.9%
Wines	11.59	69.15	206.6%
Rum/Brandy	19.28	69.39	
Jewelry	0.56		
Leather gds	4.58		
Eggs	4.89		
Silk Fabric	28.64		
Tobacco		94.80	843.3%
Tea		186.30	114.1%
Wood		115.70	14.0%
Other-FR	34.35		15.2%
Other-RW		842.20	15.2%

French Imports	From Britain	From RoW	Tariff
Wool Fab.	0.465	0.285	50.0%
Cotton Fab.	19.470		50.0%
Coffee		26.300	100.8%
For. Sugar		10.000	155.4%
Col. Sugar		83.900	71.9%
Fats/Lard		5.200	
Silk	7.790	52.210	
Wool	2.00	44.040	22.1%
Raw Cotton	1.620	106.700	12.1%
Coal	6.440	20.400	16.5%
Hides/Pets	1.697	25.620	2.2%
Flax/Linen	27.900		
Oleag.	2.790	34.770	3.3%
Wood		39.200	
Copper/Iron	14.900	0.910	
Livestock		10.600	21.8%
Other-BR	7.740		76.9%
Other-RW		397.300	13.5%

Sources: France, Direction Générale des Douanes, 1870; McCloskey, 1990; and Nye, 1991b

TABLE A.2
Import/Export Data for 1854

British Imports	From France	From RoW	Tariff	French Imports	From Britain	From RoW	Tariff
Coffee		22.18	52.8%	Silk	44.46	77.85	0.0%
Sugar		213.8	52.5%	Wool	16.78	35.72	17.9%
Wood		131.5	4.8%	Raw Cotton	0.66	99.14	14.3%
Tobacco		24.95	479.0%	Wood		57.2	0.0%
Tead		100	119.5%	Coal	8.85	56.65	10.2%
Rum/Brandy	8.94	24.26	201.8%	Hides/Pets	1.98	36.12	1.6%
Cereals	0.54	546.9	1.9%	Livestock		21.1	3.8%
Cotton Fab.	9.92	437.6	0.0%	Coffee		23.3	78.5%
Wines	8.88	47.37	84.9%	Flax/Linen	1.61	21.09	0.0%
Silk Fabric	103.3			Oleag.	1.85	15.95	14.6%
Wool Fab.	33.45			Wool Text.	0.14	0.56	50.0%
Leather gds	14.59			Cotton Text.	0.0018	0.7982	50.0%
Other	90.7	1531	8.1%	For. Sugar		16.6	107.2%
				Col. Sugar		48.7	62.2%
				Fats/Lard		6.2	0.0%
				Other	56.556	427.14	8.0%

Sources: France, Direction Générale des Douanes, 1870; McCloskey, 1990; and Nye, 1991b

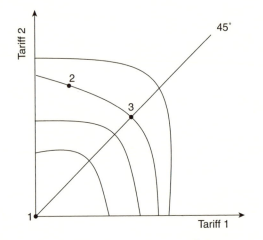

Figure A.3. TRI Existence and Uniqueness for a Small Country.

MODELING PROTECTION: TRI AND THE LARGE COUNTRY PROBLEM

The Trade Restrictiveness Index is based on the concept of a Uniform Tariff Equivalent (UTA), which is illustrated in figure A.3.

The graph shows a country's, or rather its representative consumer's, welfare level curves with respect to tariffs on two goods. For a small country, the optimal tariff, represented by point 1, lies at the origin. If the historic tariff structure is represented by point 2, then point 3, on the 45 degree line, represents the uniform tariff that generates the same welfare loss as the historic tariff.

Things go wrong, however, if we drop the small country assumption. The intuition is shown in figure A.4.

If a country is large, the optimal tariff vector, represented by point 1, lies in the interior of the positive orthant, with iso-welfare curves concentric around the optimum. We can now visualize three cases: (1) the actual tariff is given by point 2, whose welfare curve does not intersect the 45 degree line, hence the UTE is not defined; (2) the actual tariff is given by point 3, whose welfare curve intersects the 45 degree line twice at points 4 and 5, causing the UTE to be not uniquely defined and hence ambiguous; and (3) the actual tariff is given by point 6 with UTE at point 7. This last case, however, appears to be nongeneric.

THE FORMAL MODEL

The world economy consists of three regions: Britain, France, and the rest of the world. We identify sectors of activity by indices $s, t \in S$ with

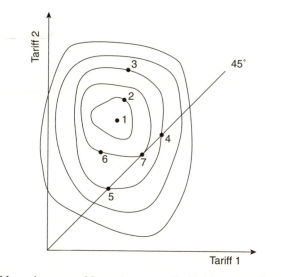

Figure A.4. Nonexistence or Nonuniqueness of a Uniform Tariff Equivalent.

$S = \{1, 2, \ldots, S\}$ representing the set of all industries. Regions are identified by indices i, $j \in W$, with $W = \{Br,Fr,RW\}$. To keep track of trade flows, we follow the usual practice that identifies the first two indices with, respectively, the region and the industry supplying the good and the next two with the client region and industry. Production uses three types of input: fixed capital, mobile labor, and imported intermediate inputs. Output consists of the nontraded good and exported goods. None of the exportables are consumed at home. Consumers are endowed with labor, a nontraded input, and receive all profits and tariff revenue. They consume imported final goods and their nontraded good.

CONSUMPTION

Each region i has a representative consumer who values a large variety of imports as well as a generic, nontraded, domestic product. This specification, also used by Anderson/Neary for their TRI computations, conforms to the available records, which are rich on import and export data but scarce on nontraded commodities.

A two-level nested CES utility function allows us to specify different elasticities of substitution within bundles of goods as well as among bundles. The malleability of nested CES offers an attractive compromise between realism on the one hand and computational expediency on the other. The first utility level combines bundles of consumption goods c_{jsi}

TABLE A.3
Own-Price Elasticities of Demand

Elasticity of substitution	Expenditure Share							
	0%	5%	10%	20%	40%	60%	80%	100%
0	0.00	−0.05	−0.10	−0.20	−0.40	−0.60	−0.80	−1.00
−0.1	−0.10	−0.15	−0.19	−0.28	−0.46	−0.64	−0.82	−1.00
−0.5	−0.50	−0.53	−0.55	−0.60	−0.70	−0.80	−0.90	−1.00
−1	−1.00	−1.00	−1.00	−1.00	−1.00	−1.00	−1.00	−1.00
−1.5	−1.50	−1.48	−1.45	−1.40	−1.30	−1.20	−1.10	−1.00
−2	−2.00	−1.95	−1.90	−1.80	−1.60	−1.40	−1.20	−1.00
−5	−5.00	−4.80	−4.60	−4.20	−3.40	−2.60	−1.80	−1.00
−10	−10.00	−9.55	−9.10	−8.20	−6.40	−4.60	−2.80	−1.00

into aggregates c_{ki}. Wine and brandy, for instance, which can be considered substitutes, belong to the same bundle generically called alcohol. Formally, we shall partition the set S into bundles, or "nests," S_k, $k \in K = \{1, 2, \ldots, K,\}$, $K \leq S$. The second utility level determines the optimal composition of the consumption aggregates c_{ki}, such as alcohol and textiles. Formally, the consumer's preferences are thus:

$$C_i = \left(\sum_{k \in K} \rho_{ki} c_{ki}^{\frac{\sigma_i - 1}{\sigma_i}} \right)^{\frac{\sigma_i}{\sigma_i - 1}}$$

where

$$c_{ki} = \left(\sum_{s \in S_k} \sum_{j \in W} \delta_{jsi} c_{jsi}^{\frac{\sigma_k - 1}{\sigma_k}} \right)^{\frac{\sigma_k}{\sigma_k - 1}},$$

and δ_{jsi} and ρ_{ki} represent benchmark expenditure shares. The consumer maximizes C_i with respect c_{jsi} and subject to

$$p_{ci} C_i \geq \sum_{j \in W} \sum_{s \in S} \left(1 + \tau_{jsi}\right) p_{jsi} c_{jsi},$$

where τ_{jsi} are tariff rates, p_{jsi} are prices, and σ_I and σ_k are elasticities of substitution.

PRODUCTION

The representative firm of region i sector s owns fixed, sector specific capital K_{is}, while labor is assumed to be fully mobile. Hence, there are decreasing returns to labor. Material inputs, all imported, along with capital and labor enter a nested CES production function along the same principle as in the consumer's utility function. Output supply and input demands result from maximizing profit.

$$\Pi_{is} = p_{is}Q_{is} - \sum_{j\in W}\sum_{t\in S}\left(1+\tau_{jti}\right)p_{jti}x_{jtis} - w_i L_{is}$$

subject to

$$\Pi_{is} \geq 0,$$

and

$$Q_{is} = \left(\alpha_{Kis}\overline{K}_{is}^{\frac{\sigma_{ix}-1}{\sigma_{ix}}} + \alpha_{Lis}L_{is}^{\frac{\sigma_{ix}-1}{\sigma_{ix}}} + \sum_{k\in K}\alpha_{Kis}x_{kis}^{\frac{\sigma_{ix}-1}{\sigma_{ix}}}\right)^{\frac{\sigma_{ix}}{\sigma_{ix}-1}},$$

where

$$x_{kis} = \left(\sum_{t\in S_k}\sum_{j\in W}\beta_{jtis}x_{jtis}^{\frac{\sigma_k-1}{\sigma_k}}\right)^{\frac{\sigma_k}{\sigma_k-1}}$$

RESULTS: THE BIG PICTURE

Over a wide range of alternative calibrations, calculations that simulate a unilateral drop in all British tariffs show a substantial net increase in British welfare, suggesting that British tariff levels were significantly higher than would be consistent with an optimum tariff policy.[3] For our baseline case, we found that British tariffs in 1841 were roughly three times larger than the optimal tariff, leading to a static welfare loss for Britain of about 1.4 percent by removing all tariffs. For 1854, on the other hand, we found that while actual tariffs were significantly reduced, they were still almost twice the size of optimal tariffs, despite

CHART A.1

Base Case: Counterfactual Unilateral Reduction from 100 per cent to 0 per cent of a
Country's Historical Tariff Vector. Effect on Own Welfare (in percent).

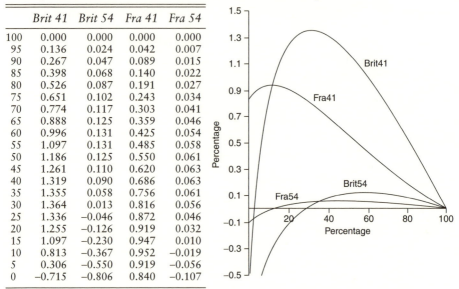

	Brit 41	Brit 54	Fra 41	Fra 54
100	0.000	0.000	0.000	0.000
95	0.136	0.024	0.042	0.007
90	0.267	0.047	0.089	0.015
85	0.398	0.068	0.140	0.022
80	0.526	0.087	0.191	0.027
75	0.651	0.102	0.243	0.034
70	0.774	0.117	0.303	0.041
65	0.888	0.125	0.359	0.046
60	0.996	0.131	0.425	0.054
55	1.097	0.131	0.485	0.058
50	1.186	0.125	0.550	0.061
45	1.261	0.110	0.620	0.063
40	1.319	0.090	0.686	0.063
35	1.355	0.058	0.756	0.061
30	1.364	0.013	0.816	0.056
25	1.336	−0.046	0.872	0.046
20	1.255	−0.126	0.919	0.032
15	1.097	−0.230	0.947	0.010
10	0.813	−0.367	0.952	−0.019
5	0.306	−0.550	0.919	−0.056
0	−0.715	−0.806	0.840	−0.107

our exaggerated assumptions on market power. Static welfare losses for
Britain, however, fell to a negligible 0.13 percent of national income.[4]
Thus, while Britain did indeed significantly reduce its tariffs, thereby
greatly eliminating associated welfare losses, those tariffs were still too
high to be consistent with a policy of free, unfettered, trade. Indeed, the
tariff levels still exceeded those that would have been consistent with an
optimal tariff policy.

In comparison, French tariffs led to much smaller static welfare losses,
which, in 1841, represented less than 1 percent of income. Those tariffs
were about 10 times the magnitude of optimal tariffs, reflecting, in part,
France's smaller market power. In 1854, French tariffs fell to a very negligible 0.06 percent loss of welfare even though, here too, tariffs were
still about twice the size of optimal tariffs. We note that the French results were robust to quite severe respecifications of the tariff equivalents
on cotton and woollen textiles, given the relatively small share of French
trade that was taxed.

Chart A.1 (see end of chapter for charts) summarizes these findings by
plotting welfare, the utility of the representative consumer, against percentage of the original tariff vector. The graph is best read from right to
left. We start with 100 percent, the full norm of the historic tariff vector,

and then observe changes in welfare as we scale the norm of the tariff vector down to 0 percent.

Issues of country size notwithstanding, readers familiar with O'Rourke's spectacularly high uniform tariff equivalents might wonder how his results, which are based on similar data, can be reconciled with our relatively small welfare effects. We speculate that the explanation lies in the high variance of British customs duties. In addition to having high levels of tariffs on a small but important set of imports, the highly discriminatory nature of these duties would distort British trade beyond what would seem indicated by the high levels alone. Hence, any uniform tax designed to mimic the welfare results of such a tariff profile would have to reflect both the effects of the tariffs themselves and the welfare losses due to the uneven imposition of customs duties. Since a uniform tax has little distortionary effect, even less so if the proceeds are returned to the consumer, it takes a very high uniform tariff indeed to obtain a small change in welfare. O'Rourke's work also took no notice of the fact that the measures he uses for French tariff levels from Nye (1991b) were purposely biased upward to demonstrate the relative openness of French trade. A more realistic set of figures would show results even more favorable to France vis-à-vis Britain than O'Rourke found.

SENSITIVITY ANALYSIS

As expected, the simulation results are sensitive to calibration, in particular, to the specified elasticities of substitution. First, according to our data, Britain was mainly an importer of consumption goods. France's imports were dominated by inputs. Since we typically assume an elasticity of substitution of 0.7 among inputs and 2.0 among most consumption goods, this asymmetry clearly lowers Britain's optimal tariff relative to France. To see how much of our result rests on this asymmetry, we performed simulations with identical calibrations for both the supply and the demand side. Specifically, we assumed that both elasticities of substitution were equal to 1, which corresponds to Cobb-Douglas specifications for both tastes and technology.

As can be seen in chart A.2, increasing the elasticity of substitution among inputs from 0.7 to 1.0, and decreasing the elasticity of substitution among consumption goods from 2.0 to 1.0, somewhat diminishes Britain's potential gains from a counterfactual reduction of tariffs in 1841, even if those potential gains are still higher than France's potential gains. For comparison, the same change in elasticity assumptions has an even larger effect on 1841 France, whose potential benefit of trade liberalization is reduced by 75 percent. More remarkably in 1854, while still

CHART A.2
Using the same elasticities of substitution in consumption and production. Effect on Welfare (in percent).

1841	Br 1/1	Br 0.7/2.0	Fr 1/1	Fr 0.7/2.0
100	0.000	0.000	0.000	0.000
95	0.086	0.136	0.019	0.042
90	0.170	0.267	0.033	0.089
85	0.256	0.398	0.051	0.140
80	0.337	0.526	0.070	0.191
75	0.418	0.651	0.089	0.243
70	0.495	0.774	0.107	0.303
65	0.568	0.888	0.131	0.359
60	0.637	0.996	0.149	0.425
55	0.701	1.097	0.168	0.485
50	0.757	1.186	0.191	0.550
45	0.804	1.261	0.210	0.620
40	0.841	1.319	0.229	0.686
35	0.860	1.355	0.243	0.756
30	0.860	1.364	0.257	0.816
25	0.835	1.336	0.266	0.872
20	0.777	1.255	0.271	0.919
15	0.665	1.097	0.266	0.947
10	0.482	0.813	0.247	0.952
5	0.167	0.306	0.210	0.919
0	−0.423	−0.715	0.149	0.840

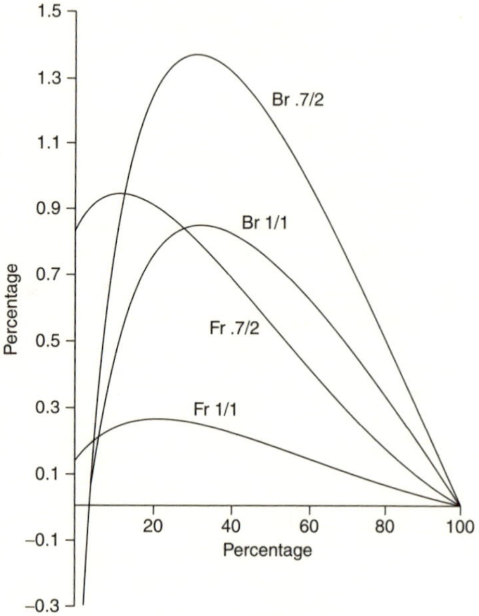

1854	Br 1/1	Br 0.7/2.0	Fr 1/1	Fr 0.7/2.0
100	0.000	0.000	0.000	0.000
95	0.005	0.024	−0.005	0.007
90	0.008	0.047	−0.010	0.015
85	0.009	0.068	−0.015	0.022
80	0.009	0.087	−0.019	0.027
75	0.008	0.102	−0.024	0.034
70	0.003	0.117	−0.032	0.041
65	−0.005	0.125	−0.039	0.046
60	−0.016	0.131	−0.049	0.054
55	−0.032	0.131	−0.056	0.058
50	−0.050	0.125	−0.066	0.061
45	−0.077	0.110	−0.078	0.063
40	−0.112	0.090	−0.090	0.063
35	−0.155	0.058	−0.105	0.061
30	−0.210	0.013	−0.122	0.056
25	−0.281	−0.046	−0.141	0.046
20	−0.369	−0.126	−0.163	0.032
15	−0.486	−0.230	−0.188	0.010
10	−0.635	−0.367	−0.217	−0.019
5	−0.837	−0.550	−0.251	−0.056
0	−1.112	−0.806	−0.290	−0.107

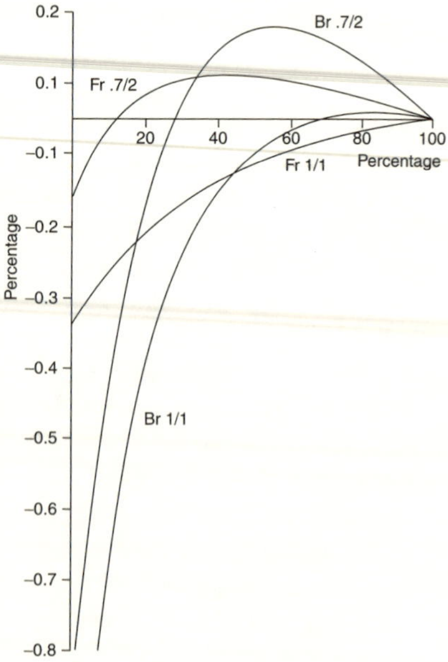

being far from being free traders, both Britain and France appear to be practicing near-optimal tariff policies under the new elasticity assumptions. While Britain's tariffs are still slightly beyond their optimal level, France actually displays a touch of magnanimity.

Second, we perform a sensitivity analysis on the elasticity of substitution among bundles of consumption goods. Chart A.3 shows the static welfare effects of a move to free trade for 1841 and 1854 in Britain and for elasticities ranging from 0.5 to 4.0. The graphs are very similar between the two years, the main difference being the relative magnitude of welfare losses. As seen earlier, for an elasticity of substitution of 2.0 among consumption bundles, Britain's high tariffs cost her close to 1.4 percent of her static income in 1841 but only 0.13 percent in 1854. Increasing the elasticity of substitution from 2.0 to 4.0 dramatically increases the welfare cost of protection to over 2.4 percent of income in 1841 and to 0.35 percent in 1854. Decreasing the elasticity lowers the welfare losses, but the critical result here is that the consumer's elasticity of substitution must be a low 0.5 before it can be claimed that 1841 British tariffs were close to welfare maximizing but only below 1.0 to make the same claim for 1854. The premise behind McCloskey's argument thus begins to hold water if imports generally faced inelastic demands. We note furthermore that for an elasticity of substitution of 0.5, a free trade policy would have cost Britain 1.7 percent of its welfare.

Third, we vary the elasticity of substitution among inputs and find our results to be particularly sensitive to this parameter. As can be seen in chart A.4, raising the elasticity from 0.7 (slightly inelastic) to 1.2 (slightly elastic) just about triples both the 1841 and 1854 static welfare losses relative to optimal tariffs. Raising the elasticity to 2.0 pushes the welfare losses to an enormous 9 percent of income in 1841 and a smaller loss of only 1 percent in 1854. More fundamentally, even a reduction of that elasticity to an almost Leontief 0.1 still places the optimal tariff below the historic tariff for either year.

Fourth, we vary the size of the rest of the world. Our baseline case tends to exaggerate British (and French) market power by assuming that the rest of the world makes up only a modest half of the world's economy. By relaxing this assumption and increasing market share of the rest of the world to 70, 90, and 99 percent, our central claim that British tariffs were too high to be consistent with an optimal tariff policy is further reinforced. The simulation results are reported in charts A.5 and A.6.

CHART A.3
Varying the Elasticity of Substitution among Consumption Bundles for Both
Britain and France: Effect on Britain (in percent).

1841	0.5	1.1	2.0	4.0
100	0.000	0.000	0.000	0.000
95	−0.017	0.070	0.136	0.206
90	−0.039	0.134	0.267	0.409
85	−0.067	0.195	0.398	0.612
80	−0.100	0.253	0.526	0.816
75	−0.139	0.309	0.651	1.013
70	−0.184	0.356	0.774	1.211
65	−0.239	0.398	0.888	1.403
60	−0.301	0.431	0.996	1.587
55	−0.376	0.454	1.097	1.765
50	−0.462	0.468	1.186	1.932
45	−0.562	0.465	1.261	2.085
40	−0.679	0.445	1.319	2.218
35	−0.818	0.406	1.355	2.327
30	−0.983	0.342	1.364	2.402
25	−1.172	0.245	1.336	2.433
20	−1.403	0.103	1.255	2.394
15	−1.676	−0.097	1.097	2.252
10	−2.012	−0.387	0.813	1.929
5	−2.435	−0.816	0.306	1.255
0	−2.992	−1.534	−0.715	−0.484

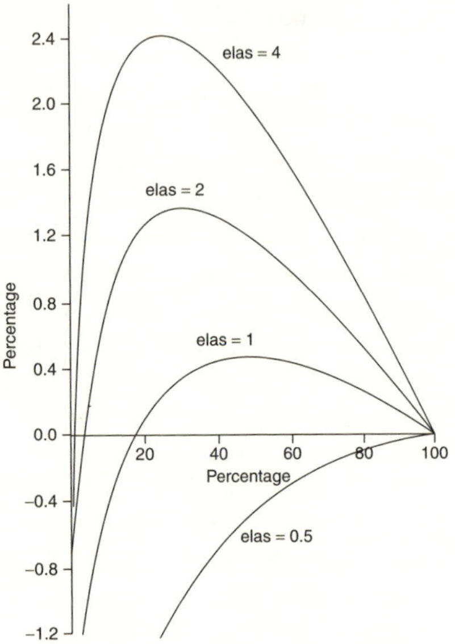

1854	0.5	1.1	2.0	4.0
100	0.000	0.000	0.000	0.000
95	−0.027	0.003	0.024	0.047
90	−0.057	0.005	0.047	0.093
85	−0.088	0.005	0.068	0.137
80	−0.123	0.002	0.087	0.178
75	−0.161	−0.003	0.102	0.216
70	−0.202	−0.011	0.117	0.252
65	−0.246	−0.024	0.125	0.282
60	−0.295	−0.039	0.131	0.309
55	−0.348	−0.061	0.131	0.330
50	−0.408	−0.087	0.125	0.344
45	−0.475	−0.120	0.110	0.350
40	−0.549	−0.161	0.090	0.345
35	−0.632	−0.211	0.058	0.330
30	−0.725	−0.273	0.013	0.298
25	−0.831	−0.347	−0.046	0.249
20	−0.951	−0.438	−0.126	0.175
15	−1.090	−0.550	−0.230	0.071
10	−1.250	−0.688	−0.367	−0.077
5	−1.441	−0.863	−0.550	−0.287
0	−1.668	−1.088	−0.806	−0.596

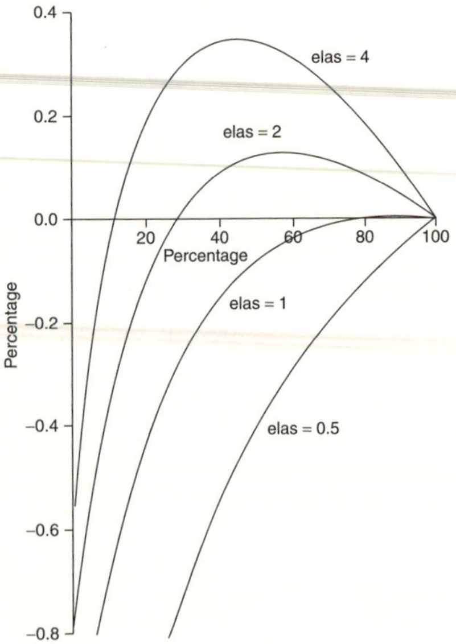

CHART A.4
Varying the Elasticity of Substitution among Input Bundles for Both Britain and France: Effect on Britain (in percent).

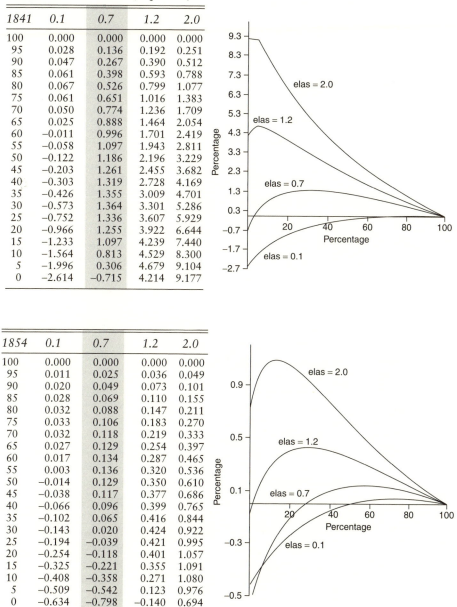

1841	0.1	0.7	1.2	2.0
100	0.000	0.000	0.000	0.000
95	0.028	0.136	0.192	0.251
90	0.047	0.267	0.390	0.512
85	0.061	0.398	0.593	0.788
80	0.067	0.526	0.799	1.077
75	0.061	0.651	1.016	1.383
70	0.050	0.774	1.236	1.709
65	0.025	0.888	1.464	2.054
60	−0.011	0.996	1.701	2.419
55	−0.058	1.097	1.943	2.811
50	−0.122	1.186	2.196	3.229
45	−0.203	1.261	2.455	3.682
40	−0.303	1.319	2.728	4.169
35	−0.426	1.355	3.009	4.701
30	−0.573	1.364	3.301	5.286
25	−0.752	1.336	3.607	5.929
20	−0.966	1.255	3.922	6.644
15	−1.233	1.097	4.239	7.440
10	−1.564	0.813	4.529	8.300
5	−1.996	0.306	4.679	9.104
0	−2.614	−0.715	4.214	9.177

1854	0.1	0.7	1.2	2.0
100	0.000	0.000	0.000	0.000
95	0.011	0.025	0.036	0.049
90	0.020	0.049	0.073	0.101
85	0.028	0.069	0.110	0.155
80	0.032	0.088	0.147	0.211
75	0.033	0.106	0.183	0.270
70	0.032	0.118	0.219	0.333
65	0.027	0.129	0.254	0.397
60	0.017	0.134	0.287	0.465
55	0.003	0.136	0.320	0.536
50	−0.014	0.129	0.350	0.610
45	−0.038	0.117	0.377	0.686
40	−0.066	0.096	0.399	0.765
35	−0.102	0.065	0.416	0.844
30	−0.143	0.020	0.424	0.922
25	−0.194	−0.039	0.421	0.995
20	−0.254	−0.118	0.401	1.057
15	−0.325	−0.221	0.355	1.091
10	−0.408	−0.358	0.271	1.080
5	−0.509	−0.542	0.123	0.976
0	−0.634	−0.798	−0.140	0.694

CHART A.5
Varying the Size of the Rest of the World: Effect on Britain (in percent).

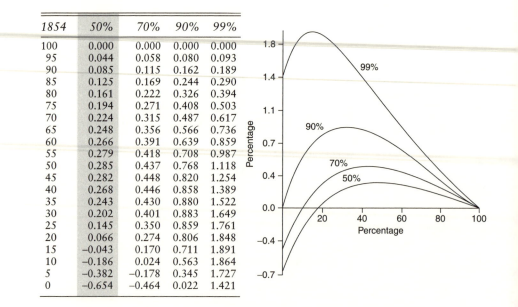

1841	50%	70%	90%	99%
100	0.000	0.000	0.000	0.000
95	0.136	0.156	0.203	0.317
90	0.267	0.309	0.409	0.649
85	0.398	0.462	0.615	0.988
80	0.526	0.612	0.827	1.342
75	0.651	0.763	1.038	1.706
70	0.774	0.907	1.253	2.082
65	0.888	1.049	1.467	2.472
60	0.996	1.183	1.681	2.870
55	1.097	1.311	1.893	3.279
50	1.186	1.425	2.101	3.696
45	1.261	1.528	2.302	4.117
40	1.319	1.614	2.491	4.537
35	1.355	1.678	2.664	4.949
30	1.364	1.712	2.808	5.344
25	1.336	1.706	2.917	5.700
20	1.255	1.645	2.967	5.993
15	1.097	1.500	2.934	6.179
10	0.813	1.227	2.758	6.179
5	0.306	0.713	2.330	5.837
0	−0.715	−0.337	1.333	4.757

1854	50%	70%	90%	99%
100	0.000	0.000	0.000	0.000
95	0.044	0.058	0.080	0.093
90	0.085	0.115	0.162	0.189
85	0.125	0.169	0.244	0.290
80	0.161	0.222	0.326	0.394
75	0.194	0.271	0.408	0.503
70	0.224	0.315	0.487	0.617
65	0.248	0.356	0.566	0.736
60	0.266	0.391	0.639	0.859
55	0.279	0.418	0.708	0.987
50	0.285	0.437	0.768	1.118
45	0.282	0.448	0.820	1.254
40	0.268	0.446	0.858	1.389
35	0.243	0.430	0.880	1.522
30	0.202	0.401	0.883	1.649
25	0.145	0.350	0.859	1.761
20	0.066	0.274	0.806	1.848
15	−0.043	0.170	0.711	1.891
10	−0.186	0.024	0.563	1.864
5	−0.382	−0.178	0.345	1.727
0	−0.654	−0.464	0.022	1.421

CHART A.6
Varying the Size of the Rest of the World: Effect on France (in percent).

1841	50%	70%	90%	99%
100	0.000	0.000	0.000	0.000
95	0.061	0.061	0.061	0.061
90	0.126	0.126	0.126	0.121
85	0.191	0.196	0.191	0.182
80	0.257	0.266	0.261	0.247
75	0.331	0.336	0.331	0.313
70	0.401	0.411	0.406	0.383
65	0.481	0.490	0.481	0.457
60	0.560	0.569	0.560	0.527
55	0.644	0.653	0.639	0.602
50	0.728	0.742	0.723	0.676
45	0.812	0.830	0.807	0.751
40	0.900	0.914	0.891	0.826
35	0.984	1.003	0.970	0.896
30	1.068	1.082	1.050	0.961
25	1.143	1.162	1.120	1.017
20	1.208	1.222	1.176	1.054
15	1.255	1.274	1.213	1.073
10	1.278	1.297	1.227	1.064
5	1.264	1.283	1.204	1.017
0	1.204	1.222	1.129	0.910

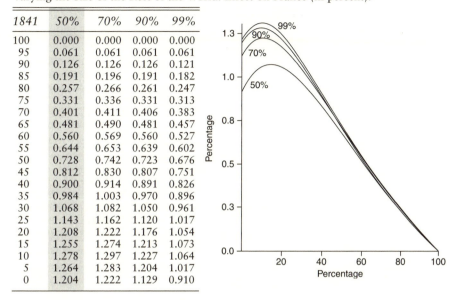

1854	50%	70%	90%	99%
100	0.000	0.000	0.000	0.000
95	0.015	0.015	0.017	0.017
90	0.029	0.029	0.032	0.034
85	0.044	0.046	0.049	0.049
80	0.058	0.061	0.066	0.066
75	0.073	0.076	0.080	0.083
70	0.088	0.093	0.097	0.097
65	0.100	0.107	0.112	0.115
60	0.115	0.122	0.127	0.129
55	0.127	0.134	0.141	0.144
50	0.139	0.149	0.156	0.156
45	0.151	0.158	0.166	0.168
40	0.158	0.168	0.175	0.175
35	0.166	0.175	0.183	0.183
30	0.171	0.180	0.188	0.185
25	0.171	0.180	0.188	0.185
20	0.166	0.178	0.183	0.178
15	0.156	0.168	0.173	0.166
10	0.136	0.149	0.154	0.144
5	0.110	0.122	0.127	0.112
0	0.071	0.083	0.085	0.068

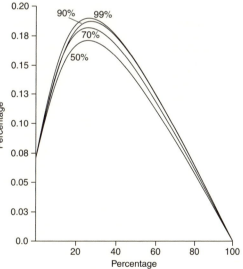

The Revenue Story

Irwin argued that Britain's high tariffs on select goods—such as wine, rum, and brandy—were levied not for protection but for revenue alone. As such, he claimed, unless given a very small weight, their inclusion into a measure of protection such as a tariff index would be misleading. His rationale was that those goods had no close domestic substitutes and, in particular, that high wine prices would have only a negligible effect on British beer consumption. However, this ignores the prohibitive effects of the tariff on certain classes of wine and spirits most likely to be in competition with domestic production of alcoholic beverages.

We should point out that these revenue maximization calculations are somewhat misleading for wine and spirits because these goods were uniquely taxed by volume rather than ad valorem. Thus, our calculations ignore the prohibitive effect of British tariffs on the cheapest class of wines, which did not enter into British consumption at all after the eighteenth century. In contrast, the finest products of Burgundy and Bordeaux naturally received much lower tariffs on an ad valorem basis for a fixed tariff. Our inability to deal with the problem of specific tariffs on wine and brandy leaves out the very important protective and distributional effects on the types of wines that were imported and on the specific protection of domestic beer.

Chart A.7
Laffer Curves: Tariff on Alcohols and Effect on British Revenue for Various Elasticities of Substitution among Alcohols, Including Domestic Beer (in percent).

1841	elas=1	elas=3	elas=5	elas=10
200	21.8	−14.4	−27.6	−40.3
190	20.5	−12.7	−24.9	−37.1
180	19.1	−10.9	−22.2	−33.7
170	17.5	−9.2	−19.4	−30.1
160	15.8	−7.4	−16.5	−26.2
150	13.8	−5.8	−13.5	−22.1
140	11.6	−4.2	−10.6	−17.7
130	9.3	−2.8	−7.7	−13.2
120	6.5	−1.6	−4.9	−8.7
110	3.5	−0.6	−2.2	−4.2
100	0.0	0.0	0.0	0.0
90	−3.9	0.2	1.9	3.7
80	−8.4	−0.4	2.9	6.5
70	−13.6	−1.9	3.0	8.2
60	−19.8	−4.6	1.7	8.2
50	−27.1	−9.1	−1.8	5.7
40	−35.8	−15.9	−8.0	0.0
30	−46.5	−26.2	−18.3	−10.4
20	−59.9	−41.6	−34.6	−27.7
10	−77.0	−64.7	−60.0	−55.4
0	−100.0	−100.0	−100.0	−100.0

CHART A.7 (cont'd)

1854	elas=1	elas=3	elas=5	elas=10
200	30.0	−11.3	−26.0	−40.2
190	27.9	−9.6	−23.5	−37.1
180	25.8	−8.1	−20.8	−34.0
170	23.5	−6.7	−18.1	−30.4
160	20.8	−5.2	−15.4	−26.7
150	18.1	−4.0	−12.7	−22.5
140	15.2	−2.7	−10.0	−18.3
130	11.9	−1.5	−7.1	−13.8
120	8.3	−0.6	−4.6	−9.0
110	4.4	−0.2	−2.1	−4.4
100	0.0	0.0	0.0	0.0
90	−4.8	−0.2	1.7	4.0
80	−10.0	−1.3	2.7	7.1
70	−16.0	−3.3	2.5	9.0
60	−22.9	−6.5	1.0	9.2
50	−30.8	−11.3	−2.5	6.9
40	−40.0	−18.3	−9.0	1.3
30	−50.6	−28.8	−19.2	−9.0
20	−63.8	−44.0	−35.4	−26.3
10	−79.6	−66.3	−60.4	−54.4
0	−100.0	−100.0	−100.0	−100.0

CHART A.8
Tariff on Alcohols and Effect on British Welfare for Various Elasticities of Substitution among Alcohols, Including Domestic Beer (in percent).

1841	elas=1	elas=3	elas=5	elas=10
200	−1.033	−1.186	−1.253	−1.311
190	−0.932	−1.080	−1.150	−1.216
180	−0.832	−0.974	−1.041	−1.116
170	−0.732	−0.863	−0.927	−1.005
160	−0.629	−0.746	−0.807	−0.888
150	−0.523	−0.626	−0.682	−0.757
140	−0.420	−0.504	−0.551	−0.618
130	−0.315	−0.381	−0.418	−0.470
120	−0.209	−0.253	−0.278	−0.315
110	−0.103	−0.125	−0.139	−0.156
100	0.000	0.000	0.000	0.000
90	0.103	0.122	0.136	0.150
80	0.200	0.239	0.259	0.287
70	0.292	0.340	0.367	0.398
60	0.373	0.423	0.445	0.470
50	0.443	0.470	0.484	0.493
40	0.490	0.470	0.456	0.437
30	0.509	0.395	0.337	0.267
20	0.482	0.200	0.070	−0.078
10	0.384	−0.178	−0.431	−0.693
0	0.164	−0.874	−1.317	−1.762

Chart A.8 (cont'd)

1854	elas = 1	elas = 3	elas = 5	elas = 10
200	−0.265	−0.319	−0.341	−0.358
190	−0.240	−0.290	−0.312	−0.334
180	−0.213	−0.262	−0.284	−0.307
170	−0.188	−0.232	−0.252	−0.278
160	−0.161	−0.200	−0.221	−0.246
150	−0.134	−0.169	−0.186	−0.211
140	−0.107	−0.136	−0.151	−0.172
130	−0.080	−0.102	−0.114	−0.132
120	−0.054	−0.068	−0.077	−0.088
110	−0.027	−0.035	−0.038	−0.044
100	0.000	0.000	0.000	0.000
90	0.025	0.033	0.036	0.041
80	0.050	0.063	0.071	0.080
70	0.074	0.091	0.101	0.110
60	0.096	0.114	0.123	0.132
50	0.115	0.129	0.136	0.139
40	0.129	0.134	0.131	0.126
30	0.140	0.120	0.104	0.082
20	0.142	0.080	0.041	−0.006
10	0.131	−0.002	−0.077	−0.166
0	0.099	−0.155	−0.290	−0.443

It is thus natural to ask whether 1841 tariffs of about 115 percent on wines and over 200 percent on rum and brandy could conceivably have been so high as to be prohibitive and not raise anywhere close to the potential revenues. Our simulations suggest, however, that for a range of plausible elasticities of substitution, those high tariffs were indeed still on the reasonable side of the Laffer curve when ignoring the problem of wine and spirits. In particular, for an elasticity of substitution of 2.0 among alcohol imports and domestic beer, the vector of tariffs on alcohol was close to revenue-maximizing. In chart A.7, the solid tariff revenue curve is flat and almost reaches its maximum at 100 percent of historic tariffs on alcohols. Only for higher elasticities of substitution would the historic tariffs have been excessive.

Finally, chart A.8 shows the welfare effects of these simulations. At an elasticity of substitution of 2.0, for which the tariffs are close to revenue-maximizing, the welfare losses remain non-negligible. While we thus agree with Irwin that tariffs—except for those on table wine—can be construed as revenue-maximizing, the associated utility loss suggests that the tariffs cannot be exempted from a protective role. Thus, our results are consistent with a trade policy aimed at revenue maximization, but only if we ignore the prohibitive effects of the tariff on wine and treat them as ad valorem rather than as the specific tariffs that had always been in practice.

Notes

CHAPTER 1
PROBLEMS OF PERSPECTIVE: THE MYTH OF FREE
TRADE BRITAIN AND FORTRESS FRANCE

1. See Roehl (1976), O'Brien and Keyder (1978), Cameron and Freedeman (1983), Nye (1987), and Friedenson and Strauss (1987).

2. The use of average tariff levels as a basis from which to denote the size and timing of the move to free trade is standard in the literature. Both Imlah's classic discussion and McCloskey employ some version of tariff revenues as a percentage of importables to indicate how free British trade was (Imlah, 1958; McCloskey, 1980).

3. The British figures are not entirely reliable before the 1820s (and indeed before the 1840s) due to the inappropriate valuations of the commodities imported and exported. An extensive reworking of the trade statistics was produced by Imlah based on the work of Gayer, Rostow, and Schwartz and has remained the basis for all further research, although Davis expanded further on the commodity series (Imlah, 1958; Davis, 1979).

4. Baldwin (1985) has used it for the United States, as have Magee, Brock, and Young (1989) in their respective cross-sectional studies of international trade.

5. In particular, I believe that McCloskey's numbers for Britain do not come close to reflecting the true barriers to French wine. The century and a half of prohibition and protection from 1700 to 1860 left their imprint on the period that followed, causing an underestimate of what imports would be under free trade and thus underestimating the British average tariff. This will be looked at in the subsequent discussion.

6. Moreover, it is my belief that Lévy-Leboyer and Bourguignon's (1985) figures may not be best for making comparisons to the work of Imlah (1958) and McCloskey (1980). If anything, their average tariff rates for France are too high. Going back to the Tableau Decénnal du Commerce, I obtain the following decadal average tariff rates for France:

1827–36	1837–46	1847–56	1857–66	1867–76
20.82%	16.86%	13.03%	6.89%	4.93%

Those seeking further details should consult Nye (1991b).

7. I have simplified the calculations by focusing only on French prohibitions, again with an eye toward refuting the hypothesis that British trade was uniformly freer. A more detailed calculation would make corrections for redundant British tariffs.

8. The more extreme protectionist case is represented by the following example from France, *Enquête: Traité de Commerce* (France, Ministre de l'Agriculture, du commerce et des travaux publics, 1860, p. 59).

A rather biased comparison of spinning costs in Oissel and Oldham that appears in testimony before the 1860 inquiry comes to the conclusion that British spinners have a cost advantage of about a third relative to French spinners (and this information was challenged vigorously by the English and numerous Frenchmen). The witnesses presented average total costs per spindle for Oissel and Oldham and found that

For Spinning Industry

For Oissel, the price per spindle	41^f	16
Per spindle for Oldham	26^f	35
Price difference per spindle	14^f	71

Therefore, even accepting that this cost per spindle fully represented differences in the marginal costs in both industries and taking the above as a high upper bound, it seems that a tariff of 50 percent strictly applied would have served to maintain existing rents of the protected industries even if transportation costs were ignored. These figures were subsequently challenged by various officials and some observers maintained that no such difference existed at all (Fohlen, 1956).

9. The question of how to determine how far a nation has deviated from free trade is covered more rigorously in the technical appendix to this book. There we have constructed a computable general equilibrium model to assess the relative importance of the tariff in distorting the trade of Britain and France. The interested reader will observe that—consistent with the more intuitive estimates in this chapter—British tariffs were more distortionary than those of the French, underlining the fact that British trade policy was far from that of a pure free trader even decades after the repeal of the Corn Laws.

10. To push the argument further let us digress a bit by briefly considering another analogy. Imagine a small, prosperous European nation today that produced virtually nothing in the way of consumer electronics but imported most of its computers and televisions from Japan. Now imagine that this nation, angered by Japan's unwillingness to buy many of its own products in return decided to raise the tariff on Japanese televisions to the point where TV imports fell to some 5 percent or less of their previous level. If the hypothetical European nation could still not produce TV sets its actions would nonetheless be inconsistent with our conceptions of free trade even if it had no domestic industry to "protect."

Now, all one need do to make this story useful is to substitute eighteenth-century Britain (and more precisely, England) for the hypothetical European nation, France for Japan, and wine and spirits, and to a lesser extent, silks and luxury manufactures, for the consumer electronic products.

11. As we will see, however, the customs tariffs did play an important, albeit indirect, role in making possible increased revenue collection through excises on protected domestic products.

12. It should be noted that total British trade was greater than that of France throughout the nineteenth century. However, it is interesting that exports as a share of GDP were not very much higher in Britain than in France and did not remain so after the Second Empire. After 1870 the ratios for the two countries were quite similar and France's export/GDP figure was even higher on occasion in the 1890s (based on independent calculations using figures in Mitchell [1980] and Lévy-Leboyer and Bourguignon [1985]).

13. The other officially protected commodity was colonial sugar. Both colonial and foreign sugar were taxed at high rates, though the latter paid much higher duties than the former. As we will see later, the sugar tariffs did play an important role in the overall tariff levels for both countries.

14. As Williams noted:

Ever since the year 1660, a positive prohibition had existed and been enforced, against the importation from the Netherlands and Germany, in any ships whatever, of wines, spices, groceries, almonds, currants, dates, ginger, liquorice, pepper, raisins, figs, prunes, sugar, tobacco, potashes, pitch, tar, salt, rosin, timer, olive oil and numerous other articles. Then silk manufactures of every kind, except silk lace were absolutely prohibited to be imported, as also were embroidery, buttons, band strings, cutwork and fringe made of thread, beef, cattle, ground corn (except wheatmeal, wheatflour and oatmeal), mutton, lamb, pork, sheep, swine, malt, foreign fish (with a few exceptions), cards, chocolate, cocoa paste, gloves, thread of copper and brass, manufactured tobacco (except from the plantations of Spain and Portugal, and except snuff), whalebone cut, wines, and woolen cloths. Besides these absolute prohibitions other considerable categories of goods could only be imported by license; others only in a few ports; others only in particular kinds of packages. (Williams, 1972, pp. 38–39).

15. The system whereby resident British merchants in foreign countries could organize as factories with a measure of independence from the local authorities was well known in Portugal and Spain. These factories were an important special interest in British trade policy; quick to respond to changes in commercial legislation and quick to lobby for change. For example, the large British communities of the Lisbon and Oporto Factories only became heavily involved in wine and spirits in the early 1700s, when the tariffs favoring Portugal and Spain over France came into effect. They quickly became important actors in the wine trade and worked to preserve and control the advantages they derived from preferential treatment (Francis, 1972, pp. 179–224). This British-controlled wine trade "was a principal factor in stabilizing Anglo-Portuguese relations" (p. 179). British and Portuguese wine concerns played a major role in blocking all attempts at liberalizing trade with France at the end of the War of Spanish Succession in 1710 and 1713 and solidified British ties to the Portuguese that would persist for over a century after (p. 129). Given the extent of Britain merchant's interests in wines from Spain and Portugal one could say that the wine trade involving the three nations was as much domestic British trade as it was international trade.

16. Although the figures here are not precise, British and French observers agreed that French wine production constituted some 40 to 50 percent of the world's total and that France's representation in internationally traded wine was

usually greater than this. Portuguese exports were overwhelmingly sent to the British market and were themselves an anomaly of British tariff policy. Thus French wine imports into Britain, at 5 percent of those from Spain and Portugal, were seen as virtually prohibitive by the French and some members of the British Parliament. Even given the tendency of wine to be a preferred source of customs and excise revenues, no other country in the world came close to having such an odd pattern of wine imports (France, Archives Nationales, [1858?]).

17. The French *viticulteurs* had long considered all drinks together and worried not only about the effects on their trade of the obvious substitutes such as sherry, port, or beer, but also about the growth in consumption of tea and coffee. After all, in the eighteenth century tea was as much a luxury as wine, though it had become the poor man's drink while wine remained an expensive luxury in the nineteenth century (France, *Archives Nationales*, n.d.; France, *Archives Nationales*, [1858?]). In addition, to the extent that there is a "learned" component of the taste for beer or wine, British tariffs and excises helped form British tastes to the detriment of French wine during the period when rising incomes provided a new consumer base; this required several decades of lower prices to readjust.

18. Throughout the first half of the nineteenth century, the report notes, "the high duty on brandy tended not only to restrict consumption of that article to a comparatively small quantity, but—which was far more serious—it encouraged smuggling to any extent which all the efforts of the customs authorities, and of the revenue cruisers failed to put down" (Great Britain, 1898, p .166).

19. The tariffs on wine and spirits played an especially important role in commercial history because Britain's unwillingness to risk a revenue shortfall through lowered liquor tariffs caused it to rebuff initial French overtures toward bilateral liberalization in the 1840s (Dunham, 1930).

20. Entirely typical is the discussion of the coming of the Anglo-French Treaty of Commerce by Leone Levi in his classic work, *History of British Commerce* (1880). Levi has a fine though brief discussion of the changes in French tariff policy leading up to the 1860 treaty and includes the full text of the treaty. However, to compare tariffs between nations he presents a table of comparative tariffs on textiles: cotton, woolens, and linens (433). He uses this as an indication of the differences in the openness of trade among nations and as a guide to the size of the changes ushered in by the era of commercial treaties. As France had rather severe prohibitions on most subclasses of these items, French trade around 1854 appears extremely protectionist.

In a different context, though Bairoch's recent account of commercial policy discusses tariff restrictions on all classes of items, he still describes the period of "European free trade, 1860–79" primarily in terms of trade in manufactures. His central comparative table of tariffs in Europe is based on a comparison of the average level of duties on fourteen manufactured products in 1875 (Bairoch, 1976, table 5, p. 42).

21. It is amusing to see how similar protectionist claims were in both countries. The French objected that Britain had such natural advantages and such hard-working laborers that French spinners could offer no serious competition to British cotton and linen. Thus from Douai in 1838 came a letter to the President and Members of the Chamber of Deputies arguing that linen spinners would suffer privation and harm if faced with unbridled British competition:

A Messrs les Président et Membres de la Chambre des Deputés.

Les maires soussignés au nom des fileurs de lin, au rouet, ont l'honneur de vous exposer que ces très nombreux industriels, se trouvent maintenant dans une situation tellement misérable que si le gouvernement n'intervient point en leur faveur, le travail va leur manquer, partant du pain; situation cruelle; intolérable; ayez pitié de leur détresse.

. . . le gouvernement de nos voisins d'outre manche n'oublie rien pour tuer cette industrie de famille, par cela donc éssentiellement nationale sa manière est vraiment libérale, pour atteindre son but plus surement et sans bruit et accorde aux fils de lins mécaniques, une prime ad valorem de 15 pour cent, (France, Archives Nationales, [1838]).

To the President and Members of the Chamber of Deputies:

The undersigned mayors, in the name of the wheel-spinners of linen, have the honor to inform you that these numerous industrial workers now find themselves in such a miserable situation that if the government does not intervene in their favor, they will lose work, and [must] go without bread—a cruel and intolerable situation. Have pity on their distress.

. . . the government of our neighbors across the Channel have lost no chance to kill this family industry, which is essential to our nation, through its liberal policies. To attain our ends more surely, [we need to impose] a surcharge of 15 per cent ad valorem on machine spun linens (France, Archives Nationales, [1838])

In contrast, British manufacturers upset by French silks and fine woolens argued as late as 1855 that,

The French produce . . . goods which by their intrinsic beauty of texture and dye leave every competitor hopelessly in the rear. The prices . . . are such that we have long since abandoned their manufacture; and the Deputation, unable to find out the cause of this undeniable superiority were obliged to ascribe it to the well-known truth that a trade once established in a certain locality cannot be carried on with the same success at another place, though the latter may, to all appearances, possess even superior advantage. (Clapham, 1952, p. 18)

CHAPTER 2
THE HISTORY OF BRITISH ECONOMIC POLICY

1. Schumpeter (1954, p. 357) expands on this by breaking the claim into three related propositions and arguing that the rest of mercantilist analysis can be fruitfully separated from this central error. Whether mercantilism had a coherent core that would survive modern analytical scrutiny is a subject for an entirely different discussion.

2. Schumpeter (1954) did believe that Smith had gone too far and deliberately ignored the other substantive insights of the mercantile writers in focusing on this error.

3. One might think that the argument is improved by observing that the British needed to protect their exports because the French protected their domestic

industries. But this is exactly the fallacy that Adam Smith later denounced. Modern day research has only confirmed that in most circumstances, responding to another's tariffs by imposing your own constitutes the proverbial nose-cutting to spite one's face.

4. In the *Wealth of Nations*, Smith said:

> Higher duties are imposed upon the **wines** of France than upon those of Portugal, or indeed of any other country. By what is called the impost 1692, a duty of five and twenty per cent of the rate or value was laid upon all French goods; while the goods of other nations were, the greater part of them, subjected to much lighter duties, seldom exceeding five per cent. The **wine**, brandy, salt and vinegar of France were indeed excepted; these commodities being subjected to other heavy duties, either by other laws, or by particular clauses of the same law. In 1696, a second duty of twenty-five per cent, the first not having been thought a sufficient discouragement, was imposed upon all French goods, except brandy; together with a new duty of five and twenty pounds upon the ton of French **wine**, and another of fifteen pounds upon the ton of French vinegar. French goods have never been omitted in any of those general subsidies, or duties of five per cent, which have been imposed upon all, or the greater part of the goods enumerated in the book of rates. If we count the one third and two third subsidies as making a complete subsidy between them, there have been five of these general subsidies; so that before the commencement of the present war seventy-five per cent may be considered as the lowest duty to which the greater part of the goods of the growth, produce, or manufacture of France were liable. But upon the greater part of goods, those duties are equivalent to a prohibition. (Smith, 1776, Book IV, Chapter 3)

5. Mokyr (2003) tries to grapple with these ideas in the context of his retrospective analysis of the work of Eli Heckscher. He both lays out a concise view of the mercantilist way of thinking and outlines an agenda for exploring the extent to which the Industrial Revolution was accompanied or caused by a more fundamental intellectual transformation that took the greater part of a century to become fully operationalized.

6. Crouzet (1987) points to the costs to the French of their persecution of the Huguenots as a significant example of the secondary effects of the war. Mokyr also argues that "the direct impact of these individuals on the aggregate economy may not have been vast, but that is less important than their significance as a symptom of the open-minded attitude of agreeing to disagree that flavors the British enlightenment" (1999, p. 39).

Chapter 3
The Unbearable Lightness of Drink: Assessing the
Effects of British Tariffs on French Wine

1. The Methuen Treaty stipulated that Portugal's wines were to receive favorable treatment with tariffs (by volume) never to exceed two-thirds of French tariffs.

2. It is curious that in the eighteenth century through the first half of the nineteenth century, Great Britain—so often cited for her liberalism during this period—was so illiberal with respect to trade policy. While more mercantilist than liberal in the late 1600s, Britain's tariffs on most goods averaged about 5 percent ad valorem, while routinely exceeding 50 percent in the late eighteenth century and still averaging thirty percent by the 1840s when the move towards freer trade began (cf. Schlote, 1952; and Thomas and McCloskey, 1981). The seeds of these policies lay in the various wars Britain entered into in the late 1600s, inducing Albion's use of trade war as a complement to her increasing use of military force.

CHAPTER 4
THE BEGINNINGS: TRADE AND THE STRUGGLE FOR
EUROPEAN POWER IN THE LATE 1600s

1. North and Weingast (1989) made the strongest and most direct arguments about the value of this standoff both in limiting the extent of political predation, while paradoxically permitting stronger state control in those areas where there was agreement by enhancing credibility and enforcement. Brewer (1988) placed greater weight on the creation of a central administration that effectively collected taxes at low cost, but he relied more on the role of geography and small population size to explain Britain's success at creating such an administration, while the French had to rely on an entirely different structure. Such an explanation—which would not explain the timing of the change—needs an argument such as that of North and Weingast to make clear how and when such a dramatic shift in governmental structure was possible.

2. Twentieth-century historians have often reflected this mercantilist view in discussing the rationale for British policy. Thus McLachlan gives us:

> There remained the trade in luxuries which could not be produced in Great Britain or her colonies, and as this usually involved the export of bullion, it was always a source of anxiety to British statesmen and economists. . . . The best example of this dangerous luxury trade was that carried on with France. English consumers were eager for brandy, wines, silks, velvets, laces and lawns, but the French, being blessed with a climate as mild and a government as efficient as those of Great Britain, had been able to develop their own agriculture, manufactures and foreign trade. (1940, p. 5)

3. A notable exception is a recent book on the internal wine trade in France, *Burgundy to Champagne: The Wine Trade in Early Modern France*, by Thomas Brennan (1997). Here too, Brennan notes the profession's relative lack of interest in wine and ascribes part of the reason to the relatively small role that wine played in total output when compared to the rest of agriculture. But this is not much of an excuse given wine's importance in commercial trade as well as its significant role in the political economy of Anglo-French relations.

4. Shillington and Chapman write:

> English economists saw in the rising Portuguese wine trade a possible means of compensation for the lost commerce with France, and were eager to point

out its advantages. The wines of France had to be bought with money; those of Portugal might be exchanged for goods, and should this market be open to the English, it might serve to check the recently established Portuguese cloth manufacture, and English might again send cloth to Portugal, as she now sent bays, and serges, and other worsted goods. The cloth trade, strictly so called, had indeed almost disappeared from Portugal at the end of the seventeenth century. . . . Many merchants, however, thought that the removal of the restrictions which had stifled the trade might be secured by diplomacy. Certain prominent English traders in Lisbon wrote in 1697 that they believed this could be done, if a strong complaint was made of the treatment of the English themselves, who were forbidden to wear their own cloth and fined for so doing. "Yet Portuguese gentlemen," they declared, "will never bear to see us wearing fine cloth, and they be denied it." Therefore, if redress on this point was stoutly demanded, the Portuguese government might admit English cloth freely again rather than grant a fresh privilege to the English residents in Portugal (1907, p. 222).

5. This preferential treatment was also discussed by Shillington and Chapman, who state:

The trade, however, on which the Oporto factory chiefly depended, was that which the French wars had called into existence, and which the Methuen Treaty had firmly established—the trade in wine. The endeavour to nullify the Methuen Treaty and the Treaty of Utrecht was, as has been shown, unsuccessful. Portuguese wines continued to be favoured at the expense of the French: in 1742 the duties on wines imported to London in English ships were, in round figures, £25 per ton for Spanish wines, £31 for German, £52 for French, and only £24 for Portuguese. For the six years from 1736 to 1741 inclusive, the import of wines from Portugal was greater than that from any other country, averaging more than twenty times that from France; and though the trade with Portugal was said ultimately to depend on that of Brazil, it was generally admitted that the trade in wine was the only means by which that in cloth could be preserved. (1907, p. 255).

6. Of course, the commercial interests aligned against France were not the only consideration in the rejection of the commercial treaty. Disapproval of the Tory peace negotiations and concern about Henry St. John Bolingbroke's association with the Jacobite movement also provided grounds for strong opposition.

7. In this vein one such pamphlet argues:

It is in vain therefore to say . . . that France by this Treaty has taken off more of the Dutys upon our Exports, than we have done upon their Imports . . . for if the Dutys upon their Imports were 500 per Cent. here, and those upon our Exports not one per Cent. in France; yet if with the easy Dutys there we could export no Goods at all hither, and notwithstanding the heavy Dutys in England they will be able still to import great quantities hither; if by this means a greater Balance in Mony shall be issu'd hence than was before; if the Value of our Lands shall fall, and greater Numbers of poor People shall be brought upon the Parish; all that the Mercator can say, will never be sufficient for his purpose. (Anonymous, 1713a)

8. The pamphlet, *Reasons humbly offer'd by the Portugal, Spanish, and Italian Merchants, against admitting French Wine to be Imported into Great-Britain*, argued:

> There are three sorts of People, whose Interest combine to endeavour a free Admission of French Wine into this Kingdom. First, Such as can make a private Agreement with the Farmers of Tobacco in France, or their Agents here; and thereby monopolize the whole Exportation of all Tobacco from hence into that Kingdom; and by that means be the sole Importers of Wine into this. Secondly, Such as would drive a clandestine Trade with France, by exporting Wool and contraband Goods thither, and bringing from thence Alamodes, Lustrings, Linnen, and others Manufactures of that Nation . . . and thereby overthrow a great Manufacture of Silks here, now it is brought to Perfection. And, Thirdly, Such as would be glad of an Opportunity to convey and receive Intelligence detrimental to the Government. (Anonymous, 1713c)

The pamphlet further noted:

> If there would hereby ensue no Damage to private Merchants, or to the Trade and Woollen Manufacture of this Kingdom to other Parts, yet the Advantage to the French Nation, by having such a Vent for their Wines, and the Mischiefs to this Government, and to the Nation in general, can never be avoided. . . . No doubt but the French King, as much as his Treasury is exhausted, would give a Million of Money to procure such a Liberty, which all the Parliaments since the late happy Revolution have with great Care, and by many Acts, endeavoured to prevent. (Anonymous, 1713c)

9. The pamphlet, *Reasons Humbly Offer'd by the Merchants Trading to Spain and Portugal against the Bill for suspending the Duty of 25 £. per Tun on French Wines*, claims

> [F]ormerly the King of Portugal prohibited the importation of Cloth into his Kingdom. . . . Which Prohibition by Treaty was taken off, on Consideration that Portugal Wine should pay one third less Duty than French Wine . . . should the Duty on French Wines be lower'd to less than the Treaty with the King of Portugal, of Course when that Treaty is broke, the Prohibition of our Cloth again commences; and with humble Submission, in such case, we very much fear that the French King will take that Opportunity of introducing his Subject's Cloth into Portugal . . . by which means we may for-ever lose the Cloth Trade in that Kingdom. (Anonymous, 1713b)

10. Though Braddick refers to the period prior to 1660, it is clear from his discussion that he paid little attention to the substitution and, consequently, protectionist possibilities inherent in raising duties and restrictions on the imports of wine.

11. It is also noteworthy that he, as did many contemporaries, saw the French wines as being in direct competition and, hence, substitutable with the ales of Britain. An anonymously authored set of *Political Essays Concerning the Present State of the British Empire* answered Hume by stating that France was unlikely to have taken up a sufficient amount of British cloth in exchange for her wine (Anonymous, 1772). Surveying the change in trade since the mid-1600s, the

author cited approvingly the immense decline in Anglo-French trade by arguing, "if we consider that the great end of trade is the exportation of labour, or, in other words, the employment of our poor at the expense of foreigners, we shall not have any reason to think our ancestors acted unpolitically in laying such restrictions on the trade to France, since all benefits of that nature result from it, not to us, but to our enemy" (essay VI, p. 468).

12. Colbert's exact phrasing was, "Il faut prendre garde . . . à ne point trop obliger étrangers á rechercher les moyens de se passer de nos vins" (Malvezin, 1892, p. 285).

13. Colbert noted "La joye que l'on temoigne en Hollande des nouvelles impositions que le parlement d'Angleterre a mises sur nos vins . . . ne sera pas de longue durée . . . estant bien difficile, voie même impossible, que les Anglais se passent de boire de nos vins" (Clement, 1863, pp. 524 and 359).

14. We pass over the question of Colbert's success in promoting or harming the French economy in general. Certainly, the oft-repeated claim that Colbert's efforts succeeded in promoting the fiscal health of the state at the expense of national economic well-being is entirely plausible, but at present, mostly unproven. On the other hand, the facile claims by some (e.g. Ladurie, 1991) that Colbert's overt desire to encourage manufacturing and industry and his evident success in one or two areas (such as wool and linens) indicates successful economic policy, demonstrates the standard aggregation fallacy—which confuses the well-being of a protected industry with the success of the national whole.

CHAPTER 5
COUNTERFACTUALS OR WHAT IF?

1. The economist is especially concerned with all forms of evidence regarding the substitutability of various goods and the extent to which demand for any products is elastic or inelastic. One of the more telling pieces of evidence is how changes in price affect total revenues. It is therefore quite revealing that when the English spirit duty (more accurately, the excise) was reduced from 11/ 8.25 d to 7/ per gallon, official statistics show an increase in measured consumption and a jump in revenue from under £4,000,000 in the early 1820s to over £5,000,000 by the 1830s (Harrison, 1971, p. 66).

2. It is difficult to get precise ranges on the actual income elasticities of wine and beer for modern economies. It is well known that income elasticities tend to decline with rising incomes, but estimates are very sensitive to the choice of underlying model, and are difficult to compare in situations where the good in question is heavily taxed and highly regulated. Demand analysis by Clements and Selvanathan (1987, pp. 240–41) for twentieth-century United Kingdom, Australia, and the United States gives income elasticities in the range of about .5 to 2.2, with the United Kingdom having the highest income elasticities of wine at around 1.7 to 2.2 for the period from 1955 to 1982 and Australia the lowest at about .48 to .76.

CHAPTER 6
WINE, BEER, AND MONEY: THE POLITICAL ECONOMY OF BREWING
AND EIGHTEENTH-CENTURY BRITISH FISCAL POLICY

1. Also, see Nye (1997) for an overview of a general theory that encompasses many of these contributions.

2. It is unclear whether taxes on land were not higher simply because of the possibilities provided by the excise or whether the state was already extracting close to the maximum from land and property. However, it is worth reiterating that taxes on alcoholic beverages also seemed to have been near the maximum in the late 1600s before political circumstances made the new rise in revenue possible. We cannot know with certainty what political configuration would have prevailed if the excises had not been forthcoming and if fiscal pressure had remained centered on the landed classes.

3. This is merely the legal incidence of course. As we know, it is likely that much of the tax was eventually passed on the consumer, who was a passive player in this whole process.

4. Mathias notes: "Great knowledge, enterprise and skill, both in the actual brewing and in management, were needed for success. For those with such qualities, and sufficient capital, . . . the 'Profits returned are proportionately considerable' " (1959, p. 24).

5. It is notable that the department in charge of the excise was viewed as "the good boy" by the Finance Committee of 1797, praising it "for the speed with which the revenue reached the Exchequer, and the negligible amounts misappropriated or lost" (Binney, 1958, pp. 40–41).

CHAPTER 7
THE POLITICAL ECONOMY OF NINETEENTH-CENTURY TRADE

1. Krasner's "State Power and the Structure of International Trade" (1976) is a classic statement of the realist tradition in the analysis of trade relations.

2. Kindleberger (1978) is useful for laying out the "conventional" view of trade history. Kindleberger dismissed the claims of Britain desiring free trade imperialism, since the political economists "believed in buying in the cheapest market and selling in the dearest"—which is flatly contradicted by British policy on French wine (pp. 51–52). He also was forthright in his description of France after 1815 as "a high-tariff country . . . with tariffs . . . for all," thanks to the discrediting of the physiocratic ideas of Turgot (p. 53). This view, again, needs dramatic revision, given France's rather liberal showing when comparing tariff levels to Britain's in the first two thirds or so of the nineteenth century.

3. George Skene Keith illustrates this complication in writing, "as long as a bounty was allowed on exportation, all importation should be prohibited, and as soon as corn rose to such a price that a bounty was unnecessary, a number of high, but not prohibitory, duties should be imposed on foreign corn imported into this kingdom" (1792).

4. D. G. Barnes's (1961) *A History of the English Corn Laws from 1660–1846* is also instructive in showing how the various taxes, duties, and regulations on agriculture in Britain went from primarily supporting regulations on domestic trade in the seventeenth century, to export taxes that were designed to limit overseas sales of grain by the British in the eighteenth century, to the more common import tariffs in the early nineteenth century. Throughout, the political claims were said to have been about the maintenance of a fair price for both the consumer and producer and were especially invoked when international economic conditions, harvest variability, or technical progress threatened to induce rapid changes in the market, changes which in the end could not be held off by any of these policies.

5. Although there is no doubt that British leaders' adherence to the doctrines of Adam Smith played an important role, one should not exaggerate the importance of the stated pronouncements of contemporaries. There were always many influences on policy, most of which were not observable or recorded. Indeed, a cynical observer of British tariff policy might argue that the overall trend matches a simple strategic actor model that focused on overall welfare. We could see that early on in the century, when British market power as the pioneer industrializer was at its height, British tariffs were higher and consistent with the idea that a true market leader might benefit strategically from a moderate set of tariffs. Later on in the century, when competitors such as France and Germany had emerged and effectively undercut British monopoly on modern industrial products, Britain chose to move to freer trade because they benefited from such a policy. Such an interpretation would not be inconsistent with economic theory. It is not common simply because we so often observe that nations choose to engage in trade policies that are politically desirable but that are harmful to the nation as a whole (cf. Nye, 1991c).

Chapter 8
Trade and Taxes in Retrospect: Were British Fiscal Exceptionalism and Economic Success Linked?

1. The rejection of the widespread but inaccurate views of earlier economic history that assigned causal significance to certain sectors because they happened to be the fastest growing was perhaps the most important outgrowth of the cliometric work on the Industrial Revolution in the quarter century from 1960 to 1985, and marks one of the most significant divides between the findings of the generation of McCloskey, David, Crafts, Harley, Mokyr, von Tunzelmann, and the other post-1960s cliometricians and the development theories of Rostow and Gerschenkron, who placed great stock in the idea of a sudden discontinuity rooted in the development of technologically advanced sectors of the economy.

2. This point emerges as a secondary theme in Braddick's investigation into the transformation of the British fiscal system at the end of the seventeenth century, where tax authorities always had to be concerned with how a tax was perceived and received, and whether it would in fact produce the revenue gains promised by the raise (1996).

APPENDIX
MODELING THE EFFECTS OF BRITISH AND FRENCH TARIFFS
ON NATIONAL INCOME

1. This section is based on Dakhlia and Nye (2004).

2. In 1854, for example, Britain imported 8.88 million francs (MF) worth of wine from France and 47.37 MF worth of wine from the rest of the world. In our standard calibration, we would thus assume that the rest of the world also imported 8.88 MF worth of wine from France and produced an additional 47.37 MF for its own consumption. Alternative specifications of market shares are explored as part of our sensitivity analysis.

3. It is important to point out that we restrict our attention to equiproportional reductions of the historic tariff vector. Our computed "optimal tariffs" are not global, but rather constrained to the segment connecting zero tariffs to the historic tariffs. As a consequence, we likely to underestimated the welfare losses associated with protection.

4. To use modern examples for comparison, Krugman and Obstfeld (1997) report welfare costs of protection at 9.5 percent for Brazil, 5.4 percent for Turkey, 5.2 percent for the Philippines, and 0.26 percent for the United States.

References

Anderson, James E. 1995. "Tariff-Index Theory." *Review of International Economics* 3:2 (June): 156–73.

Anderson, James E., and J. Peter Neary. 1994. "Measuring the Restrictiveness of Trade Policy." *World Bank Economic Review* 8:2 (May): 151–69.

Anderson, James E., and J. Peter Neary. 1996. "A New Approach to Evaluating Trade Policy." *Review of Economic Studies* 63: 107–25.

Anonymous. 1709. *Reasons Humbly Offer'd by the Portugal, Italian, and Spanish Merchants Against Importing French Wines, in Return for Tobacco.* London. Microfilm [Hanson 1018]: 1350: Reel 275; no. 4555.

———. 1713a. *The Consequences of a Law for Reducing the Dutys upon French Wines, Brandy, Silks, and Linen, to Those of Other Nations.* London.

———. 1713b. *Reasons Humbly Offer'd by the Merchants Trading to Spain and Portugal Against the Bill for Suspending the Buty of 25 £. per Tun on French Wines.* London. Microfilm. [Stanford]: Reel 297; no. 5041.1.

———. 1713c. *Reasons Humbly Offer'd by the Portugal, Spanish, and Italian Merchants, Against Admitting French Wine to be Imported into Great Britain.* London.

———. 1713d. *The Trade with France, Italy, Spain, and Portugal, Consider'd & c.* London. Microfilm [Hanson 1859]: Reel 297; no. 5047.

———. 1772. *Political Essays Concerning the Present State of the British Empire.* London.

Bairoch, Paul. 1989. "European Trade Policy, 1815–1914." In Peter Mathias and Sydney Pollard, eds., *The Cambridge Economic History of Europe*, vol. 8, *The Industrial Economies: The Development of Economic and Social Policies.* Cambridge: Cambridge University Press.

———. 1976. *Commerce extérieur et developpement économique de l'Europe au XIXe siecle.* Paris: Mouton.

Baldwin, Robert. 1985. *The Political Economy of U.S. Import Policy.* Cambridge, MA: MIT Press.

Barnes, Donald G. 1961. *A History of the English Corn Laws, from 1660–1846.* New York: A. M. Kelley. Reprint of 1930.

Barzel, Yoram 2001. *A Theory of the State.* Cambridge: Cambridge University Press.

Binney, J.E.D. 1958. *British Public Revenue and Administration 1774–92.* London: Oxford University Press.

Bonney, Richard, ed. 1995. *Economic Systems and State Finance.* New York: Clarendon Press.

Bosher, J. F. 1964. *The Single Duty Project; A Study of the Movement For a French Customs Union in the Eighteenth Century.* London: University of London Athlone Press.

Braddick, M. J. 1996. *The Nerves of State: Taxation and the Financing of the English State, 1558–1714.* Manchester: Manchester University Press.

Brennan, Thomas. 1997. *Burgundy to Champagne: The Wine Trade in Early Modern France*, in Johns Hopkins University Studies in Historical and Political Science. 115:1. Baltimore: Johns Hopkins University Press.

Brewer, John. 1988. *The Sinews of Power.* Cambridge, MA: Harvard University Press.

Briggs, Asa. 1985. *Wine for Sale: Victoria Wine and the Liquor Trade, 1860–1984.* Chicago: University of Chicago Press.

Bright, John, and J. E. Thorold Rogers, Eds. 1908. *Speeches on Questions of Public Policy by Richard Cobden.* London: T. Fisher Unwin.

Brown, Lucy. 1958. *The Board of Trade and the Free-Trade Movement 1830–42.* Oxford: Clarendon Press.

Burnett, John. 1999. *Liquid Pleasures: A Social History of Drinks in Modern Britain.* Routledge: London.

Burnette, Joyce, and Joel Mokyr. 1995. "The Standard of Living Through the Ages." In Julian L. Simon, ed., *The State of Humanity.* Malden, MA: Blackwell Publishers Inc.

Cameron, Rondo, and Charles Freedeman. 1983. "French Economic Growth: A Radical Revision." *Social Science History* 7:1: 3–30.

Clapham, John H. 1952. *An Economic History of Modern Britain. Volume 2, Free Trade and Steel 1850–1886.* Cambridge: Cambridge University Press.

Clark, G. N. 1923. *The Dutch Alliance and the War Against French Trade, 1688–1697.* Manchester: Manchester University Press.

Clark, G. N., and Barbara Mary Tanner Franks. 1938. *Guide to English Commercial Statistics, 1696–1782.* London: Offices of the Royal Historical Society.

Clay, C.G.A. 1984. *Economic Expansion and Social Change: England 1500–1700. Volume II: Industry, trade, and government.* Cambridge: Cambridge University Press.

Clement, Pierre. 1863. *Lettres Instructions et Mémoires de Colbert, Vol. II.* Paris: Imprimerie.

Clements, Kenneth W., and E. Anthony Selvanathan. 1987. "Alcohol Consumption." In Henri Theil and Kenneth W. Clements, eds. *Applied Demand Analysis: Results From System-Wide Approaches.* Cambridge, MA: Ballinger Publishing Company.

Coleman, D. C. 1977. *The Economy of England, 1450–1750.* London: Oxford University Press.

Corden, W. Max. 1971. *The Theory of Protection.* London: Oxford University Press.

Crouzet, François. 1987. *L'economie britannique et le blocus continental, 1806–1813.* Paris: Economica.

Crowhurst, Patrick. 1977. *The Defence of British Trade, 1689–1815.* Folkestone: Dawson.

Dakhlia, Sami, and John V. C. Nye. 2004. "Tax Britannica: Nineteenth Century Tariffs and British National Income." *Public Choice* 121 (December): 309–33.

Dakhlia, S., and A. Temimi. Forthcoming. "An Extension of the Trade Restrictiveness Index to Large Economies." *Review of International Economics.*

Davenant, Charles. 1695. *An Essay Upon the Ways and Means of Supplying the War*. London: Printed for Jacob Tonson.

Davis, Lance E., and Robert A. Huttenback. 1986. *Mammon and the Pursuit of Empire: The Political Economy of British Imperialism, 1860–1912*. Cambridge: Cambridge University Press.

Davis, Ralph. 1979. *The Industrial Revolution and British Overseas Trade*. Leicester: Leicester University Press.

Douglas, Roy. 1999. *Taxation in Britain Since 1660*. New York: St. Martin's Press.

Dunham, A. L. 1930. *The Anglo-French Treaty of Commerce of 1860 and the Progress of the Industrial Revolution in France*. Ann Arbor, MI: The University of Michigan Press.

The Economist. 1865, April 22. London: The Economist Newspaper Ltd.

The Economist. 1865, June 24. London: The Economist Newspaper Ltd.

Ekelund, Robert B., and Robert D. Tollison. 1981. *Mercantilism As a Rent-seeking Society: Economic Regulation in Historical Perspective*. College Station, TX: Texas A&M University Press.

Fisher, Harold E. S. 1971. *The Portugal Trade: A Study of Anglo-Portuguese Commerce, 1700–1770*. London: Methuen.

Fogel, R. W. 1967. "The specification problem in economic history." *Journal of Economic History* 27. 283–308.

Fohlen, Claude. 1956. *Lindustrie Textile au Temps du Second Empire*. Paris: Plon.

France, Administration des Douanes. 1858. *Tableau Décennal du Commerce de la France, 1847–56*. Paris: Imprimerie Nationale.

———. 1878. *Tableau Décennal du Commerce de la France, 1867–76*. Paris: Imprimerie Nationale.

France. 1894. *Annuaire Statistique de la France*. Paris: Imprimerie Nationale.

France, Archives Nationale. [n.d.]. AN F12 2484.

———. [1828?]. AN F20 744.

———. [1838?]. AN F12 2537.

———. [1858?]. AN F12 2525.

France, Direction Générale des Douanes. 1870. *Tableau Général du Commerce de la France, 1869*. Paris.

France, Ministre de l'Agriculture, du commerce et des travaux publics. 1860. *Enquête: Traité de commerce avec l'Angletterre, Vol. IV*. Paris.

Francis, Alan D. 1972. *The Wine Trade*. London: A&C Black.

Friedenson, Patrick, and André Strauss, eds. 1987. *Le Capitalisme français XIXe–XXe siècle*. Paris: Fayard.

Gilpin, Robert. 1971. "The Politics of Transnational Economic Relations." *International Organization* 25:3 (Summer): 398–419.

———. 1987. *The Political Economy of International Relations*. Princeton, NJ: Princeton University Press.

Gordon, H. S. 1971. "The Ideology of Laissez-Faire," in A. W. Coats, ed. *The Classical Economists and Economic Policy*. London: Methuen.

Gourvish, T. R., and R. G. Wilson. 1994. *The British Brewing Industry, 1830–1980*. Cambridge: Cambridge University Press.

Great Britain, Parliament, House of Commons, Select Committee on Police of the Metropolis. 1817. *First Report; With Minutes of Evidence Taken Before the Committee; and an Appendix*. London.

Great Britain, Sessional Papers, House of Commons. 1898. *Customs Tariffs of the United Kingdom, 1800–1897*. Vol. 85. London.

Great Britain. 1965. *Statistical Abstract for the United Kingdom 1846–78*. Vol. nos. 8–26. London: Kraus Reprint.

Hancock, David. 2000. "Law, Credit, the Supply of Labour, and the Organization of Sugar Production in the colonial Greater Caribbean: A Comparison of Brazil and Barbados in the Seventeenth Century," in John McCusker and Kenneth Morgan, eds. *The Early Modern Atlantic Economy*. Cambridge: Cambridge University Press.

Harper, William T. 1997. *Origins and Rise of the British Distillery*. New York: Edwin Mellon Press.

Harrison, Brian. 1971. *Drink and the Victorians: The Temperance Question in England 1815–72*. Pittsburgh: University of Pittsburgh Press.

Heckscher, Eli F. 1935. *Mercantilism*. London: G. Allen & Unwin Ltd.

Higounet, Charles, ed. 1962. *Histoire de Bordeaux*. Bordeaux: Federation historique du Sud-Ouest.

Hilton, Boyd. 1989. *Corn, Cash, and Commerce*. Oxford: Oxford University Press.

Hoffman, Philip T., and Jean-Laurent Rosenthal. 1997. "The Political Economy of Warfare and Taxation in Early Modern Europe: Historical Lessons for Economic Development." *The Frontiers of the New Institutional Economics*. 31–55.

Howe, Anthony. 1997. *Free Trade and Liberal England, 1846–1946*. Oxford: Clarendon Press.

Huetz de Lemps, Christian. 1975. *Géographie du commerce de Bordeaux*. Paris: Mouton.

Hume, David. 1777. *Essays, Moral, Political, and Literary, Part II: Political Discourses*. London: Printed for T. Cadell. Reprint of 1752.

Imlah, Albert. 1958. *Economic Elements of the Pax Britannica*. New York: Russell and Russell.

Irwin, Douglas A. 1988. "Welfare Effects of British Free Trade: Debate and Evidence from the 1840s." *Journal of Political Economy* 96: 1142–64.

———. 1993. "Free Trade and Protection in Nineteenth-Century Britain and France Revisited: A Comment." *Journal of Economic History* 53:1 (March): 146–52.

James, M. K. 1951/52. "The Fluctuations of the Anglo-Gascon Wine Trade During the Fourteenth Century." *Economic History Review* 4:2.

Jones, Ronald W. 1971. "Effective Protection and Substitution." *Journal of Industrial Economics* 19:1 (Feb.): 59–81.

Keith, George Skene. 1792. *Tracts on the Corn Laws of Great Britain*. London.

Keohane, Robert. 1984. *After Hegemony: Cooperation and Discord in the World Political Economy*. Princeton, NJ: Princeton University Press.

Kindleberger, Charles P. 1978. *Economic Response: Comparative Studies in Trade, Finance, and Growth*. Cambridge, MA: Harvard University Press.

Koehn, Nancy F. 1994. *The Power of Commerce: Economy and Governance in the First British Empire*. Ithaca and London: Cornell University Press.

Krasner, Stephen. 1976. "State Power and the Structure of International Trade," *World Politics* 28 (April): 317–47.

Krugman, Paul. R., and Maurice Obstfeld. 1997. *International Economics: Theory and Policy.* Reading, MA: Addison-Wesley.

Langford, Paul. 1989. *A Polite and Commercial People: England 1727–1783.* New York: Clarendon Press.

Ladurie, Emmanuel Le Roy. 1991. *L'Ancien Régime: de Louis XIII á Louis XV, 1610–1770.* Paris: Hachette.

Levi, Leone. 1971 [1880]. *History of British Commerce.* Shannon, Ireland: Irish University Press.

Levi, Margaret. 1988. *Of Rule and Revenue.* Berkeley, CA: University of California Press.

Lévy-Leboyer, Maurice and François Bourguignon. 1985. *L'Économie Française au XIXe siècle.* Paris.

Macfarlane, Alan. 1997. *The Savage Wars of Peace: England, Japan and the Malthusian Trap.* Cambridge, MA: Blackwell Publishers.

Macpherson, David. 1805. *Annals of Commerce,* 4 Vols. London: Nichols.

Magee, Stephen, William Brock, and Leslie Young. 1989. *Black Hole Tariffs and Endogenous Tariff Policy.* New York: Cambridge University Press.

Malvezin, T. 1892. *Histoire du commerce de Bordeaux depuis les origines jusqu'à nos jours,* t. II. Bordeaux.

Marczewski, Jean. 1965. "Le produit physique de l'économie française de 1789 à 1913." *Cahiers de l'ISEA* 4 (July): VII–CLIV.

Mathias, Peter. 1959. *The Brewing Industry in England, 1700–1830.* Cambridge: University Press.

Mathias, Peter, and Patrick K. O'Brien. 1976a. "Taxation in England and France, 1715–1810." *Journal of European Economic History* 5: 211–13.

———. 1976b. "Taxation in England and France 1715–1810." *Journal of European Economic History* 5: 601–50.

McCloskey, D. N. 1980. "Magnanimous Albion: Free Trade and British National Income, 1841–1881." *Explorations in Economic History* 17:3: 303–20.

———. 1981. "The Industrial Revolution 1780–1860: A Survey." In Roderick Floud and D. N. McCloskey, eds. *The Economic History of Britain Since 1700,* vol. 1. Cambridge: Cambridge University Press.

McLachlan, Jean O. 1940. *Trade and Peace With Old Spain, 1667–1750: A Study of the Influence of Commerce on Anglo-Spanish Diplomacy in the First Half of the Eighteenth Century.* Cambridge: Cambridge University Press.

McLean, Iain, Robert Pahre, Cheryl Schonhardt-Bailey, and Fiona McGillivray, eds. 2002. *International Trade and Political Institutions: Instituting Trade in the Long 19th Century.* Cheltenham: Edward Elgar.

Mitchell, B.R. 1980. *European Historical Statistics, 1750–1975,* 2nd. rev. ed. New York: Facts on File.

———. 1988. *British Historical Statistics.* Cambridge: Cambridge University Press.

Mokyr, Joel A. 1999. "Editor's Introduction: The New Economic History and the Industrial Revolution." In Joel Mokyr, ed. *The British Industrial Revolution: An Economic Perspective.* Boulder: Westview Press.

———. 2003. "Mercantilism, the Enlightenment, and the Industrial Revolution." Working paper presented to the Conference in Honor of Heckscher. Stockholm.

———. 2005. "The Intellectual Origins of Modern Economic Growth." *Journal of Economic History* 65:2 (June): 285–351.

Monckton, Herbert Anthony. 1966. *A History of English Ale and Beer.* London: Bodley Head.

Le Moniteur Industriel. 1856. 6 July. Paris.

Morgan, Kenneth. 2002. "Mercantilism and British Empire: 1688–1815." In Donald Winch and Patrick K. O'Brien, eds. *The Political Economy of British Historical Experience 1688–1914.* Oxford: Oxford University Press. 165–91.

North, Douglass C., and Barry R. Weingast. 1989. "Consitutions and Commitment: The Evolution of Institutions Governing Public Choice in Seventeenth-Century England." *Journal of Economic History* 49:4 (December): 803–32.

North, Douglass C., and Robert P. Thomas. 1973. *The Rise of the Western World.* Cambridge: Cambridge University Press.

Nye, John V. C. 1987. "Firm Size and Economic Backwardness: A New Look at the French Industrialization Debate." *Journal of Economic History* 47:3 (September): 649–69.

———. 1991a. "Changing French Trade Conditions, National Welfare, and the 1860 Anglo-French Treaty of Commerce." *Explorations in Economic History* 28: 4 (October): 460–77.

———. 1991b. "The Myth of Free Trade Britain and Fortress France: Tariffs and Trade in the Nineteenth Century." *Journal of Economic History* 51:1 (March): 23–46.

———. 1991c. "Revisionist Tariff History and the Theory of Hegemonic Stability." *Politics and Society* 19:2 (June): 209–32.

———. 1993. "Reply to Irwin on Free Trade," *Journal of Economic History,* 53: (March): pp. 153–58.

———. 1997. "Thinking About the State: Property Rights, Trade, and Changing Contractual Arrangements in a World with Violent Coercion." In John Drobak and John V. C. Nye, eds. *Frontiers of the New Institutional Economics.* San Diego: Academic Press.

O'Brien, Patrick. 1988. "The Political Economy of British Taxation, 1660–1815." *Economic History Review* 41:1 (February): 1–32.

———. 2002. "Fiscal Exceptionalism: Great Britain and its European Rivals from Civil War to Triumph at Trafalgar and Waterloo." In Winch and O'Brien, eds. *The Political Economy of British Historical Experience 1688–1914.* Oxford: Oxford University Press.

———. 2006. "Provincializing the First Industrial Revolution." Working Papers of the Global History Network (GEHN).

O'Brien, Patrick K., and P. A. Hunt. 1993. "Data Prepared on English Revenues, 1485–1815." European State Finance Database. Accessed at: http://www.le.ac.uk/hi/bon/ESFDB/frameset.html. Files used: \obrien\engd001-010.ssd and \obrien\engm001.ssd. (accessed Jan. 15, 2006).

O'Brien, Patrick, and Caglar Keyder. 1978. *Economic Growth in Britain and France, 1780–1914.* London: G. Allen & Unwin.

Olson, Mancur 1984. *The Rise and Decline of Nations: Economic Growth, Stagflation, and Rigidities*. New Haven: Yale University Press.

Ormrod, David. 2003. *The Rise of Commercial Empires: England and the Netherlands in the Age of Mercantilism 1650–1770*. Cambridge: Cambridge University Press.

O'Rourke, Kevin. 1997. "Measuring Protection: A Cautionary Tale." *Journal of Development Economics* 53: 169–83.

Paul, Ellen Frankel. 1980. "Laissez-Faire in Nineteenth Century Britain: Fact or Myth?" *Literature of Liberty* Iii:4.

Roberts, David. 1960. *Victorian Origins of the British Welfare State*. New Haven: Yale University Press.

Roehl, Richard. 1976. "French Industrialization: A Reconsideration." *Explorations in Economic History* 13:3 (July): 233–81.

Samuelson, Paul A. 1971. "An Exact Hume-Ricardo-Marshall Model of International Trade." *Journal of Industrial Economics* 19:1 (Feb.): 1–18.

Schlote, Werner. 1952. *British Overseas Trade From 1700 to the 1930s*. Trans. by W. O. Henderson and W. H. Chaloner. Oxford: Blackwell.

Schonhardt-Bailey, Cheryl. 1997. *The Rise of Free Trade*. London: Routledge.

Schumpeter, Joseph A. 1986 (1954). *History of Economic Analysis*. Oxford: Oxford University Press.

Shillington, Violet Mary, and Beatrice Wallis Chapman. 1907. *The Commercial Relations of England and Portugal*. New York: E. P. Dutton & Co.

Sideri, S. 1970. *Trade and Power; Informal Colonialism in Anglo-Portuguese Relations*. Rotterdam: Rotterdam University Press.

Simon, André. 1909. *History of the Wine Trade, Vol. 3*. London.

Smith, Adam. 1776. *An Inquiry Into the Nature and Causes of the Wealth of Nations*. London: W. Strahan and T. Cadell.

Stasavage, David. 2003. *Public Debt and the Birth of the Democratic State: France and Great Britain 1688–1789*. Cambridge: Cambridge University Press.

Thomas, R. P., and Deirdre McCloskey. 1981. "Overseas Trade and Empire, 1700–1820." In Roderick Floud and Deirdre McCloskey, eds., *The Economic History of Britain, 1700–Present*, vol. 1. Cambridge: Cambridge University Press.

Viner, Jacob. 1948. "Power vs. Plenty as Objectives of Foreign Policy in the Seventeenth and Eighteenth Centuries." *World Politics* 1.

Williams, Judith Blow. 1972. *British Commercial Policy and Trade Expansion 1750–1850*. Oxford: Clarendon Press.

Winch, Donald, and Patrick K. O'Brien, eds. 2002. *The Political Economy of British Historical Experience 1688–1914*. Oxford: Oxford University Press.

Young, Arthur. 1770. *The Expediency of a Free Exportation of Corn at this Time: With Some Observations on the Bounty, and its Effects*. London: Printed for W. Nicoll.

———. 1772. *Political Essays Concerning the Present State of the British Empire particularly respecting: I. Natural Advantages and Disadvantages, II. Constitution, III. Agriculture, IV. Manufactures, V. The Colonies, and VI. Commerce*. London: Printed for W. Strahan and T. Cadell.

Index

British manufactured goods, 53; British trade deficit with, 45; commercial treaty of 1713 with, 34; and Continental Blockade, 29; economy of, 56, 107; and Eden Treaty, 27–28; excise tax in, 57; exports of *vs.* British exports, 8–9; and free trade, 5, 9–10, 89, 107, 109, 117, 155n2; GDP of, 7–8; industry in, 107; internal commerce of, 11; and luxury goods, 53, 57, 58; market power of, 122; mercantilism in, 78; and the Netherlands, 58; and Nine Years War, 47, 49; perspective of, 55–59; and post-war resumption of trade (1713), 52, 54; and property rights, 28; protection by, 94; punishment of, 11, 42, 114; regulation in, 76–78; as rival of Great Britain, 51, 53, 106, 114; role of in British trade, 47–49; Smith on, 27; Spanish alliance with, 50; tariffs of, 1; tariffs of *vs.* British tariffs, 3–7, 8, 9; taxation in, 86; trade levels of, 11; trade openness of, 7–9, 13, 106; trade policy of *vs.* British trade policy, xiii, 1, 3–7; and wine exports, 32; wine in economy of, 47; working class in, 107. *See also* wine, French

Francis, Alan D., 33, 38, 61, 62

Franks, Barbara Mary Tanner, 54

free trade: and Anglo-French Treaty of Commerce, 31, 89, 108–9; and beer brewing, 83, 84; and Corn Laws, 30; at end of 19th century, 28; and exports *vs.* imports, 25; and France, 5, 9–10, 89, 107, 109, 117, 155n2; and free-riders, 92; generalized *vs.* specific, 12–13; and Germany, 109; and Great Britain, xiii, xiv, xv, 3, 5, 9–10, 31, 89–90, 92–94, 95, 97, 104, 109, 110, 114, 117, 122, 123, 151n2, 155n2, 156n5; and laissez-faire, 26, 118; measures of, 121; and repeal of Corn Laws, 93, 94–98; and revenue, 104, 114; revised understanding of, 109; Smith on, 27; and taxation, 10; as term, 9–10. *See also* liberalism

French Indies, 22

French privateers, 21, 22

French Revolution, 14, 28, 58, 88, 116, 119

gabelle, 75, 85

Gayer, Arthur, 145n3

George II, 36

George III, 36

Germany, 89, 94, 109. *See also* wine, German

Gerschenkron, Alexander, 156n1

Gilpin, Robert, 93–94

gin, 17, 40, 49, 55, 61, 64, 87

Gin Act, 86

Gin Age, 42, 87

Gironde region, 37

Gladstone, William, 30–31

Glorious Revolution, x, 20, 79, 113, 119

Gordon, H. S., 118

Gourvish, T. R., 99

grain, 12, 30, 95

Great Britain: and Bordeaux exporters, 57; budget of, 72–73, 100–105, 106; commercial policy of, 22; as commercial power, 89; and Continental Blockade, 29; and Eden Treaty, 27–28; exports of *vs.* French exports, 8–9; fiscal policy of, xvi, 68–88, 90, 113; and free ports, 86; and free trade, xiii, xiv, xv, 3, 5, 9–10, 31, 89–90, 92–94, 95, 97, 104, 109, 110, 114, 117, 122, 123, 151n2, 155n2, 156n5; French role in trade of, 47–49; GDP of, 7–8; GNP of, 72; as hegemon, 92–94, 95, 109; and interest-group politics, 90; international power of, 90–91; investment of, in Portugal, 15, 16, 25, 41, 46, 49–50, 53, 59, 147n15; investment of, in Spain, 15, 16, 41, 46, 50, 53, 59, 147n15; liberalism in, 2–3; market power of, 96, 97, 121–22, 123, 124, 156n5; and mercantilism, 23–25, 89, 151n2 (chapter 3), 151n2 (chapter 4); and Methuen Treaty, 50; and Napoleonic Wars, 29; and Nine Years War, 46–47, 49; and property rights, 29; regulation in, 76–78; rivalry of with France, 51, 114; security of, 111–12; as shaping world trade, 93, 94; tariff policy evolution in, 156n4; tariffs of *vs.* French tariffs, 3–7, 8, 9; tax policy evolution in, 156n4; trade deficit of, 45, 46; trade levels of, 11; trade openness of, 7–9; trade policy evolution in, 20–31; trade policy of *vs.* French trade policy, xiii, 1, 3–7

Hallay, Casaux du, 37

Hancock, David, 22

Harper, William T., 41, 42, 43